WHAT I CAME TO SAY

D0351315

WHAT I CAME TO SAY

Raymond Williams

Edited by Neil Belton, Francis Mulhern
and Jenny Taylor

HUTCHINSON RADIUS

Hutchinson Radius
An imprint of Century Hutchinson Ltd
20 Vauxhall Bridge Road, London SW1V 2SA

Century Hutchinson Australia (Pty) Ltd
20 Alfred Street, Milson's Point, Sydney NSW 2061

Century Hutchinson New Zealand Limited
PO Box 40-086, Glenfield, Auckland 10, New Zealand

Century Hutchinson South Africa (Pty) Ltd
PO Box 337, Bergvlei, 2012 South Africa

First published by Hutchinson Radius 1989

Paperback edition first published 1990

© The Estate of Raymond Williams 1989

British Library Cataloguing in Publication Data

Williams, Raymond, 1921-1988
    What I came to say.
    1. Culture — Sociological perspectives
    I. Title
    306
    ISBN 0 09 174441 5

Typeset in 10/12 Times by Avocet Marketing Services, Bicester, Oxon.
Printed and bound in Great Britain by
Mackays of Chatham PLC, Chatham, Kent

Contents

Preface

Raymond Williams has been described in many ways, but his own preference was clear: he called himself a 'writer'.

Economy alone justified this choice. In a working career of more than forty years, he pursued his intellectual and political concerns across a range that included virtually every major cultural form and institution, and many major political movements and structures of the modern period – and this in a repertoire that included not only extended historical and theoretical analysis, but also regular journalistic commentary, a substantial amount of prose fiction and drama too. Summaries like this are dispiriting to compose and to read: pedantic yet inexact, managing to be both incomplete and redundant. They gesture at the remarkable scope of Williams's achievement, but fail to mark the way he remapped the fields he entered and redesigned the instruments he found to hand. They overlook, in this mass of printed material, a strong, deeply reflected practice of *writing*.

The findings of academic research are conveyed by a process known as 'writing *up*', but we should expect literature specialists, and above all critic-novelists, to perform this hydraulic operation with a lighter touch ... Williams's conception of 'writing' worked against all such commonplaces. In his usage, the term overrode the received classification of kinds (literary/non-literary, imaginative/intellectual, and so on), emphasizing the basic continuities within a specific means of cultural production. The most significant unities and divisions within writing were not necessarily of the traditional or official type; they were rather 'conventions' or 'ways of seeing', historically formed, often deeply felt *social understandings* of the world we inhabit. Now, to approach writing (and cultural practice generally) in this light is to see our history and situation in a different and often surprising way. Inherited analyses must be reviewed; new kinds of analysis must be attempted, remaking or simply displacing the existing terms of intellectual (and social) interest. These are among the most familiar procedures in Williams's work, and they are amply represented in this volume, especially in part II, which brings together analysis of some key contemporary institutions – 'high' and 'popular', dominant and oppositional, formal or not. However, this perspective on writing has further implications, which have not been so fully appreciated.

Our routine definitions of the public and the private, and of personality and impersonality in writing, are historical conventions, no less so for all the intuitive force with which we respond to them. It was Williams's habit to think and write across them, tracing the patterns of feeling that can never be wholly repressed, even on the most rigorous intellectual and political occasions, and clarifying the social meanings that cluster around even the smallest, most idiosyncratic or intimate personal particulars. The cruces of identity – the spontaneous answer we give to the question, Who or what are you? – are the moments at which subjectivity must be acknowledged but also understood as historical. The frequent autobiographical reference in Williams's work is the simplest example of this double conviction. The essays in part I have been gathered – in most cases from ephemeral or remote publications – to illustrate fully the rare quality of his attention to questions of individual and collective identity.

It is striking how readily such analyses turn to matters of cultural form, of *composition*. But not surprising: for Williams's understanding of writing positively entailed a high degree of formal self-awareness. (As he looked over the final version of the book-length interview, *Politics and Letters,* in which I had a part, his first comment was: 'It feels like a quite new form'.) 'Realism' (naive) and 'moralism' (earnest) are terms that have been applied to his work. They are scarcely apt. Acute as an analyst of written forms, Williams was equally 'critical' in his use of them. The ironies, the constant self-reference and (more and more marked in later years) the mobility of voice and manner – these and kindred features of his texts suggest quite another temperament and practice.

Of course, there was nothing simply modernist in this. The last part of the volume brings his central practice into explicit and pointed relationship with his fundamental value. Williams wrote as a socialist, for socialism. *That* is 'what he came here to say'. Properly enough, we think of his bequest to socialist culture and politics as one of 'ideas' – concepts, analyses, judgements. But it is greater still. Perhaps this volume of essays – in important ways the most *characteristic* set of his writings yet put together – will encourage us to read the 'ideas' as they actually take shape and move, in the work of a very remarkable writer.

Francis Mulhern

I

My Cambridge

It was not my Cambridge. That was clear from the beginning. I have now spent eighteen years in the university, in three distinct periods. In each of them I have started by being surprised to be there, and then, in time, made some kind of settlement. But this has always, even in the longest period, felt temporary.

The surprise can be related to the fact that, in each of the three periods, I didn't ask or apply to come here. When I became an undergraduate, at Trinity, it was the first time I had seen Cambridge and I knew virtually nothing about it. My headmaster in Abergavenny had spent a year at Trinity, after taking his degree at Aberystwyth. I took the old Higher School Certificate at sixteen and was awarded a State Scholarship. There had been no talk of university before that time. My headmaster and my father met and talked about it, and the headmaster wrote to Trinity. They said I could come up in October 1939, and that is what happened. Then, since other more important things had been happening meanwhile, I had only two years as an undergraduate, before I was called up into the Army. Just over four years later, in mid-October 1945, I was with my regiment on the Kiel Canal, and next in line on the list of Captains to be posted to Burma. What was then called BLA, the British Liberation Army, was generally translated as Burma Looms Ahead. One morning I was called to Headquarters, and I expected it to be the posting. It was a notification of what was called Class B Release, with instructions to report to Trinity College, Cambridge, where the first term of my third student year had already begun. That period lasted till the following June. I was offered a graduate scholarship at the end of it, and considered staying for research. But I wasn't much interested, and in any case now had a family to support. I got a job in adult education, from Oxford, and that was the next fifteen years. I visited Cambridge only once during that period, to give a lecture at a summer school. I walked around and, though I knew my way, it seemed wholly strange.

3

Then, in the spring of 1961, I went down one morning for the post and opened a letter informing me, in three official lines, that I had been appointed to a Lectureship in the English Faculty at Cambridge: a job I didn't even know was vacant and certainly hadn't applied for. The adult education job had been changing, in ways I didn't like. Over the next two days I had other letters, which had been meant to arrive first and explain the situation. These included requests that I would consider accepting the appointment, but the die had already been cast and in fact I was glad. A bizarre episode followed, in which I visited Jesus College to be considered for a Fellowship. That eventually came through, and so in the summer of 1961 I was back. I shall presumably stay until I retire.

Each of the three periods presented a very different Cambridge. The image of the place includes persistence, duration, stability, and this is obvious enough from most of the buildings. Some spirit also may be said to persist. Certainly I have noticed its radical difference from Oxford, in spite of the obvious similarities. But to see this long-run Cambridge means standing back. I feel it most when I am away, or sometimes when I am showing a visitor around. What comes through then is very general and probably in its own way true. But in each of these three periods I have known the place in quite different ways, from close up and within what I suppose is a sub-culture. These sub-cultures vary at the time and over the years. Some are projected as the essential Cambridge, or as the Cambridge of particular years. I don't know. In these three periods I have found the place quite different. What sticks is what you were doing, and particular individuals and groups. But memories are selective. This is clear even in those cases in which people profess to be remembering a group (it is usually brilliant; it is always unique). What I have noticed about these memories of groups is that they are at least partly determined by what happens to the people afterwards. The successful, obviously, are more easily remembered; the others, equally important at the time, can be made to fade. There is a close parallel in external images of the intellectual life of the university. People talk of the Cambridge of Moore and Russell, or of Wittgenstein and Richards, and so on. Yet at any time such figures are a tiny minority in the whole intellectual life of the university. It is falsifying, in a particular way, to project the place through these few figures, who are as often as not relatively isolated, or quite uncharacteristic. It is the same, though less obviously, with the buildings. Often, when I am showing someone around, I am told how beautiful the place is, and I can stop and look and agree that it is so. But hurrying through and past the same places in the ordinary buzz and rush, it is extraordinarily difficult to see this. Buildings materialise as memories of meetings, or as unwanted appointments. Changed places, changed uses, carry odd mixed memories. And as these change through time, for someone who comes back and works here the effect is bound to be different from the images and memories carried by people who were here for three years and then left. One obvious difference is that when you live here for any time you get to know the town, as a town, as well as the university, and that whole added dimension makes many of the more local memories very different.

When I came up in 1939 the war had just started and the feeling of temporariness was bound to be strong. It was my first view of the place, though my parents had visited my lodgings, in Maid's Causeway, and a box of food – ham, marmalade and honey – had been sent ahead with my trunk. I was told by a porter where to buy a gown, but spent much longer hunting the streets for a lavatory. On the next morning there was an address in hall by the Senior Tutor: scriptural and familiar. Later that day I discovered that though I had come to read English, the college had no arrangements for teaching it. I had to go down the road to Dr Tillyard of Jesus College, who sent me on to Mr Elvin of Trinity Hall. I was given an essay assignment on Shakespeare's sonnets, and a lecture-list. That worked out well enough. There were others in the college reading English, and these were my first friends. I put my name down for rugby, and played a few games. I joined the Union, as a life member, but only after some embarrassment, since I knew no one who could propose me. In this and in other ways, over the first week, I found out what is now obvious: that I was arriving, more or less isolated, within what was generally the arrival of a whole formation, an age-group, which already had behind it years of shared acquaintance, and shared training and expectations, from its boarding schools. I was reminded of a conversation my father had reported to me, from his advance visit. The porter had asked him, rather haughtily, whether my name was already down. 'Yes, since last autumn.' 'Last autumn? Many of them, you know, are put down at birth.' I try to be charitable, and find it easier now. But I remember sitting on the benches in hall, surrounded by these people, and wishing they *had* been put down at birth. There was little personal difficulty or dislike, but the formation was easy to hate – is still easy to hate – and I have to record that I responded aggressively. The myth of the working-class boy arriving in Cambridge – it has happened more since the war, though the proportion is still quite unreasonably low – is that he is an awkward misfit and has to learn new manners. It may depend on where you come from. Out of rural Wales it didn't feel like that. The class which has dominated Cambridge is given to describing itself as well-mannered, polite, sensitive. It continually contrasts itself favourably with the rougher and coarser others. When it turns to the arts, it congratulates itself, overtly, on its taste and its sensibility; speaks of its poise and tone. If I then say that what I found was an extraordinarily coarse, pushing, name-ridden group, I shall be told that I am showing class-feeling, class-envy, class-resentment. That I showed class-feeling is not in any doubt. All I would insist on is that nobody fortunate enough to grow up in a good home, in a genuinely well-mannered and sensitive community, could for a moment envy these loud, competitive and deprived people. All I did not know then was how cold that class is. That comes with experience.

There was soon an alternative, or what seemed at the time an alternative. I was already active in politics, and I joined what was then called CUSC – the Socialist Club. It was an extraordinary political situation. From the mid-'thirties the club had been dominated by student communists, but the CP was now against the war and the coming split was obvious. In those first months of what is now called the phoney war there was in fact less tension than there should have been. The open split didn't happen until later in the year, when the son of a Labour MP wrote to a schoolfriend in Oxford, setting out the plans of a new Labour Club. It seemed very funny at the time that the schoolfriend had meanwhile become a communist. But what mattered more than these inevitable manoeuvres was the intense sub-culture of CUSC. I have seen nothing like it since, even in the days of the strong student Left of the late 'sixties. To begin with, there was a clubroom, which served lunches. This became the effective centre of social life; much more so than the college. It was above what used to be MacFisheries, in a passage off Petty Cury. The room later belonged to the Footlights, and I have seen other nostalgic memories of it. The whole area has been pulled down now, and replaced by a shopping centre. But it is one place I still remember vividly. The lunches through the hatch on the right of the door as you came up the stairs. The posters on the walls, including the inevitable 'Your Courage, Your Resolution... will bring Us Victory', altered either by underlining Us or by changing Resolution to Revolution. The wall newspaper, on which I pinned my first political article, done on my new typewriter, on which I could get only the red part of the ribbon to work. But more than anything the films. Virtually the entire sub-culture was filmic. Eisenstein and Pudovkin but also Vigo and Flaherty. Someone said it was only in the 'sixties that undergraduate culture became cinematic rather than literary. In some ways this may be true; the literary culture was then also there. But the lunches and the films were, I now think, the real organising elements of CUSC, with the Cosmo in Market Passage as an out-station. Much of the politicking was internal: a fairly persistent feature of the Left. But we intervened actively in the Union. I spoke regularly in debates, but in the middle of the first term was suspended for speaking ill of the Curator of the Fitzwilliam Museum, who was on the opposite side in a debate on the rights of women. I insisted that he was not a curator but an exhibit, until the bell stopped me.

One other thing that had happened was the evacuation of the London School of Economics to Cambridge. This eventually affected the politics, making it more varied and considerably more sophisticated, though also more to the Right. One fortunate effect of the evacuation was that I met my future wife, who was an LSE student. She came with a birthday party to a CUSC dance in the Dorothy Ballroom, at which I was taking the admission tickets. I don't know whether it was just that night, but I was certainly then talking with an American accent. It was at about the same time that I dropped out of playing rugby. My last game was for Trinity against the LSE.

There were several magazines, and I contributed a short story called *Mother Chapel* to one of them. In some way that I have never understood it got back to Wales and caused a good deal of embarrassment to my parents, though they were not chapel people. I also wrote a story called *Red Earth*, which interests me now because half of it was a satiric presentation of avant-garde students. All these incidents, now obviously enough, show confusion and division of feeling. But over that whole first year, and indeed the first term of the second year, I was an active student militant, as it is now called, and this took up most of my time, the academic work going along in what seemed like a separate existence; indeed as a sort of routine job, or, put the other way round, a hobby. The special conditions of Cambridge academic life, especially for arts students, seem to produce this situation again and again. When I read other reminiscences – especially now as what other people call a don – I am continually surprised at the relative absence or minor interest of work. Yet some work got done; I found a packet of it recently. Examinations were passed. It was just that all the real life was this other.

In my third term I became editor of the student newspaper, then called the *Cambridge University Journal*, commonly *CUJ*, printed by Foister and Jagg in another building, near the Lion Yard, which has gone down under the shopping centre. It was no term to be an editor. The war became real suddenly, but there was still general surprise that the Proctors banned a debate, which was announced as comic, on a motion welcoming the imminent collapse of Western Civilisation. The date was May 1940. I printed summaries of the speeches in the *CUJ*. There was some trouble, but more important things were happening. We left Cambridge expecting invasion, not expecting to come back. In Wales I went with my father to the first shooting practice of what became the Home Guard. There is an infinite capacity, at that age and especially in certain conditions, to live several merely nominally connected lives.

The second year, understandably, was more serious. The politics could not continue as a privileged extension of the 'thirties. CUSC was now in a basement on the corner of Peas Hill and Benet Street; it is a clothes shop today. Slowly, through the year, a different mood became dominant. In my own case it meant mixing more with the group in CUSC who were called the aesthetes. We published a magazine, for which I wrote a story called *Sugar*, and worked hard and, we thought, stylishly, at other writing, and in theatre and film. I still spoke regularly in the Union, and in the Easter term was elected Chairman of Debates, the wartime equivalent of President. But the most important thing that happened, intellectually, during the year, was that I had to relate the active cultural interests, and the radical theories that seemed to go with them, to my academic work in English, which in the first year had seemed separate and formal, like school. Now, as they say in examination papers, I had to compare and contrast, bring the two kinds of interest into useful relation. I didn't succeed. I could have done with some help, but, unsurprisingly, looking back, there was none available. There was plenty of sound academic teaching, but it had no connection at all with the problems of our own writing and with our arguments about new forms and new audiences. Moreover, in the relatively self-contained and often arrogant atmosphere of our group, we didn't know how to frame questions that might have provoked answers. We had an activity and an affiliation, and we knew what we thought about others.

At the same time, conditions were becoming harder. Friends back on leave from the Army were contemptuous of the undergraduate life-style which they had shared only a few months before, but while that contrast was obvious, the style itself was becoming more cramped. I think it was at this time that some of us founded, in Trinity, against considerable senior opposition, a college students' union. The flashpoint in the origin of this now highly-respectable body was the appearance at meals of a hitherto unknown meat dish called bitok: a peculiarly nasty kind of rissole. It is curious how persistent this kind of student complaint about college food is, and how very seriously it is taken at the time. I recall also that this was happening to an undergraduate generation which, as a matter of course, assumed an upper-class life style. Parties were like that, and there were regular visitors from literary London and the London theatre who kept up the style. Our group drink, as I remember, was the especially potent gin and cider. I think I can still taste it, though I have not drunk gin since the war.

As a condition of finishing our year's course we were required to enrol in military training, as officer cadets. I remember Bren gun sessions on the Rifle Range beyond Grange Road. I had now been moved to be supervised by Tillyard. When I came back to Jesus College, fifteen years later, he had recently retired as Master, and we talked on High Table. 'All I can remember about you, Williams,' he said gruffly, 'is boots.' I at once related this to the character of our supervisions, where he was kind and quiet over a cup of tea and I was pushing hard and probably rudely with questions I couldn't properly formulate. Then the memory came back, and the more prosaic explanation. My supervision hour with him came immediately after this weekly drill. I had to rush back on my bike, still in uniform, and clump up his stairs. The slightly comic situation is still symptomatic, however, of the displacement and disconnection which, through no fault of his, were now evident. I was indeed running hard all the time to stay still, or rather, since stillness would have been welcome, running hard, desperately improvising, into the same deep-seated muddle. When I thought I had got out of the muddle, many years later in *Culture and Society* or in *The Country and the City*, I found looking back on that time exceptionally embarrassing and even painful. I came to feel the same way about many of the earlier political naiveties. This has now almost, if not quite, gone. It was so mixed up with problems of personal development, which included every kind of emotional confusion, that I was probably the last person to realise that the tensions and contradictions, messy as they were, belonged to a phase of quite general transition. Certainly that is what many students now tell me, though with the advantage of knowing answers that, to the extent that some are real, were in practice dearly bought. It was this whole experience, and one later experience, in 1948, that I had in mind when, years later, I described Burke as 'one of that company of men who learn virtue from the margin of their errors, learn folly from their own persons'. I would not put it like that now. I think the angry thrust was necessary, and moreover that it was substantially right. The errors it involved, of a general kind, followed from its insertion into the preformed and only partly connecting world of the public-school Left and the late Bloomsbury avant-garde. Yet these, where I found myself, were the only formed alternatives to the much larger and more dominant public-school Right, deeply embedded in the colleges, and to the depressed academic literary establishment. It took me much longer to get out of the alternative formations; the orthodox formations had, for obvious reasons, never seemed even plausible.

That is to look back. At the time it all simply spiralled downwards. When I left Cambridge, in the June, I sold my typewriter, my gown, my bicycle and most of my books. This was only partly a symbolic gesture. I was in debt, and in a couple of weeks I was going into the Army. But I remember thinking, beyond these practical reasons, that it was goodbye to all that. We read golden reminiscences of Cambridge so often, from the successful, of course. Remembering 1941, and having seen scores of cases since, I have to include this other kind of fact. Cambridge can break you up, to no good purpose: confuse you, sicken you, wring you dry. In the 'sixties, now on the side of authority, I used to see young men to whom this had happened, and always, beyond that uncomfortable figure in the chair, I saw a strange and at least equally impossible young man of 1941. I was once taken, on an academic outing, to a performance in King's College Chapel, on the safe theme of the Biblical writing on the wall. Our party responded aesthetically, but they approved the theme as a matter of course. Outside, on the sacred wall of the chapel, two young men had written, in paint, 'Free Nelson Mandela'. I went to court to give them character references. In the general shock, which I could indeed understand, everyone else had left them to fend for themselves. After this and other similar cases, including going weekly to a prison to supervise a young man unreasonably convicted in what was called the Garden House Riot, I got the reputation – the phrase is still used – of being 'soft on students'. I even had this said to me by one of the former leading activists in CUSC, now a respectable Professor. In the ordinary sense I think I am hard on students; certainly I have found that I am a harsh examiner. But I have good and continuing reasons for knowing that the challenge Cambridge offers is not only to achievement; it is often, necessarily, to dissent. The university prides itself on being liberal to dissenters, and in comparative terms this is often true. But there are kinds of dissent which are beyond its terms: inarticulate, incoherent, and then often raging or messy. It is at times like this that I wonder whether any of my colleagues has ever been young, or young in ways which did not repeat those of their fathers or prefigure their own rounded maturities. My complaint against students, in fact, is that too many of them fade from their tensions, or go whoring after any authority but their own possible futures.

Anyway, it seemed to be over. But then the ironies began. Everywhere

MY CAMBRIDGE

I went in the Army I found that Cambridge – not my painful flux, but the clear distant sound of the place – was an admission ticket; indeed, as it used to be called for the families of railwaymen, a privilege ticket. Once, only once, this was because it indicated that I was clever. A future General decided that, having been to Cambridge, I could learn anything, and sent me to train as an instructor on the machinery of a new type of tank; I indeed learned the manual but I am mechanically one of the stupidest people ever born, and the fitters, with their usual loyalty, had to clear up after me. Mostly, Cambridge mattered because it showed I was the right sort of person. Shades of 1941, when a future Peer, then the most active of our Tory opponents in student politics, called out of the window as I was leaving: 'Remember, I'll get you, Williams.' Anyway, to my brother officers on the Kiel Canal, when the release came instead of the posting, the pattern seemed correct: the first words after 'lucky bastard' were that I was 'going back where I belonged'.

It didn't feel like that, in a demob suit in the autumn of 1945. All the familiar centres had gone. I had lost touch with all my previous friends and acquaintances. And the atmosphere had changed, beyond recognition. Eventually, through a chance contact, I found the new alternative sub-culture, which in English but also in Anthropology was the group around F.R. Leavis. I had known virtually nothing of him before, and I was not now to be taught by him; Trinity had a young Indian Research Fellow, B. Rajan. In that whole year I heard Leavis talk once. But I had two close friends who were taught by him, both also socialists, and we spent much time together planning a magazine – it was eventually two magazines – which would bring together *Scrutiny* criticism and Left politics. We also collaborated on other writing projects, and this lasted for a few years after we went down. I lived in my third lodging in Cambridge (Malcolm Street had followed Maid's Causeway): a house at the top of Victoria Road. My wife, until I finished my course, lived with our daughter at her mother's home. It was a quieter, if, in retrospect, no less confused and confusing time. But one of the differences was that I got back to intensive academic work: losing myself for many months in Ibsen and then spending an Easter vacation reading George Eliot against the clock. This is the prototype of the hardworking ex-serviceman student, but there were also the long hours in the Indian Restaurant opposite St John's and the planning of the magazines. When we thought we couldn't raise any money beyond £20, we even considered going to Newmarket and putting it all on an outsider. Eventually, as an ex-serviceman, I got a paper allowance, under the rationing scheme, and we made our way for a time. But what I think mattered most – it would have been strange to that young man of 1941; it is a much more common choice now – was the Tripos. I became extraordinarily involved with the examination itself; emotionally involved. I remember walking down from Victoria Road and across Jesus Green on the morning it started, and all I saw was my home village, which in a strange way now seemed at stake. One of my examiners told me, years later, that mine was one of the two sets of papers she clearly remembered after many years of examining. Certainly I put a strange intensity into what, after all, is a relatively distant and formal exercise. But English Part Two makes more room than any other examination I know for that kind of commitment. My first two books, and parts of others, started with that work. Alongside it the influence of Leavis, indirect as it was, proved extraordinarily invigorating. For some time it seemed a solution to the unresolved problems of 1941, to which it appeared to speak so directly.

Sorting that out, and eventually rejecting it, took the next ten years, and during that period, as for so many people at a distance, Cambridge was Leavis, though with the paradox – which supported much of our indignation, and which was an important element of the affiliation – that Cambridge, established Cambridge, had rejected him. It was very strange, after 1961, returning as a colleague when he was about to retire, and with many of my own positions changed, to get to know him directly for the first time: with a persistent respect, but with the changes rapidly hardening. I wish, looking back, that I had come into contact with him in 1941, when his questions and some of his answers would have been directly relevant. But the moment had passed, and although we tried to talk, very little got said on either side. What I mainly remember is a curious incident when we were sitting side by side in a crowded meeting and our hands were on the table in front of us. The backs of my hands are covered with hair, and I noticed him staring at this, with his marked physical intensity, and then looking at his own very different hands. The trivial incident sticks in my mind because it is a fair enough instance of how deep, when it came to it, all the differences really were.

The return in 1961 was as strange as might be expected. The Lectureship seemed a very good job at the time, though within a couple of years I was being offered Chairs elsewhere. But for reasons that should be apparent, it was very important to me to work out my particular argument in Cambridge. The lecturing of that first five or six years had the intensity of a culmination; also, as was later to appear, of a rapidly deepening isolation. All my friends and acquaintances were now a generation younger than myself. My contemporaries and seniors, some of whom showed me kindness (which was as readily offered), were colleagues at work but in little else, for we were thinking all the time about different things, and in that sense living in quite different places. I took and have since taken rather more than a full share in the business of the English faculty, but after fifteen years I am intellectually more isolated from it, and from anything at all likely to happen in it, than I was when I came. The key moment, perhaps, was my rejection of literary criticism: not only as an academic subject but as an intellectual discipline. I have argued that case elsewhere; it involves a parallel rejection of the specialisation of literature. But nobody quite believes I mean it, and the Faculty, for its own good reasons, has literary criticism as its heart and soul. I spend much of my time in Cambridge writing, but beyond that it is a great crossroads, where I am glad to keep meeting people, especially from other countries. What is formed and forming, at the centre of it, is as alien now as at any time in my life.

This is especially evident in my college. But that began on the wrong foot. I was asked to stay a few days, with a Fellowship in mind. In Cambridge a University Lectureship is the key appointment; to a married man, anyway, a Fellowship is at best a social convenience. What was in mind for me was a Teaching Fellowship, involving direction of studies and up to twelve hours supervision a week. This is paid for, but partly in kind, and one lives, mainly, on the Lectureship salary. Now if in these circumstances a college wants you, the favours, it seems to me, are at least even-handed. But it was not like that. The atmosphere of most colleges, more so then than now, indicates privileged admission beyond the terms of the already achieved intellectual appointment. I was surprised to find, when I arrived, that I had sponsors, and that they were necessary because I had a number of opponents. I was wheeled round to be looked over, by enemies and by the all-important neutrals. I was asked to breakfast, a Cambridge custom I had forgotten, by a senior Fellow who told me, over the toast, that he was himself a 'good Labour man', and that he had for years been trying to persuade the college to celebrate (with a feast) the feast-day of the Old English patron saint of domestic servants, who were quite insufficiently regarded. I replied that I must be a different kind of Labour man, since this would surely mean only more work for the staff. 'Servants we call them here,' he explained, genially. I went out of that and another encounter to tell my sponsors I didn't give a bugger what they did with their Fellowship. But the hours of cross-talking had had a different effect, and I was eventually elected. In the light of later events, with my dropping out of the dining and most of the social life, though I kept up the teaching, I am sure the original opponents believe they were right all along. And indeed I was welcomed back to Cambridge by a front-page editorial in the *Cambridge Review*, written by a colleague and entitled, with a cold acidity that became clearer as it continued, 'Mr Raymond Williams'. Another meeting, I have heard, summoned to discuss my arrival, decided that I was a prime instance of what was happening in State education, where you feed these boys and then they bite your hand. Of course, this wasn't all that happened. When I have been doing Faculty and university business, I have found the element of Cambridge that nobody outside seems to know, and that is in any case obscured by the very different figure of the more public don, as it is or was also invisible to the undergraduate intent on his own absorbing sub-culture: the extraordinarily plain, hard-working, cool centre. This is congenial enough, for business. When I went to my college I found I could manage best by thinking of it as the officer's mess which, in surprising ways, it so closely resembled. In the university it is more like any English public body, and like all English public bodies coping intelligently and efficiently, in local ways, with problems and contradictions so deep-seated that any possible solution, other than hand-to-mouth, goes wholly beyond their terms: their terms of reference, as they would call them, in their essentially incorporated way.

So then, as I look across the fields to this strange city it is both easy and difficult to remember how much has happened to me here, and how important, at different times, it has been in my life. Easy because I still work here, with certain traceable continuities, and with so many places reminding me of past and present. Difficult because, over all these years, it still seems no more than an intersection; never a possession, of or by. There are specific reasons for that, but as I read the history, and the recent history, it seems to me a more common case than is usually acknowledged. So many things have been done here, and so often they have been done quite against the grain.

1977

Seeing a Man Running

One February afternoon in the hard winter of 1963 I was walking south on King's Parade, wrapped and hooded in an army sheepskin against a driving crosswind full of grain snow. The street was empty until, a hundred yards ahead of me, a man came running around the corner from Pembroke Street. As he came nearer I could see that he was only lightly protected against the weather, his shirt collar wide open, his jacket flapping as he ran.

There was never any difficulty in a physical recognition of Leavis. I could already see the deeply tanned skin and the strong set face. But it was only a few weeks since I had been told, pointedly, by two separate elderly dons, that in Cambridge you didn't speak to an acquaintance you happened to meet in the street. I had felt rebuked. In my own country, along the Welsh border, we do not think of passing anyone, friend or stranger, without a salute or a greeting. If we are not busy we usually stop for a talk. I had been back in Cambridge, as a senior member, for less than two years. The social coldness, I supposed, went with the intellectual atmosphere and the east wind. So what should happen with this respected acquaintance, who had now stopped running and was walking towards me?

As he came close he looked intently into my face. I nodded and raised my arm. The intent look hardened. He passed without a word. My instructors had evidently been right. Then there were sudden running steps behind me and as I swung round a hand was laid on my arm.

'I'm sorry, Williams. I didn't mean to cut you.'

I had read that expression often, but I had never before heard it used.

'That's all right. It's a terrible day.'

'It isn't that,' he said, his look hardening again. 'But I have to get to the bank before it closes.'

'Of course.'

He took his hand from my arm and ran on. I crossed the road, though I had no need to.

Twenty years later, after many hours spent with Leavis, in meetings, in passing conversations, in longer talks, both before and after that day in the snow, I remember this incident more sharply than any other. It is very small in itself, but I think of it as symptomatic of such relationship as we had. Many people working on Leavis, as it is called, and an increasing number working on the relationship between his work and my own, come to ask the answerable questions, about what is in the books, and then find it difficult to believe that there are further questions I cannot answer at all: what our relationship was like, as colleagues seeing each other quite often; what we said to each other about the themes we shared and the issues which so evidently divided us. Faced by polite but insistent disbelief, when I have said, truthfully, that we never really discussed them, I have sometimes tried recounting this small incident, but to find it meaning nothing to them.

'Surely? Surely?'

'But no.'

When I came to a lectureship in Cambridge in 1961, Leavis was not far off retirement. His attitudes to the English Faculty, and those of most of the Faculty to him, were set rock hard. Yet that image alone will not do. There were regular eruptions: a reported remark about a colleague that he had made at a lecture; a combative letter to the Chairman; a fierce argument at a meeting. I have never known a social situation in which a group seemed so obsessed by one man. Everybody, it seemed, had a Leavis story, and made it his first business to pass it on. His contemporaries, especially, dispensed such stories, at least to me, in the tone of that advice of the elderly dons about talking in the street. Meanwhile I, in effect, knew nothing. Whenever I met him he was unfailingly polite. In most cases, in the Faculty arguments, he seemed to me to be right. At the same time, you cannot come in on the last couple of chapters of a history like that and delude yourself that you understand any of it as well as those who had been living it through, with all their circumstantial though also (I found as I went on listening) largely uncertain and contested accounts. It was not my shared history, though I had an oblique and unavoidable relation to it, through the work.

Of course among the stories I was sedulously told were some which included what he or one of his circle – the more usual word was 'gang' – had said about me. Since at that time, just after *The Long Revolution*,

I was getting stick from almost everybody, I was merely curious. Could it really be the case, as I was confidently told, that someone very close in that circle had said that I was a prime example of the boy educated at state expense who had turned to bite the hand that had fed him? This was so incongruous with what I had understood of the work that I was unwilling to believe it, though I would have enjoyed some relevant analysis of that 'state expense'. Yet many people did again and again misunderstand, at times almost wilfully, their actual relations with Leavis and some of his most basic attitudes. I was much later told that he had demurred at this description of me. Yet the politics were a problem, as I discovered much later again, when a left-wing lecturer, in trouble at his university, asked me to collect some eminent supporting signatures, and insisted that I approach the Leavises. I spoke to Mrs Leavis on the 'phone. She refused angrily and in political terms.

As I look back now I see a gradual unfolding, in my own mind, of what the full Leavis position had come to be. The young researchers now upbraid me for being so slow in seeing it. They may be right. But what I get, to the end, in the work but even more in my direct contacts with the man, is a sense of something wholly unresolved, into which that fierce energy was still being poured. At the surface level there was a very strange mixture of the deliberate and the reckless, but below that again there was a condition I have only ever seen in one or two other men: a true sense of mystery, and of very painful exposure to mystery, which was even harder to understand because this was the man of so many confident and well-known beliefs and opinions. Perhaps I merely mistook this. But it was the sense I always got from those infrequent but unforgettable hard and lost stares into some distance.

No memoir can touch those levels; certainly no memoir of mine, who as I got to know him knew that I was not getting to know him. It was easier at a relatively public level. At one of the first Faculty meetings I attended almost the entire business was a very long argument between Leavis and the Chairman of the day about the propriety of asking a question about one of the previous summer's examination papers. He was repeatedly told that the question was not admissible, and repeatedly, with extraordinarily forensic skill, he kept asking it. I look back on that now from a Faculty still riven by disputes but in which there is a special annual meeting to discuss the examiners' reports and, where necessary, the papers. It was how it so often went. I could align with Leavis because of what I took to be the position from which he was arguing. Then at another meeting it would be wholly different. There is a mood which sometimes grips university teachers of English, when they take on a fierce collective existence as examiners: a hard pleasure strengthened by an unchallengeable sense of duty as they mark, mark, mark people; execute extraordinary intellectual exercises of grading. The common pursuit, the collaborative spirit, I would think, looking across at Leavis and expecting some shared sense of the problem: the marking had to be done, while the system was there, but was this mood necessary to it? It was a shock when I sometimes saw him going along, though clumsily, with the cold distance of the exercise. Standards, standards. It was a shock comparable with that moment, which impressed some others, when during a discussion of a man proposed for an invitation to lecture he suddenly said, extending his hands: 'He is not one of us.'

The official business in which I had most to do with him was when a new paper on the novel had been proposed for Part II of the Tripos, and I, as secretary, had to convene a committee on it. I spent, in all, hours on the 'phone and in the street persuading Leavis to join it. He was quite sure he would not be wanted; I insisted that he especially was. He joined, eventually, and was very sensible and helpful. It is true that there was one major argument, but it was conducted in my view – others disagree – in a wholly appropriate university spirit. The crux was whether the paper should be the English novel, or the novel in general. He wanted the English novel only. A majority were against him. The example of the Tragedy paper was raised: to understand English tragedy it was useful or even necessary to set it beside the Greek and the French. Leavis would not budge. A general paper on the novel would amount to radical misdirection.

'But Dr Leavis', someone said, 'to understand the twentieth-century novel we have, for example, to read Proust and Kafka.'

'I have read them.'

'Then should not the students have the chance to read them!'

'It would be a misdirection. There is nothing relevant there.'

'But surely that would be for them to decide.'

'It would be a misdirection.'

'Because of reading in translation?'

'That too.'

'Then what about American novelists? Faulkner, for example.'

At this point I have to hold on to my seat. I have the clearest memory of what was said next, and of the mood in which it was said: one of fierce pleasure in the argument but also of surprising conviction.

'Faulkner!' Leavis said. 'When the Americans moved in on Europe, after the War, they had to have a great novelist. That's who they chose, Faulkner.'

Nobody knew, at the time, what to say after that. The general argument continued. Leavis could see that he was losing. Finally, with that open pleasure which usually accompanied what he supposed a decisive point, he turned to me in the chair.

'I put it directly to you, Mr Secretary. The coherent course would be the English Novel from Dickens to Lawrence.'

He knew quite well that this was the title of my main current lecture course. He knew also, I think, that the course was an attempt at a sustained argument against *The Great Tradition*.

'All right', I said, 'I think it is a coherent course. But a majority of the committee want some foreign novelists included, and I think their arguments are strong. Part II, after all, has that important extending dimension.'

'No, I am putting it to you, directly.'

'I could vote for either. They would be very different. But at the moment I'm an officer of the Faculty, trying to get the committee's decision.'

'To you,' he repeated.

The meeting resumed. Eventually a compromise was arrived at: broadly what Leavis wanted as a core, but the other works admitted. He wrote after the meeting and said that I had 'done wonders with that committee'. But when, through a later group, a specimen paper was produced, and it became clear that the compromise wasn't going to work easily, or perhaps at all – as has indeed proved the case – he denounced the whole idea, attacked it in print, said less about the early history of the proposal than I thought he might have done, built the case, as so often, into a general indictment of this misdirecting and excluding Faculty. He had lost, as so often, in a cause that meant everything to him. It was then difficult for him to admit how much, in practice, he had taken part and tried to take part. Long after he had publicly admitted general defeat, in his proposals for an English course, he went on trying to influence more local directions, and by the 'sixties, by some of the younger lecturers, was being positively invited to contribute. But it was too late, in all important ways. He wanted such collaborative work; it had been his ideal. But though he was often helpful at meetings, he both hated and projected the repeated experience of being in a minority.

'If you had voted for Dickens to Lawrence,' he said later, 'it would have turned the committee.'

'I said I would vote for it.'

'You said for either.'

'Because that is my position. What I mainly wanted was a paper on the novel. Either would make a great difference to the Tripos.'

'You could have turned it.'

'No. The majority was clearly the other way.'

'You were not prepared to stand out and be isolated.'

'I have done that often. But on this it didn't apply. I wanted that paper, in either version.'

'I am taking the sense of your work.'

'Yes, and it is nearly all in a minority position. But isn't that the problem, working in any institution? So long as I can teach as I want, I have to accept a framework built by a majority I don't agree with.'

'No, you don't have to accept it.'

'Accepting it as you have. To continue the work. To put these other ideas in.'

He shook his head. He would not accept what he took as a mere excuse, nor apply the general point to himself. There was this kind of barrier, again and again, whenever the central issues were approached. He had worked a lifetime in a Faculty he opposed and despaired of. In a different mood and from different positions I was starting something of the same. I don't blame him for finding the problem insoluble. I have found it increasingly insoluble in these latest years. But we couldn't share that sense, at any time. Everything came out from him directly and *ad hominem*, while I was trying to talk about systems and structures, and of the problems of choice while we were inevitably inside them. He at least couldn't question that 'inevitably', having made the same kind of choice, but neither could he admit it. The whole cast of his mind was that of the heroic isolated individual who was nevertheless appealing, in terms, for Cambridge, for the common pursuit, for more open discussion, for taking part; always appealing and acting in both ways, in a very complex whole situation. It is that figure, and that problem, that I see as real, by contrast with the distantly idealised version of the lonely and punished hero, and more especially with the popular version of the intensely disagreeable, uncooperative and troublemaking man.

I have one other substantial memory. During a later episode of contested Faculty business he invited me to tea at his house. Though that was the supposed occasion, none of my attempts to discuss the

business was responded to. Instead he told me the whole story which I
know he told to so many: of the War, of the Faculty in the 'twenties, of
Wittgenstein, of Richards, of the reception of his wife's first book, of
the years of *Scrutiny*, of his increasing exclusion, of the illnesses and
the problems of money, of other (named) people losing or renouncing
their way. Most of those who have heard it will know how
compellingly it was told. It was a sustained structure of feeling through
the only apparently random episodes. It was essentially composed, in
a literary sense. I responded to the events, though remembering the
other versions I had heard of some of them. But I also responded, for
myself and as he and others had taught, to their telling.

'You should write this', I said.

'That has been said before.'

(Always that edgy kind of reply. I once wished him happy birthday,
and he said: 'I see you've been reading *The Times*', and I said: 'No, I
don't read *The Times*; I just knew it was your birthday.')

'It has the involving strength of one particular kind of novel', I said.

He looked away.

'With this difficulty', I added. 'That one is wholly convinced by this
powerful single-perspective account, until one remembers the
possibility of appearing oneself as a character in one of the later
chapters.'

He looked across at me, angrily. It seemed an entirely impertinent,
even insolent remark. Was not the real feeling all back there, in the
account he had given me? What kind of pretension was it to suppose
oneself as mattering in it? I was speculating all this from the look, but I
hadn't mainly said what I had as a personal point; it was meant to be a
point about the method, about the composition, about what that kind
of self-centredness is when it reaches a certain intense generality,
enfolding and apparently addressed to a special and consenting kind
of reader, and then the inevitable surprise of finding actual people and
events – oneself or others – absorbed and presented in this same
powerful procedure.

'I must tell you . . .', he resumed, and the complex story began again,
in a new episode.

There is not much else to tell. Thinking about method disturbs this
whole process. Whose story is it anyway, as we are all seen and by that
famous method 'placed'? Yet among mainly sad or baffled memories
there is one that still makes me laugh out loud. We often sat side by
side at Faculty Board meetings. He was mainly, in my opinion, polite
and attentive, though the rows that also occurred are more strongly

remembered. Often, through the duller business, we would both look out through the huge window. We once whispered to each other, simultaneously, that the wind had changed. In one very dull patch I looked down and saw him intently examining the backs of my hands, which are covered with hair. He had spread his own hands out in front of him; the backs were quite smooth. At the other end of the table they were trying, as I remember, to nominate an examiner for the Winchester Reading Prize. He went on staring at our hands and when he saw that I had noticed, he smiled.

'Nothing scriptural, for God's sake', I said under my breath. I don't think he heard, but he nodded, and there was a 'Good' from the other end of the table. The examiner for the Winchester Reading Prize had been appointed.

In the year that Leavis died I gave an unofficial memorial lecture for him. Nothing official had been arranged in the Faculty, but I wanted the occasion to be marked. I set down simply 'F.R. Leavis' on the Faculty List. I see from the notes that I spent most time discussing his kind of Practical Criticism and the phase it had offered to represent in Cambridge. I tried to describe the largely unrepeatable combination of close verbal analysis and intense moral argument. There is a sharp, underlined note rejecting what seemed to me the retrospective accommodation: 'a marvellous critic, pity about the man and all those "extra-literary obsessions"'. For the man was all intense concern and conviction, at levels inaccessible to separated argument, though vigorous argument and demonstration often proceeded from them. I took my own theoretical distance from this, as a method, and argued that in any case imitation of the method, without that original constitutive centre, must be weak. I emphasised his quite exceptional wholeness of response, but took that commonplace phrase to its relevant source: a lived, serious and intransigent project, which could not and would not be theorised in any of the positions and terms it claimed. Thus the man was not separable from the critic: for him a virtue, but for the rest of us a problem. *Ad textum, ad hominem*: the personal method that had been offered as a whole educational project had to be taken back or forward, to quite other kinds of history, argument and analysis (especially of language). It is not what might be said at an official memorial lecture, but it was the recognition I wanted to make of a unique and irreplaceable man, taking those two adjectives more seriously and more literally than in their use in tributes.

The last time I actually saw him he was running along the

Madingley Road with a fistful of letters to post. I had often seen him doing this, in his last years, and thought about the wide correspondence into which he put so much vigorous writing, idiosyncratic and impersonal in that wrought, intense, precarious fusion one keeps recognising, at every level, but not in ordinary terms understanding. I was in a car and there was traffic about, but I slowed down and waved. His face was set hard with the effort of the run. He did not look across, as he continued running.

1984

Fiction and the Writing Public

Do your friends say 'You ought to
write a novel' when you tell them
an anecdote?... If so, post this form.

When Thomas Huxley first spoke of an educational ladder, he was
not, I suppose, thinking directly about Jacob and the angels, but about
democracy and the needs of an industrial society. But the moon has
been shining for some years now, and the number of those who have
gone up the ladder and down the wall has steadily increased. Not
many, of course, have come out to play: the majority have done what
Huxley expected of them; a few, like Richard Hoggart, have stood and
looked around, preoccupied. The moon, after all, takes its light from
elsewhere; the wall is still high, the ladder narrow; back there, where
we came from, an extraordinary party seems to be in progress, and
Hoggart stands listening to it, like a sober son watching his family get
drunk. In a serious group, he is an unusually serious person. And what
this group manages to get said, in its own accents, has a major directive
importance. When others are giving up democracy, or defining culture
as its antithesis, the strains in this group are crucial, for here, as in any
future England, there must be loyalty to both. Hoggart is particularly
admirable, because he sees the ladder as Jacob saw it, and neither as a
convenience nor a technique.

The real importance of *The Uses of Literacy* is not that it is a
comprehensive and intelligent account of contemporary commercial
writing. As such, certainly, it is welcome: a natural successor and
complement to say, *Fiction and the Reading Public*. But Hoggart has
attempted to go beyond this, to issues in which the methods of
professional criticism (in which he is fully competent) do not serve. It
is fair to say of Mrs. Leavis's admirable book that the reading public is
really only present in the title; the documents in the case are her real

24

centre of attention. Hoggart, similarly, attends to the documents, but he also seeks to see the reading public as people, and to judge the documents with this reference. The result is not a better book than *Fiction and the Reading Public*, for the concentration on documents at least made questions of form and procedure more simple. But in extending the range of the discussion, Hoggart has encountered literary problems – which I do not think we can say he has solved – that are of exceptional contemporary interest.

The distinctive world of the writers of Richard Hoggart's generation and background is a complex of critical habit, recording ability, and imaginative impulse. This is, I think, the current mainstream of English writing, and one which is likely to broaden and deepen. The effect it is having on the forms of contemporary writing has not yet been assessed, although the symptoms have been noticed. A common reaction to many of the poems in *New Lines*, for example, is the complaint that the 'poetry' is muddled or inhibited by critical judgments, critical itches, theories of communication, observations on a culture. Certainly these elements are visible in some of the poems of Enright, Wain, Davie, Larkin and Holloway. Or again, in a novel like Amis's *That Uncertain Feeling*, there are times when the ordinary progress of the fiction is cut across by similar judgments, observations and itches, often in the significantly popular form of parody. Now in Hoggart's book, which is primarily a critical work, the analysis of documents is cut across by pieces which are very like this kind of fiction: sketches of 'allegorical figures' in the cultural situation; wry accounts of personal feeling; parodies and generalised comments, in a similar feeling-tone. What has been normally observed about this apparent confusion of forms takes a heavy pejorative emphasis. There was the same thing in Leavis, where the outbursts towards the end of *D.H. Lawrence, Novelist* were quite widely thought to disfigure an otherwise sound critical work. In Orwell, again (from whom Hoggart, in terms of literary method, seems to have learned a great deal), there was a curious amalgam of personal observation and social generalisation, which offered itself as a whole but which was not, in its parts, uniformly valid or even uniformly assessible. It has in fact been easy for academics (the real literary historians, who treat literature as documents) to blame this group of mixed critics for getting distracted by life and politics and the British Council and other irrelevancies, which disturb the sweet clear line of an exposition. Similarly it has been easy for novelists and poets of an older minority tradition to blame the new novelists and poets for having got mixed up with literature and education and cultural questions ('some of them, good God, actually have experiences *while reading*') which again disturb that sweet clear line. It is a curious situation, complicated by the undoubted fact that there are radical differences of skill and integrity among writers of this kind. Thus Leavis's outbursts, while sometimes private or matters of rote, are normally the pressure-points of the whole body of his work. It is for just this capacity to get angry about situations which it might be convenient to class as 'not my field' that we respect him. On the other hand, Orwell's similar capacity to get angry, on personal evidence, about whole institutions, is sometimes valuable, sometimes silly and even harmful. In the poems of *New Lines*, sometimes the pressure of this complex produces honesty or even intensity; at other times, silliness and pose. The novels in this category are critically simpler to assess: uniformly entertaining, uniformly inadequate in any permanent respect. But, when these distinctions have been made, it seems to me to remain true that the attempts to express and articulate this particular complex of interests and pressures are in fact the vital contemporary mainstream. The gaucheness and posing are not always failures of integrity; sometimes, at least, they are the by-products of the most honest attempts we have to communicate new feelings in a new situation.

The feelings and situation with which Hoggart is concerned are in fact relatively new in writing. The analysis of Sunday newspapers and crime stories and romances is of course familiar, but, when you have come yourself from their apparent public, when you recognise in yourself the ties that still bind you, you cannot be satisfied with the older formula: enlightened minority, degraded mass. You know how bad most 'popular culture' is, but you know also that the irruption of the 'swinish multitude', which Burke had prophesied would trample down light and learning, is the coming to relative power and relative justice of your own people, whom you could not if you tried desert. My own estimate of this difficulty is that it is first in the field of ideas, the received formulas, that scrutiny is necessary and the approach to settlement possible. Hoggart, I think, has taken over too many of the formulas, in his concentration on a different kind of evidence. He writes at times in the terms of Matthew Arnold, though he is not Arnold nor was meant to be. He has picked up contemporary conservative ideas of the decay of politics in the working class, for which I see no evidence at all: the ideas merely rationalise a common sentimentality – the old labour leaders were noble-hearted, less materialist, fine figures of men, but they are seen thus because their demands are over. (It is worth remembering that working-class materialism is, objectively, in our circumstances, a humane ideal.) He has acquiesced, further, in ideas of the working class as a bloc. He says, for instance, that 'in working-class speech "I" sounds like ae (as in "apple")', though in fact there is no such thing as 'working-class speech': the only class speech in England is that of the upper and middle classes; the speech of working-class people is not socially but *regionally* varied. Finally, he has admitted (though with apologies and partial disclaimers) the extremely damaging and quite untrue identification of 'popular culture' (commercial newspapers, magazines, entertainments, etc.) with 'working-class culture'. In fact the main source of this 'popular culture' lies outside the working class altogether, for it was instituted, financed and operated by the commercial *bourgeoisie*, and remains typically capitalist in its methods of production and distribution. That working-class people form perhaps a majority of the consumers of this material, along with considerable sections of other classes (all, perhaps, except the professional), does not, as a fact, justify this facile identification. In all of these matters, Hoggart's argument needs radical revision.

Yet Hoggart's approach, though involving a relative neglect of ideas, admits very valuable evidence which a concentration on ideas alone would neglect. The analytic parody of commercial writing, which most of us can now do, quickly becomes mechanical unless it is deeply correlated with personal and social observation of a feeling kind. The value of Hoggart's book is the quality of this observation, but here again we must make a distinction. There is social observation, which can properly be generalised, as for instance in Hoggart's chapters, 'There's no Place Like Home', 'Self-Respect', and 'Living and Letting Live'. Hoggart is much more reliable on all this than Orwell: he writes, not as a visitor, but as a native. But this is an observation of *mores*, which can properly be spoken of in class or group terms. The correlation between this and the newspapers and magazines is, as a result, exceptionally valuable: in particular Hoggart's note on the exploitation of 'neighbourliness'. Yet, beyond *mores*, there are further regions of social and personal fact – the world, shall we say, of the novelist, rather than of the sociologist. It is when he enters these regions that Hoggart tends to enter fiction. It is not that he becomes unreliable (though in one or two instances I think he does), but that he is now dealing with whole situations involving individuals rather than with the structures of such situations which are the *mores*. It is less easy to see this distinction because so much recent fiction, particularly the work of this general group, often offers a kind of personalised account of *mores* rather than a whole account of individuals within social situations. I will take some instances where I think Hoggart is thus mistaking his material.

The section on 'Mother' is satisfactory, and moving, in a way that the section on 'Father' is obviously not. The successful section is partly observation of *mores*, partly personal re-creation: the interaction of these produces something almost comparable with successful imaginative creation in its own right. The section on 'Father', on the other hand, is meagre and generalised, and the false personalisation – the usual position at the mirror – at once enters: the 'small ... dark ... whippet' of a man (the generalised caricature) becomes, in feeling, as a kind of mediation, Lucky Hoggart, trying on a cap and neckerchief. A more serious instance is the section 'Scholarship Boy', which I think has been very well received by some readers (and why not? it is much what they wanted to hear, and now an actual scholarship boy is saying it). Certainly we can generalise in some respects about scholarship boys as a group, but the portrait which Hoggart offers goes very far beyond these, and becomes, in the wrong way, personal (wrong, because offered as a general account). The problems of sexual delay, of the intellectual's isolation, of unease and the sense of exile, of the constrained smile at the corner of the mouth, of nostalgia, careerism, phantasy: these, certainly, are socially affected, but I cannot imagine where Hoggart has been if he has not noticed these things as characteristic of a group much wider than that which he offers to describe. They are familiar to us in fiction, from Gissing and Joyce to Huxley, Orwell, and Greene, and in life the spread is as wide. Moreover, while some of these matters can be socially characterised, others are clearly individual, in the full sense, and need a fully individualised substantiation to be read with much respect. At such moments in the book one feels Hoggart hesitating between fiction or autobiography on the one hand, and sociology on the other. The sociological method worked for matters apparently close to this, but once matters involving the myriad variations of individual response are in question, it breaks down. It is when this happens that one wishes Hoggart had written an autobiography or a novel: even if unsuccessful, it would have been an offering in relevant terms.

My argument returns to an earlier point: the confusion of forms which the new complex of feeling has affected. In *The Uses of Literacy* we find, first, the professional critic, who gets through his work with a really intelligent mastery; second, the social observer, who has a fine, quick descriptive talent which lends a background and depth to the critic's observations; then third, the man, the writer, seriously committed to the recall and analysis of first experience, seriously concerned with personal as well as social relationships, and with their interaction; involved, finally, in imaginative creation, as he draws figures from the world he has experienced and attempts to set them in a theme. I am not blaming Hoggart for this variety, but since the condition is general, I am trying to insist on the distinctions we shall all have to make, if the voice of this generation is to come clear and true. We are suffering, obviously, from the decay and disrepute of the realistic novel, which for our purposes (since we are, and know ourselves to be, individuals *within* a society) ought clearly to be revived. Sound critical work can be done; sound social observation and analysis of ideas. Yet I do not see how, in the end, this particular world of fact and feeling can be adequately mediated, except in these more traditionally imaginative terms. Of course it cannot be George Eliot, again, not even Lawrence, though the roots are in both. But there, I think, is the direction, and there, under the fashionable lightness of parody and caricature, this solemn, earnest, heavy voice that one hears, at the crises, in Hoggart, is a voice to listen to and to welcome.

1957

Review of *The Uses of Literacy* by Richard Hoggart (1957)

Desire

The simplest autobiographies are those which are ratified, given title, by an achieved faith or success. Among these, what passes for success has come to predominate. It is then not surprising that most are either written by ghosts or by the equally ghostly figures of acknowledged reputations. Many of the harder kinds of achievement are too full of other kinds of content, to say nothing of contradictions and uncertainties, to pass easily into a Life. A memoir of some event or experience is one thing; the composition of what can be seriously taken as a whole life experience quite another.

Within these difficulties, in one of the byways of Modernism, autobiography is beginning to be widely used as a deliberately uncertain, self-exploratory form. Record and narrative are not renounced, but their threads are loose, within a different intended effect. The difference from fiction of the same apparent kind is, however, still crucial. Always, within the autobiographical form, a figure can emerge from the cloud of uncertainty to say, offering a special kind of conviction: 'this is what I know (now know) happened' or at least 'this is what (I now believe) I actually felt.' The massive shift, as popular forms, to biography and autobiography can then in part be understood as a response to the corresponding but unsolved difficulties of Modernist fiction. The last threads of an attested verisimilitude are not cut.

The most available apparent form for this kind of writing is a model derived from psychoanalysis, in which the nominal self of the account is temporarily divided into an uncertain object and an analytic subject. This is strongest when the analytic subject has access to other evidence than simple memory – for example, in the records and recollections of others. The degree of admission of real others is often an evident lifeline: not an overriding but at least a moderately verifiable account. Yet taken seriously it is full of surprises, which in the end decide which side we come down on: authentic and therefore open self-exploration, or that more widely shared self-absorption which is the main communicative link of internal, inner-directed autobiographical writing. It is a matter in the end, I suppose, of which projection of the self – uncertain object or analytic subject – is really the ghost.

Yet there is also another available form: a model of self-accounting drawn from history or from critical sociology. Here the analytic subject has seriously verifiable general evidence, but its forms can be so strong that the uncertain object is merely placed within them: made representative with only marginal personal evidence. This form has been especially important in our own period because of the preoccupations of class. There has been a demand for accounts of class formation and class transition supported by the substance of individual experience. Even the strangest of us, within this form, can be made emblematic, by others if not by ourselves. Yet what becomes apparent, as the diverse accounts come in, is that even the true generalities of class formation and class transition are crossed by specific circumstances of different kinds: both the specifically personal, as in family situation, family size, the characters of parents, siblings and neighbours, and the specifically social, in types of settlement, forms of local culture, orientations towards work and education. If we then add, as must now be the case, the specificities of gender, as a radical factor within the other diversities and complexities, the very strengths of the earliest examples, which have become models, can become obstacles. For the most available analytic subject is then not even our own ghost.

These points are one way of introducing the questions and uncertainties which both provoked Carolyn Steedman's book and in some important ways survive it. At an intellectual level, but one supported from her own experience, she wants to challenge the accounts of working-class childhood which have been written by men, within a particular mode. She has especially in mind Richard Hoggart's *Uses of Literacy*, which she describes as representing a 'passivity of emotional life in working-class communities', where 'the streets are all the same; nothing changes.'

More sharply, Carolyn Steedman also challenges Jeremy Seabrook's *Working-Class Childhood*, where a similar passivity is also the lost solidarity of the 'old working class', by contrast with post-war 'materialism', but which in the very form of its analysis 'denies its subjects a particular story, a personal history, except when that story illustrates a general thesis ... All of Seabrook's corpus deals ... with what he sees as "the falling into decay of a life once believed by those who shared it to be the only admissible form that life could take". I want to open the door of one of the terraced houses, in a mill town in the 1920s, show Seabrook my mother and her longing, make him see the child of my imagination sitting by an empty grate, reading a tale that tells her a goose-girl can marry a king.'

'The child of my imagination': that again is the uncertain object, in what is offered as the story of two working-class childhoods, her own and her mother's. Yet in context, and in this strand of the book, the challenge is still primarily intellectual. She is rejecting a version of working-class culture which has also been challenged, by men as well as women, on more general social and political grounds. Rhetorically, however, she rejects a *masculine* mode, in which 'the sons of the working class ... put so much effort ... into delineating a background of uniformity and passivity.'

Yet her most significant challenge is broader, or at least the question that initiates it is broader. She relates the 'refusal of a complicated psychology to those living in material distress' not only to what she calls (misleadingly because too generally and flatly) 'cultural criticism' but also to 'the positioning of mental life within Marxism'. This is little developed, theoretically, and is based on what seems very limited reading, but the general challenge is clear and important. She argues convincingly that 'a notion of consciousness as located' – solely or primarily – 'within the realm of production' reduces even the class-consciousness, let alone the whole lives, of most women and all children. In fact, she might have added, following a wider perspective on this heavily contested area, that it reduces the consciousness and lives of many men, who were all also (it has sometimes to be noted in following some styles of contemporary women's writing) children.

More positively, on the basis of these challenges, she is concerned to emphasise and value a kind of radicalism which she sees as neglected by the solidarities of production and as misrepresented and maligned by the retrospective accounts of a passive, undemanding 'old working class': 'I take a defiant pleasure in the way that my mother's story can be used to subvert this account. Born into the "old working class", she wanted; a New Look skirt, a timbered country cottage, to marry a prince.' Of course this is an element in her attempt to understand and relate to the specific life and development of her mother, on which more must be said. Yet since she offers the point as general, it is worth some general reflection.

There is indeed an extraordinary muddle, now very damaging

politically, in those accounts of the 'old working class' which celebrate, by contrast with their post-war successors, the lack of what is called 'materialism'. The term is taken from a tendency in conservative thought, ultimately with a religious reference. But within that perspective, both the collective movement of defence and of aspiration for better living conditions, and the many millions of private desires within and beyond that movement, were alike condemned: almost always, in practice, by the already comfortable. It doesn't then help if the distortions of one kind of retrospective account, emphasising only a decent, self-denying solidarity and excluding more private ambitions, envies and fantasies, are to be matched by the elevation of these private desires to the status of a more authentic radicalism. Carolyn Steedman never goes quite that far, but others are doing so: indeed it is a central rationalisation of the rejection of socialism, in the enchanting name of a generalised 'desire', by a whole group of French intellectuals.

The class factor in what is blurred as 'materialism' is relatively simple. The disadvantaged come to learn, almost always in practice before principle, that their best chance of getting material benefits, over a range from subsistence through comfort to pleasure, is by combining as and where they can. Always, within this, there are diverse private ambitions, but the ethical test – of course often difficult to apply – has to do with the relation of any of these to the common project. The fiercest condemnations, often now seen as 'moralistic', are in practice of those short cuts to affluence which can be seen either as careerism or as personal collaboration with enemies of the class. To present the class ethic as if it were in practice and exclusively 'the map of an upright and decent country' is to ignore the pressures, the complications, the specificities, of many actual lives. But what happens if, responding only to these difficulties, we dilute the principle of 'an upright and decent country': for example, that immediate post-war world, which Steedman convincingly celebrates, in which, through the common action of the Labour movement, the poor got a health service and a generation of children got better care than ever before in history?

This is where the mode of autobiography and the mode of intellectual and historical argument cross, with real difficulties for both. For it is not only Steedman's radicalism – her robust and welcome assertion that poor people justifiably want things they see others much like themselves enjoying, and that this is not to be put down by anyone as some shameful 'envy' – which follows from this general intersection. It is also, and more influentially, the now rampant politics of the Right, which seeks to substitute such individually-shaped desires for the difficult practices of common and sharing provision: a substitution made easier, ironically, both by the reduction of radicalism to individual desire and by the retrospective melancholy of accounts of the 'old working class', where what is always being said, falsely, and by way of excuse as often as exhortation, is that the 'upright and decent' project has been lost.

In an autobiography it comes down to the question of how the story is told. Steedman is acutely conscious of this. Her book hesitates, theoretically, before, during and after the simplest narrative: to significant effect, at least for one kind of reader. Yet the theoretical questions cannot be separated from the aching personal questions, in approaching a life as close as that of a mother. There are ways of telling and reflecting on a story, but also, it sometimes seems, of avoiding it: the quick transitions between uncertain object and analytic subject become elements of a deeper hesitation.

Thus, in a straightforward narrative mode, we read: 'It was two weeks before her death that I went to see her that time, the last time: the first meeting in nine years, except for the day of my father's funeral. The letter announcing my visit lay unopened on the mat...' The mother 'looked like a witch': a 'Lancashire face', and 'the illness made her thinner and gaunter.' It is a situation, a moment, which produces, in this reader at least, a longing, even an envy, for a fully developing narrative: that mode which the Modernist hesitation interrupts or displaces. Has the displacement, then, anything to do with those nine years? And is that a theoretical or an autobiographical question? Why do I track this moving narrative through its reflective and fragmentary revelations, until its substance can give perspective to the intellectual arguments? 'I was really,' Steedman writes, 'a ghost who came to call.' The local and passing observation indicates all the central questions about this hesitant autobiographical exploration of *two* lives.

To pull out the bones of the story is of course to simplify it. What does it mean to say, summarily, that the mother grew up in a poor Lancashire mill town, working in its marginal trades, and that she went away to London with a man who was leaving a wife and a child, and who later in effect moved away from her, so that the new family was technically illegitimate, and within the terraced streets of South London, in part for these reasons, avoided family and neighbours and the ordinary habits of community? That in London, eventually, the mother became a manicurist, serving rich women? That there was then both radical resentment and a kind of envy, so that it can be said (but pushing the period back) that 'she learned selfishness in the very landscape that is meant to have eradicated it'? Is that 'selfishness' too abrupt, too conceding a word for what is more sympathetically and convincingly described as 'a profound sense of insecurity and an incalculable longing for the things she didn't have'? Isn't her precise social situation, so clearly evoked, one of the specific areas in which, relatively isolated and exposed, desire narrows to the immediately or visibly attainable, the older common longings impatiently pushed away? Isn't the highly educated daughter then committed to doing more than admitting her mother's 'desire for the things of the earth to political reality and psychological validity', as if that were a contrast to the real project of her class?

I put these questions to this book because in its problems as much as in its complicated substance I believe it to be important. It can be recommended for elements which I have not discussed, notably the chapter on 'reproduction and refusal' which explores, through her relations with her mother, profoundly physical questions, in ways that compel attention. But its central theme is how we understand and try to relate to each other once we have admitted the diversities and the pressures of our actual rather than our projected lives, and it is one that confronts us with the formal problems of that hybrid of autobiography and argument which is now so clear a consequence of the shifting class relations of our time and within these, shaping the mode, of the specific situation of the intellectual from a working-class family. We are already in a position to separate some versions of this form from others, just as we need urgently to separate different kinds of 'working-class novel'. *Landscape for a Good Woman* is pulled and strained within these crucial divergences, and it would be an evasion to give it only the simple acknowledgment and welcome which it deserves. What it most deserves, for its exceptional openness and honesty, is hard questioning: against some of its implications and seeking to develop others.

1986

Review of *Landscape for a Good Woman: A Story of Two Lives* by Carolyn Steedman (1986)

Distance

The most arresting image on television, in recent weeks*, has been the stylish map of the world which introduces *Newsnight*. It does not show the Falkland/Malvinas islands.

The problems of television during this crisis can be referred to familiar frames: the issues of control and independence; of the quality of reporting; of access and balance in discussion. All are important, but underlying them are some more difficult questions: latent for many years but made very sharp and specific by these events and their representation. They can be summarised as problems in the culture of distance.

The central technical claim of television is that it can show us distant events. The hybrid name selects this quality, following *telescope, telegraph, telephone, telepathy*, with *tele* as the combining form, from the Greek for 'afar', related to *telos*, 'end'. Yet in most everyday television, distance, in any real sense, is not the leading factor. We are in one place, usually at home, watching something in another place: at variable distances, which however do not ordinarily matter, since the technology closes the gap to a familiar connection. The familiarity can be an illusion, but the qualitative change when we see really distant events is usually obvious. We have been shown men walking in space and on the Moon. We have seen our whole planet from outside. And from time to time, indeed often, we have seen men fighting in wars.

The strangest quality of these last weeks has been an absence. That is why the incidental omission of the now famous islands from *Newsnight*'s diagram map sticks in the mind. Certainly it reminds us how selective, and then how differently selective, the television picture of the world can be. But what is much more significant is the revealed

*Written during the Falklands War, 1982.

36

distance between the technology of television, as professionally understood, managed and interpreted, and the political and cultural space within which it actually operates.

Of course from the beginning there were two linked factors which changed what had been understood as the ground rules of television news. The great distance of the islands from Britain, and the fact that in all its early stages this was a naval and long-distance air campaign, led to almost insuperable logistical problems. At the same time there were genuine security requirements: disclosure of the identities and positions of various forces could have exposed them to attack. Yet these factors were then extended. The Ministry of Defence, which has more press and information officers than any other government department, produced a spokesman of such stunning formality that televising him seemed in itself a new form of communication. Deprived of its actualities, television stood its reporters in the streets outside closed doors, constructed models and panels in its studios, and showed film from Argentina.

This strange and protracted sequence was in itself a novel representation of the culture of distance. It has led to much impatience, but then it may eventually be seen that the systematic exhaustion of patience has been part of the inner history of these events. The long, slow approach to the islands was a material reality. But then: to go all that way and do nothing? To hear those discussions night after night, as in an unusually extended pre-match analysis? To want at least something to happen, as in the ordinary rhythms of television?

'We have been discussing this now for six or seven weeks.' The Zimbabwe negotiations lasted six or seven months. Behind both issues there had been argument and attempted negotiation for many years. But then, in the absence of more familiar rhythms, a new and particular rhythm was eventually established. Its principal elements were slowness and inevitability. Its supporting factors were that for many different reasons, and enclosing many different opinions, most capacities for long-term attention and for any substantial patience were indeed exhausted. The slow movement reached its bloody climax. 'Let's get it over with,' many were saying and had been effectively rehearsed to say.

Yet this is still only part of the culture of distance. Suppose, for contrast, that this had been an American operation. There can be little doubt that the film would have been got back, quickly, and would have filled our screens. But film of what? It is said that what was eventually the nightly exposure of ground fighting, and of fires and corpses, turned public opinion, in the United States and elsewhere, against the war in Vietnam. There is no certainty that this is true. That war lasted so long that patience was exhausted with quite other political consequences than the present action is likely to give rise to. But it was in any case the representation of a close-up war: physically distant on the earth but physically close in the lens. What has been happening in the South Atlantic, up to the point where British troops went back on the islands, has been a war of technical distance: of buttons pressed and missiles fired from distances often beyond the range of normal vision; moreover, in many cases, of missiles programmed to direct themselves to their targets. It is the kind of destruction which many of us have been trying to think about in a nuclear exchange, but with two effective differences: that it is on a comparatively small scale, and that it is (as the long slow rhythm had assured us) at a very safe distance.

At a reputedly safe distance, but the precise images of this war of distance had been strongly built into the culture. In every games arcade we can press buttons and see conventionally destructive flashes on targets: 'the invaders'. Television already has, in its library footage, film of excitingly named missiles – side-winders, rapiers, sea wolves – streaking towards exercise targets, which flash and disintegrate and fall. If (but more strictly when) the film of the South Atlantic fighting gets back, it will be important to ask what difference there is, what difference is represented, when the flash of a hit can be remembered to contain and to be destroying a man. Deprived of actuality film, television has been inserting film of these exercises, intermittently subtitled. Is it second best? Who can say? The representation of spectacular destruction may already, in many minds, have blurred the difference between exercise and action, rehearsal and act. For it is one of the corroding indulgences of the culture of distance that to the spectator the effect at least offers to be the same.

Some of us will therefore be cautious in supporting the merely professional complaints of some people in television. Already the language of certain reporters indicates an impatience for colour and action, the prepared modes of filing a war story. Then can any of us be sure there is no television director waiting to say 'Cue Harrier', 'Cue Marines'? Watching the studio war-games has already indicated that this is more than a technical problem. There has been a model of the islands with ships and planes on stalks surrounding it. The proportional size of the ships and planes, and of the dark shadows they cast under the studio lights, has been so exaggerated that it is obvious that the discussion is being controlled by the culture of distance, and indeed at times reaching its morbid last phase, in the culture of alienation. The television professionals, in these constructions, have been so deeply integrated with the out-of-action military professionals they have been interviewing that it felt like suddenly entering another country. Yet it was already there in the flow: programmes such as *Sailor* and *Fighter Pilot* had laid in the view that war is a profession. The Army's own advertising slogan had been taken over, as routine, when troops were used in a labour dispute: 'with dustcart drivers still on strike, Glasgow Corporation called in the Professionals' (23 March 1975). In these and other ways there were the elements of an integrated viewpoint: a good clean shot; well-ordered sequences; professionals understand professionals.

It happens that I came in on the current run a little late, after the programme had started. When the Argentines invaded, I was in Ireland at the Festival of Film and Television in the Celtic Countries. I heard the first House of Commons debate on a transistor above Killarney. Distance in that form had particular effects. Every contradiction seemed heightened. The invasion had been ordered by a brutally repressive military regime to which Labour and Conservative governments had supplied advanced weaponry. The use of force to resolve a long-standing problem was being countered by the threat or use of force to resolve it back again. The rhetoric of an expedition against a fascist military government did not exclude the possibility of active co-operation with Chile. An enterprise to restore the democratic rights of the islanders was being launched with the means and symbols of old imperialist actions. The cynical culture of late capitalism, which had used a national flag for underwear or for carrier bags, switched, as it seemed overnight, to an honorific fetishism which at the same time, though in different colours, was on the streets in Buenos Aires. In a culture which had celebrated *Monty Python*, heroic stances and ripping yarns were being played or at least offered for real.

While I still read the cool and informative Irish newspapers, and watched Irish television, I got some supporting sense of the real complexity of the events. These seemed to hit every contradiction at its most exposed point, making any simple opinion or position impossible. In this peripheral problem which had suddenly become central, everything was off-balance. The House of Commons debate confirmed rather than recognised this. It was only when I got back to Wales, and saw the English papers, that I heard the screeching.

Turning away to cool, low-voiced television, I found the long slow rhythm – the professional presentation of a dragging but limited time, the long march to the models – that I have been trying to describe. After several days of it, feeling the rhythm soaking in, I happened to pass a bonfire of rags and oil in the village and suddenly, in an overwhelming moment, I was in a field in Normandy and the next tank, with my friends in it, was burning and about to explode. I think I then understood the professional culture of distance. Its antiseptic presentation of the images of war was skilled but childish. This sense was deepened by the fact that, in the perspective of my generation, the professionalism being offered was not of fighting but of exercises and models. Throughout the crisis, across different opinions, I have not heard any talk of that distant calculating kind from friends who had been in actual battles.

This seems to me the determining issue. There have been some genuine attempts to present some kind of balance in discussion. It is too early to offer any precise account: that will come later. But such interviewing of dissenters and doubters as there has been has taken place within the general unreality of the presentation of war. Moreover even the important and sustained discussion of negotiating positions and possibilities, which in the early weeks played in counterpoint to the war-games, was vitiated by the absence of hard information. Did a television reporter fly to Peru to interview its President on the precise terms of his proposals, and to question him and then others back home? If so, I missed the report. Speculation flourished in the absence of precise terms. When at last some were finally published, and the opposed positions seemed to some of us no more irreconcilable than in most serious international disputes, including many which eventually get settled, it was already the eve of the climax of that long slow rhythm. The patience of all those who, to be frank, had never sounded particularly patient was said to be exhausted.

Was said to be. One permanent element of our kind of press and television came very clearly into view during these weeks. We can call it the Corps of the Briefed. 'The feeling in Whitehall', 'Sources close to Ministers', the steady feed of these official/unofficial indications occurred alongside numerous official interviews and recordings. It is then necessary to ask what function they serve. Is it only a discreet nudging, beyond attributable public statements? Or is it also a way of enrolling parts of the media, on mutually acceptable terms, in a sense of being inside, being privy? Hopes might rise from some report of a rewording of a formula, but before the details, and before even the opportunity to consider the report with any care, 'it is felt in Whitehall that this in no way meets *Britain*'s requirements' (my italics). 'It is understood that the basic problem is one of the credibility of the people we are trying to deal with.' Indeed.

Yet some people in television, as in a few newspapers, did more than sit up and beg to be privy. One of the most ominous moments of the crisis was the angry, loose-mouthed reaction to such programmes as *Panorama* and other BBC reporting of alternative views. It is interesting that subsequent inquiry, by opinion poll, showed this reaction as the view of a minority. But it takes its place in a lengthening history of such incidents, most of which have hitherto concerned reporting and discussion of the conflict in the North of Ireland. It is as if, each time, the basic terms of an understanding of programming independence have to be reinvented. Yet the film from Argentina, and the television clips, which were also complained about, were showing quite clearly what a 'patriotic' model of television looked like. Galtieri spoke, on a triptych of stone-faced generals. Flags and leaders were paraded. Authorised voices interpreted and exhorted. Or, later, when fighting started, favourable news was rushed, unfavourable news delayed or discounted. Can this be really what anyone openly wants? Yet several of the incidental arguments apply. When our boys are in danger, can we tolerate voices which doubt what they are doing?

This problem also is affected by the culture of distance. If those crowds in Buenos Aires are only a flag-waving mob, looking remarkably like the rougher kinds of football crowd, if that nation and that people are only that uniformed Junta, perhaps it is not really *patriotism*. There was at least one telling interview with a mixed Argentine-British family, in which the son was just going to military service. For a moment the conflict became real, past the coarse official confrontations. Yet when David Frost repeated one of his characteristic programme models, with a British studio audience and several Argentines present by satellite, no communication of any value occurred. There was jeering from some in the British audience, before arguments were fully got out, while the mainly Anglophile Argentinian bourgeois at the far end of the line offered familiar national arguments in the accents of misunderstood old friends. For that was another of the contradictions which came out so plainly in the gyrations of American government spokesmen. These Argentinians were and plainly felt themselves to be 'our kind of people'. To excitedly patriotic British members of that audience this didn't apply. From a different class level they were seeing enemies engaged in doubletalk. Meanwhile, for myself, the official Argentinians I kept seeing on the screen were the enemies of my Argentinian friends: friends who at the same time would not for a moment accept the official British presentation of the dispute and of the war.

The war. But is it a war? At the time of Suez a government spokesman said we were not at war: we were in a state of armed conflict. All that is happening again. It permits the obliqueness of British television reporters still speaking from Buenos Aires, ever since the fighting began. It allows legal loopholes for what can still be said and done at this end, beyond the more general arguments for the free expression of opinion in any crisis; the worse the crisis, the more the need for free information and opinion, subject to direct security concerns. Yet it is only in this respect that it may be necessary to consider this crisis and its modes of presentation as a rehearsal: a rehearsal which then demands detailed appraisal.

The distancing of war has been the central mode: indicated by the physical distance but confirmed and developed by a specific culture. The absence of any return fire, except at those directly exposed on our official behalf, distorts the imagination and permits the fantasies of models and of convictions without experience. But beyond the specific circumstances there is a more general question of what is being rehearsed. It is a direct question about the culture of contemporary democracy. Parliament is debating and we listen. Yet none of the representatives, it seems safe to say, could have been *directly* given the views on this unforeseen crisis of those they offer to represent. This is especially true of that decisive first debate, which inaugurated the whole sequence. What then followed was the unique modern combination of a Cabinet with absolute sovereign powers, acting within a complex of parliamentary parties, opinion polls and television. It has been extremely powerful. On a neglected problem and an unforeseen crisis it has been able to set the agenda and the terms of public response and argument. The attempts of some television programmes and some Members of Parliament and others to express alternatives, to broaden the agenda, come already placed as dissident. The sovereign power to order war operates within the cultural power to distance. General discussion and voting are replaced by television discussion and opinion polls. The modes interact, for the war is fast or is made to appear fast, and there can be no hanging about when the threat is urgent and the blood is roused. Modern systems, in television and opinion-polling, alone correspond to this induced urgency. It is a new political form, latent for many years but now at least temporarily made actual. Its name is constitutional authoritarianism.

DISTANCE

If it is a rehearsal, will there be a performance? That threat hangs heavier than even these bloody events. And that perhaps is the real shock. Certain assumptions about the political culture of Britain, which has been seen since the 'sixties as relaxed, tolerant, peace-loving, sceptical, contemporary, have been shown to fail to hold. The distance between either the most serious or the most fashionable bearers of these attitudes and a latent and organisable majority of our people has been quite suddenly shown to be very wide, on issues that matter. In the early weeks dissidents claimed to be speaking for a majority. The opinion polls, within the whole operation, relentlessly refuted them. Volatility of opinion, the prospect of the morning after, may be cited for comfort. But there is very little that is tangible to give any reassurance. An unnecessary war has been arranged and distanced within a culture that had already distanced mass unemployment. The sinking of a ship shocks and grieves, but is then sealed over by the dominant mood. The argument about this war is difficult enough, and will of course continue. But the larger argument that now needs to be stated, with a patience determined by its urgency, is about the culture of distance, the latent culture of alienation, within which men and women are reduced to models, figures and the quick cry in the throat.

1982

43

Writing, Speech and the 'Classical'

The ideal of the 'classical' has been so closely associated, historically, both with the practice of writing and with the facts of educational and civil authority, that it should not be surprising that it now faces major difficulties. To those of us whose working lives have been centrally concerned with writing, the second half of this conventionally numbered twentieth century has brought many surprises. Among some these changes have occasioned distress. The old authority of writing, and more specifically of print, has in many areas been by-passed by what seem more ephemeral or more doubtful forms. 'I saw it on television', as a warrant of authority, is now more common than the comparable 'I saw it in the newspaper', though by some the authority of either ought still to be questioned . In some areas of education, prolonged practice in composition and analysis is being reduced or replaced by oral exercises, often supplemented by tests of written or at least inscribed response which closely resemble or actually are the filling-in of forms: 'delete where appropriate'; 'tick this box'.

It is then easy to feel that a long literate tradition, carrying so many of the achievements and also the hopes of civilisation, is in real danger. Many children, it is said, are already more skilled at a computer keyboard than with a pen. Modern writing, except in certain specialised areas, has rejected what it calls the longwinded in favour of the notably short and sharp breathed. The complex constructions of many older forms of writing are rejected in favour of the running impromptu of the colloquial. And if this is so, some argue, the rising generations, again apart from a few barely tolerated specialists, will be effectively cut off from that great body of writing, in a number of languages, which we have had good reason to call 'classical'.

It was obvious that the effects of these changes would be felt first among those responsible for the learning and teaching of the old classical languages. Latin has been dislodged from its position as a general requirement for entry into higher education. Greek, which never had the same privileged connections with civil authority, in the churches and lawcourts, has been pushed even further away. Yet some comparable effects have been noticed in the teaching of even English literature, and have worked their way, though less noticed, into the teaching – or should one say the abandonment of teaching, even in the English Faculties of many universities – of the English language itself. Certainly some forms of English writing, of earlier centuries, appear to have become more difficult to understand, if only because of a general lack of terms to describe, with any accuracy, forms of writing other than the contemporary or relatively recent.

It is from this general sense of a great literate tradition now under major threat that many who once associated literacy with high liberal virtues and aspirations, to say nothing of more recognisable conservatives, whose privileged learning is readily identified, at least by themselves, as a last bastion of civilisation, and who in this sense are even proud to be known as reactionary, gather what strength they can to resist the strong tides of contemporary social development, or if that is not possible at least to preserve some areas, some places of storage of learning and practice, from what they have precedents to call the barbarian onslaught.

If I do not stand with them, in the terms which they have announced – simple adhesion to what they call the 'classical', a simple affiliation to what they significantly call the 'canon' – it is not that my educational history, and indeed much of my working life, has not been bound up with theirs. In that sense I am indeed, by presumption, of their party, and we all know that the most bitter responses are regularly reserved for those who, presumed to be of a certain party and having appeared to gain advantages from it, nevertheless refuse to join it. I have often put the charge to myself, since I know that if I had not been good at school Latin I would not, from a working-class family, have entered the kind of higher education which led to my writing *The Long Revolution* and other similarly subversive works. It was not for that, it could be said, that my Latin master took me patiently through the *Georgics*, though as it happens his choice of text – for I was by that stage his only pupil – was made because he knew that my father supplemented his earnings as a railwayman by the extensive keeping of bees and by selling their honey in Abergavenny market, just down the road from the Grammar School. I wish I could say that anything I learned improved his beekeeping. It went much more into an increasingly distancing education. Yet there was one deeper lesson, though it took many years to understand. The skills of learning and of literature were not self-evidently distant from everyday labour. If they were being made to appear so, that was a fact about our educational system and, this being construed, about our social and economic system, with which the skills and the materials of learning should not be, as so often, glibly identified. I could of course see one all too probable end of that line of thinking: that resentment of these systems might eventually lead to rejecting or diminishing the skills and materials thus traditionally identified with them. Indeed, at university, I was taught that perspective: that the masses were coming, and that they would trample and destroy the fine fields of culture. On this I can only repeat what I wrote in *Culture and Society*, recalling that curious incident of the dog in the night. For the trampling which has indeed happened, and which is of course still happening, with ever more resolute and destructive thuds, did not after all come from them. It came from very different people, seeing profit rather than privilege in the exploitation of learning and eventually, by that criterion, seeing little or no profit in that humane and literate tradition which, from their narrowed understanding of a society and even of an economy, they found increasingly irrelevant and even, in its practical offering of so many diverse and alternative values, dangerous.

Yet what might then be said is that we should, as a party, as a profession, stand also against them. Whoever may be controlling these dangerous tides, it is our plain duty to resist them. I can go along with that, some of the way, in the most immediate terms, but my most general position is quite different. I believe that what must really be done, precisely from our own learning and skills, and in a much wider collaboration of the humanities than has yet been realised or even convincingly proposed, is to understand, in some new ways, what the traditions of learning and of literacy really are, and from this to find new directions for an extending practice, which our rapidly changing, indeed dislocating, society is going, on its life, to require.

One of the central problems of this necessary and now urgent reconsideration is a better understanding of the relations between writing and speech. There is a moment in the *Annals* of Tacitus (XIV,30) which for me, a Welshman reading it after some nineteen centuries, clearly dramatises the problem. There is also a different but even more revealing moment in his *Agricola*, xxx, to which I shall return.

The point of the confrontation between the Roman army under

Suetonius and the Britons crowded on what is now the island of Anglesey is quickly registered. We are not likely to forget the contrast between the scared but disciplined soldiers and, on the opposite shore, the troop of frenzied women and the Druids lifting up their hands to heaven and pouring forth dreadful imprecations. Yet what is now most striking is that this is widely represented and read as a confrontation, a violent contrast, between civilisation and barbarism, with the Britons as the barbarians, when the truth of the local case is almost exactly the reverse. It can of course be argued that behind those soldiers, who crossed the straits to kill and burn and destroy, was a high material civilisation, stretching back to the gathered and tributary wealth of Rome. Yet what was actually being destroyed on Anglesey was a distinctive native culture, with its own highly organised order of scholars, philosophers, poets and priests. It is always very difficult to see such an event, of which we have seen a hundred examples in later imperialisms, from any point of view but that of the effective conqueror. I have sometimes tried to imagine the arrival of an alien army, black or red, on the banks of Cam or Isis, and the accounts that might be given of the curiously named Dons, pouring forth in their robes and uttering dreadful imprecations. That the implied comparison can appear absurd is my point. For while there can be little doubt that, by the standards of their time, the learned order of the Celts was highly skilled in natural philosophy and in oral poetry, what it lacked was writing, and that deficit, as in many other comparable cases, has been decisive. It is not that writing alone can be made the test of a highly developed learned and artistic culture. It is that once it is introduced it confers quite disproportionate advantages on those who possess it. Theirs, above all, is the record and, if we are not careful, the verdict of history. In the history of Britain this has been especially marked. Gildas, in the sixth century, seems not to know that there had been a life of his people before the Romans arrived. His ignorance is still echoed today, qualified only, in popular accounts, by vague images of savages in skins and woad, or even, often confused with them, comparably traduced cavemen. Through most of the Middle Ages extraordinary pseudo-histories, reaching an intensity of influence in my neighbour Geoffrey of Monmouth, took as their point of origin a misreading and then an extrapolation within a frame of reference which had been defined by a version of classical literature. The false etymology of Brut and the Britons was to be joined by the fantasy of the British Israelites, from that other body of sacred and authoritative texts, in the Judaeo/

47

Christian tradition. It is a terrible irony that writing, until our own century incomparably the greatest skill of accurate record, should so often, within the realities of historical conquest and repression, have become a medium of obscurantism and falsification. And it is this fact which should now be a challenge to those of us who belong and are committed to the high literate tradition.

It is true that inspired, to an important degree, by classical and Judaeo/Christian texts, there is now a growing body of evidence of a different, non-literate kind. The evidence of archaeology, difficult as it must often be, is bringing us much nearer to an adequate understanding of that long and vast and diverse human history which is before and beyond writing. It is there, for example, in our own country, that we find apparent evidence of an even earlier, mathematically-skilled learned class, in the British Neolithic: two millennia before the Roman legions as they are two millennia before ourselves. All this is of great importance, and we can recall Marx and Engels saying that material evidence should always be preferred to literary records. Yet we have only to look at hard material evidence which has no written accompaniments to realise the limitations of their polemical point. The central example is that of the great cave paintings: major works of art if indeed, in a modern category, that is how they should be described; major human achievements, by any category or standard; yet liable, as we have seen, in the absence of any but the most general contextual evidence, to extraordinary variations of qualified interpretation, from primitive magic to target practice; few willing, it seems, to accept more directly what human hands find joy in making, by material practice, in paint or in stone or in ink.

Thus the point should never be to oppose literacy to the range of other major human skills, for a judgment either way. We have seen the disproportionate historical advantages of literate societies, but not all of these would have been realised, to their current extent, if they had not, to put it bluntly, been carried by force of arms. We have seen this clearly enough in the last five centuries, when European forces arrived in the rest of the world with both guns and texts. At a late point in that long and bloody process, after centuries of written tales of the eccentricities and barbarisms of those being attacked, there was an exceptionally interesting moment, in which what might be called the liberal mind, formed in the complex development of its own metropolitan culture, looked at and listened to the barbarians and found them fully human. This went through many phases: the important contacts with Sanskrit, for example, and with the Hindu grammarians, which were to be so vital an element in the great nineteenth-century development of European philology; or the methodological problems of the Amerindian languages, which contributed to a major new turn in linguistics. The more general contact, in our own time, with other great ancient cultures, including some notably literate, should have altered, permanently, our derived and limited sense of the canon of human civilisation as defined by our own texts, our 'humanities'.

Yet there is one particularly interesting phase of what I have called the liberal mind, when the effort is made, within a complex and sophisticated minority culture, to see the process the other way round, from the other side. The classic case of this, in English, is, I suppose, E.M. Forster's *Passage to India*. There are also the African novels of Joyce Cary. It is then worth adding at once that this liberal mind, at its best, is no substitute for the direct voice or writing which is really from the other side. We have been learning this, in interesting and deeply challenging ways, in the important and developing work of the Indian and West African and East African novelists. Yet this is at a time of a general development of literacy, in the metropolitan but also in many mother tongues. From the period of classical literature we do not have such benefits, and it is this consideration which makes puzzling for me, though it seems not for many others, that moment in the *Agricola* of Tacitus when Calgacus denounces imperialism, in words of a concentrated power which I find without equal: indeed in what can be properly called a classical statement of human values.

Raptores orbis: the Latin words still have more power than any translation I have seen: *brigands du monde*, as a French translation has it; *plunderers of the earth*, as an English. *Raptores orbis*: it is that unforgettable underlying image of hands seizing the round globe itself that, as I read it, is the source of the power. *Auferre, trucidare, rapere falsis nominibus imperium, atque ubi solitudinem faciunt, pacem appellant.* Again this surpasses the available translations. One part of the sentence has been extracted and widely quoted, with the common versions of making a wilderness of a desert and calling it peace. But it is the exposure of the double falsehood which should strike home. It is the linkage of *imperium* and *pacem*, the two false names, which should count. It goes much further than Proudhon's revolutionary challenge, *property is theft*, for here are the received conditions of civilisation, ordered government and peace, seen as covering, with false names, the real practices of theft, massacre and rape.

In their original power these are Latin words: spoken, *in hunc modum* – which may be the decisive point – by a man with a good Celtic name, Calgacus, Swordsman, before a battle somewhere west of Aberdeen, at Mons Graupius which might be Sillyean Hill east of Keith, and the Britons with their backs to the sea. Within the discriminating advantages of literacy, which archaeology in any such case can only track, that is in effect all we know.

Yet in a different sense how much it is then that we know, or can know. For what I find remarkable, within the common practice of including set speeches in narrations, is the power of this speech to surpass its occasion. It is inserted, we remember, within what is in effect a eulogy of Agricola, and nothing of that emphasis is withdrawn. Agricola's countering speech is in character with the eulogy: firm, experienced, practical, successful: prudent and moderate, as Tacitus summarises: 'a good man you would have readily believed him, and been glad to have found he was a great man'. Yet what the speech of such a man counters is not the distantly reported 'dreadful imprecations', with their impression of wild barbarism, but a close, sinewy, classical statement of the virtues of civilisation – liberty, community, justice, a plain-living self-respect – and these brought to a climax within the terrible necessity of opposing their destroyers, the *raptores orbis*.

What is usually said, as I have followed it, is that Tacitus the practised lawyer and orator is extending his skills, in this studied piece of writing, even to the speech of an enemy of Rome. Others couple this with the argument that in thus humanising the enemy, as perhaps also in the *Germania*, he is representing the old senatorial virtues against the tyranny and corruption of that stage of the Empire from which Agricola, though serving it, had suffered. I take these points, but still the actual speech of Calgacus surpasses them: his is a universal statement against the whole project that was the reputed glory of Rome. It would be good to be able to believe that what Calgacus says is really the voice of that conquered British civilisation. But we have no way of knowing that, even when we seem to hear the same voice centuries later, in the earliest Welsh poetry, where among the braggadocio of military valour and the flattery of tyrants we catch also the sad sound of a different idea of humanity, including the experience of humanity in defeat, as in Aneirin. Whether there was indeed any such continuity, or whether if there was Tacitus could have known of it, we are unable to say, barred for all time by that single deficit in writing.

Yet what we may be able to say is that we can see here, very clearly, what is really comprehended by the idea of *humanitas*. The word, as in another passage Tacitus reminds us, is easily misunderstood, in the way that *civilisation* was often misunderstood in our own late eighteenth and nineteenth centuries, leading to an important and influential if still difficult distinction between *civilisation* and *culture*. Speaking of the Britons who were adapting to Roman civilisation, by wearing the toga and frequenting the fine galleries and bath-houses and banquets of the new order, he adds, with a cutting edge: *idque apud inperitos humanitas vocabatur, cum pars servitutis esset.* We have since known very many of these eager, new-rich collaborators, but few have had the benefit of that judgment from the other side, that in their inexperience they were calling civilisation that which was a part of their submission and servitude.

It is the reach of that wider *humanitas*, against a powerful war-machine and a display of material wealth and skill, which we can at least temporarily extract. There remains, however, the specifically literary problem. As I said earlier, the insertion of speeches in historical narratives was by this time conventional. It goes back to Thucydides, whom we are not surprised, if we examine the convention, to find the contemporary of Sophocles and Euripides. In Latin it is common from Cato. Yet the imposed distance of genres, as here between drama and history, is for all its emphasis in classical literature in some important respects misleading. What we find, as we think about it, is a fundamental question about the relationships between speech and writing, which from our own period and type of education, with its accustomed predominance of print, we are rather poorly placed to understand.

So much of what is now called the literature of the world, including a large part of its greatest literature, was either written for actual speaking or in a mode of speech, that we are likely to deform it if we apply our comparatively recent norm of writing for silent reading. It is not only that so much of this work is drama or oratory (the latter including the modern forms of sermons, lectures and addresses, which as late as the nineteenth century play a most important part). It is also that through classical and medieval times, and in many cases beyond these, most reading was either aloud or silently articulated as if speaking: a habit we now recognise mainly in the slow. Most classical histories were indeed quite close to oratory, and public speech, rather than silent reading of an artefact, was the central condition of linguistic composition.

Yet within this condition and its conventions we must make

distinctions, not only, as obviously, between individual writers but more decisively between functions. Thus if with the memory of the speech of Calgacus in mind we turn to the speeches of Boudicca and Suetonius, as represented in the *Annals* (XIV, 35,36) we find a mode which is effective as an element of narration; indeed the speeches are enclosed within narrative. They are short, to the immediate point and situation, but with hardly any reference or relevance beyond these. It might then be possible to contrast the speech of Calgacus in terms of its more developed oratory, which is indeed obvious; the speech is, in that sense, evidently 'set'. But though I may be wrong I think we must see something more in the difference: something which I would myself relate to the dramatic mode. It is not only that we have to remember classical drama as a unique (though internally developing) combination of narration, speech and chorus, in which many elements are somewhere between the categories of speech and narration as we now distinguish them. It is also that remembering the dramatic mode allows me, at least, to get beyond what is otherwise the difficulty of the placing of the speech of Calgacus within a eulogy of his conqueror. For while it will not do to extract the speech as an absolute condemnation of imperialism, it will not do either to dissolve it into a eulogistic narration. What the dramatic mode made possible, in what has to be seen as a major cultural liberation, was what in fact we find here: a narration, a speech, of a number of voices; thus inherently, in its multivocal character, a way of presenting voices, which while they speak have their own and temporarily absolute power, but which because other voices will speak have to be gathered, finally, into a whole action. Of course much is changed when the narrative mode in drama is specialised from messengers and reports to a single, enclosing narrative voice: moreover, as in Tacitus, a named voice, declaring his particular relation to his subject. Yet the thrust of the mode can still be there: Calgacus can denounce imperialism, with a reference and relevance beyond the narrative occasion, yet he can then be not so much answered as followed by the very different voice of the practical, moderate, loyal servant of Empire who goes on to defeat him. And what has then to be said is that neither voice is lost; the alternative voices stick in the memory, in ways comparable to the many voices of drama.

I am not making only a technical point. The crisis of humane studies, in our own times, can be described in many ways, but one major element of it, which has been too little and sometimes not at all recognised, is the again changing relation between writing and speech. All of us likely to be taking part in the discussion have been so formed by writing and by the silent reading of print that we may come to misrepresent even our own subject, ironically in a period in which oral forms, of some new and some older kinds, are again becoming central and even decisive in our culture. To trace this full history is beyond this occasion; I have tried, several times, to write parts of it, elsewhere. But the key point is not only a change of modes. Difficult as it may be for some of us to admit it, writing has from the beginning been a special form of privilege and social discrimination. Unlike all other forms of social communication and record, it does not come to anyone in the most general processes of growing up in a particular society. It has to be carefully taught and learned, and until comparatively recently, and still in some respects today even in the most literate societies, access to this skill has been carefully and at times malignly controlled. Moreover we must remember where it started: in the bureaucratic records of centralising urban economies, and then in trading economies. What must now be seen, historically, as advantage or deficit, in this or that former culture, has to be related not to some abstraction of civilisation but to particular kinds of social order. It is then true that there developed, on this material base and again in particular kinds of social order, moving in that same centralising direction, ways of using writing which were eventually to give us what we now call the literatures of the world. Yet, given the relation of this development to the mode of public speech, what was still a minority practice had a public presence and reference.

The case was then changed with the coming of print and silent reading. Over the five centuries of print which have formed our minds, even the writing for public speaking, of earlier times, has been reclassified as what we call, barbarously, 'oral literature', and has been reified as 'texts'. Of course we would not have these at all if they had not been written down and preserved: that key function of record in writing to which scholars have primarily to attend. But there were two wider social effects.

First, when such decisive matters as history and law retreat into writing, with different degrees of retreat according to whether a dead or specialised or a vernacular language is employed, a majority of any people is cut off from knowledge of some of its most decisive conditions of life and identity. The extraordinary ignorance of the British about their own past is not mere deficit; it is again and again functional, through the effective control of print. And then none of us should really be surprised if forms of dismissal or even hatred of that book-learning spread and take effect, the more quickly of course if the print is foreign.

Nor should we be surprised, though we can be right to be shocked, when these distances are demagogically exploited. We say that we are offering the great works of the ages; others say, often with justice, that these are too bound up with distance and privilege and authority to be taken or even offered innocently.

This point becomes crucial when we include the second effect. Through the agonisingly slow development of general literacy, and then significantly in the period of rising democracy and the extension of the suffrage, received written forms were modified by innovations and pressures of several kinds. As late as Fielding's *Tom Jones* lovers can speak their extended declarations in the mode of generals before a battle, and the narrative voice is still in many ways spoken. But through the nineteenth century there developed not only the composed artefact, often of an impersonal narrative, for silent reading, but wholly novel ways – though with some precedents in parts of the drama – of representing what was not now public or semi-public speech, but conversation. I have given examples of this development, and of its conventions and difficulties, in *Writing in Society*. But what was also happening, for largely political and commercial reasons, was the development, in the newspapers, of a novel representation of public speech: one which in our own century has become, though always in conventional and sometimes in highly artificial ways, increasingly colloquial and idiomatic. The narrative voice in the novel followed the same course, though usually with more integrity.

It is then into this situation that the new oral forms of cinema and radio and television, two of them combining speech with a new power of moving images, arrived. The majority response of the highly literate, at each stage, has been deep suspicion if not horror. It was not only classicists, it was also teachers of English literature – English print – who could feel their whole world threatened. The values of high literacy, privately and clubbably evidenced by long knowledge and experience of so many major works, were taken as arrayed against what was seen as a destructive and demotic – demotic was quicker to say than democratic, though some went all the way – anyway vulgar mass culture.

I have been arguing against this conclusion through the whole of my working life, and I know I still fail to persuade. But what I have still to say, and with special point within the Classical Association, is that a major ground for my argument has always been high literacy itself. It is high literacy which shows us the remarkable historical diversity of modes of address and composition. It is high literacy which shows us the extraordinary diversity – literally as wide as the world – of the meanings and values which these works carry: a diversity which again and again is their only general value, and one which is not to be reduced to plausible singularities of consideration or conclusion, or to the use of literature, in some highly selective tradition, to ratify the habits of some temporary or self-interested group. It is again high literacy, in its only real sense, which can take us beyond those local conclusions of commonsense or necessity, as common among the generally literate as anywhere else, which override the facts of actual change and diversity, and even more the profound alternatives of belief and commitment in the long human record: facts and alternatives which at any time, and under any pressures, are necessary grounds of wisdom in complex and contending societies. It is high literacy, finally, which calls the bluffs of authority, since it is a condition of all its practical work that it questions sources, closely examines offered authenticities, reads contextually and comparatively, identifies conventions to determine meanings: habits of mind which are all against, or should be all against, any and every pronunciation of a singular or assembled authority.

But if the classics must be separated from authority, by the very process of understanding what authentic authorities are or are not, there must equally, from disciplines based on more recent material, be an attempt at honest collaboration and convergence. It is bound to be the case that the works of the classical European languages – and that formulation is meant to emphasise that there are others – are necessary elements of human culture and understanding, whatever else may be happening. Yet that you would properly expect me to say. What I have also to say may be more surprising. There are very many faults in our current uses of the new oral and oral-visual forms, some of them, in their control of access, repeating the early faults of print. Yet as forms they could be especially near to us. Some modes of public speech are again being directly attempted, within conditions which remove them from what must be seen as the decadence of oratory: conditions which have already multiplied the actually contributing voices, and might multiply them many times again; conditions moreover of dialogue, of the multivocal, which are repeatedly trivialised, under the pressures of a centralising system, but which include possibilities beyond those of silent reading. For close, sustained, checkable argument there are still few substitutes for print, but for direct exchange the new forms have advantages, and it is now in any case true that all these modes can be followed without specialised and discriminating access; the mother-tongue is again the common entry for all to hear, if not yet for all to speak.

At the same time, within the rapid and often reckless expansion of these forms, at a time of major social dislocations as well as persistent inequalities, the skills that have been learned in high literacy have much to contribute. Our working practices may seem much too slow to survive in that torrent, but it is already the case that many young scholars and analysts, with some success, have taken these skills through to the material of the new forms: forms which now in any case must be included among the humanities. The work is not for any one group to do. Only a very diverse community of writers and scholars and analysts can approach adequacy. But then that finally is my case for a reorganisation of the humanities, a new school and curriculum of humanities, which will undoubtedly include many workers whose terms and materials will be very strange to classicists, but which in including classicists will continue to assert its breadth, its depth, and, above all, its historical sense of humanity.

1984

Presidential Address to the Classical Association.

Community

Two truths are told, as alternative prologues to the action of modern Wales. The first draws on the continuity of Welsh language and literature: from the sixth century, it is said, and thus perhaps the oldest surviving poetic tradition in Europe. The second draws on the turbulent experience of industrial South Wales, over the last two centuries, and its powerful political and communal formations.

It would be possible, within an English perspective, to see these truths as of different kinds, literary and political: one or other to be emphasised or reduced to background. Yet the distinctive Welsh character of each offered truth is that it is simultaneously political and cultural. This is a mode of argument, but perhaps even more of assumption, which has often seemed alien and unacceptable east of Offa's Dyke, though its relevance to the English experience can be shown to be just as direct. Within Wales, the two truths, or those versions of them which are reciprocally dismissed as inadequate, are matters of intense and often bitter controversy. Indeed perhaps the least known fact, by others, about contemporary Welsh culture and politics is that there are harsh and persistent quarrels within a dimension which is seen from outside as unusually singular. The nearest analogy I can find is with what is known in England, more properly in London, as the Hard Left, where a confidently named sector, marked off from all others, is often riven by controversies more bitter than anything in a more established politics.

Yet there is, after all, a distinguishable Hard Left, and in the same sense a distinguishable Welsh culture. Each can be tracked in its general affiliations, but the more profound community is its area of discourse: the very specific issues which it selects for argument. For myself, when I say 'two truths', it is not from some sense of detachment or balance but because, seeing the matter in my own living conditions from both inside and outside, I am especially aware of the common elements of authenticity in each apparently alternative case.

The argument for an essential cultural continuity, informing a people long threatened by suppression, is well made in Emyr Humphreys's *The Taliesin Tradition*. At one level the book can be usefully read as a history of Welsh literature, by one of the finest of modern Welsh writers. Indeed I am tempted to a review which would simply insist that English students of literature should read it, since it remains a scandal that a body of writing of this substance, composed on this island, should be so largely unknown to readers of strict literary interests. A general impression from Matthew Arnold will not do. The major verse of Dafydd ap Gwilym and the romances of *Pedair Cainc y Mabinogi* (in English the *Mabinogion*) are evident classics in the writing of this island. Moreover the interest of several Welsh verse forms is considerable. Even polemically, one must wonder at the students of Hopkins who do not know *cynghanedd* (a set of techniques still practised).

> Fy ing enfawr, fy ngwynfd-fy mhryder
> Fy mhradwys hyfryd;
> Ei charu'r wyf yn chwerw hefyd
> A'i chasau'n serchus o hyd.

Alan Llwyd

This *englyn*, as so often, is dependent on particular Welsh assonances, but in at least some cases, and certainly in Dafydd ap Gwilym and the *Mabinogi*, the achievements are accessible in translation. Consider only this brief extract from the technique of a rapid sequence of metaphors and comparisons, the *dyfalu*, in Dafydd's poem on the seagull as love messenger: 'a piece of the sun, a steel glove at sea, and yet swift and proud and light on the wave, fish fed, foam footed, lily of the sea, contemplative of the wave, like a written page, speak for me.'

Yet Emyr Humphreys has written much more than a literary story. He argues that the continuous poetic tradition, named from the first Taliesin, the sixth-century poet of the British kingdom of Rheged (now south-west Scotland), has 'contrived to be a major factor in the maintenance, stability and continuity of the Welsh identity and the fragile concept of Welsh nationhood'. The difficulties attending this argument are almost too obvious. The land now known as Wales, the people now known as Welsh, have experienced over those long centuries so many major changes of use and condition that continuity, except in the language, and even there in eventual decline, seems a merely mythical construct. Indeed, in an earlier phase of what appears to be the same argument, in a dominant tendency within a revived Welsh nationalism between the wars, the construct was plainly ideological. Against all the modern political experience of Wales, this tendency was on the cultural Right then influential throughout Europe. Wales was offered by some as the last noble fragment of a classical and catholic world. Welshness had the function of 'Englishness' in Leavis or of 'timeless' in Eliot: a stand of old values against a destructive industrial civilisation. Its most memorable expression was a poem 'The Deluge', by the nationalist leader Saunders Lewis, which began:

> The tramway climbs from Merthyr to Dowlais,
> Slime of a snail on a heap of slag.

That industrial landscape or wasteland was accurately observed, but the sting was the judgment: 'here once was Wales.' It is then unsurprising that the inhabitants of that landscape, now the great majority of the Welsh, and with English as their main or only language, rejected a sense of Wales and of Welshness which seemed designed to exclude them.

Emyr Humphreys's argument is different, or partly different (he quotes the Saunders Lewis poem with apparent approval, or at least without dissent). He sees the myth-making that is at work in any construction of a 'timeless identity', but then argues: 'The manufacture and proliferation of myth must always be a major creative activity among people with unnaturally high expectations reduced by historic necessity, or at least history, forced into what is often described as a marginal condition. In fact this marginal condition is now the essence of the human condition, with or without material security: we can bear even less than a little reality when it hovers over our heads in the shape of a nuclear missile.' Part of this connects with an argument which I have used myself: that the long Welsh experience of a precarious and threatened identity has informed Welsh thought with problems now coming through to once dominant and assertive peoples: most evidently, in our own time, the English. Yet the argument can then move in several ways. The most common, as in much Modernist writing and very strongly in serious North American culture, is an attachment to the dynamics of mobility. Old and dissolving identities are at best raw material for an exchange of new and deliberately provisional universals, on which settled identity is the past from which there must be escape to the precarious and invigorating excitement of the new. In Wales, among otherwise different tendencies, the argument has not gone this way. This is what makes its writers and thinkers – traditionally based in a social status and obligation wholly different from the idea of the isolated artist or intellectual – a centre of opposition to the dominant literary and intellectual modes of Western Europe and North America. For the major Welsh response to the dissolutions of community and identity, which have been so repeatedly and directly experienced, has been to make, or to try to remake, communities and identities which will hold.

Emyr Humphreys finds these in a cultural tradition. Dai Smith, as a vigorous exponent of the second truth, finds them in the communal struggles and loyalties of a Welsh industrial proletariat. Yet even within this contrast there are shared assumptions. In a recent radio report on the people of the mining valleys during the present bitter coal strike, Dai Smith said that the three words he kept hearing were 'culture', 'community' and 'jobs'. The first two are not the classical words of an industrial proletariat, as universally theorised. Indeed they are words which I have been so whacked for using in England, as if they were my private inventions or deviations, that this reminder of a genuine area of shared discourse was especially welcome. Among some English Marxists this strain has been tagged as 'culturalist'. It is to be hoped that some of them at least will notice that this is the language of what has been, in the worst days so far of the strike, the most solid working class of the British coalfields.

Dai Smith, in *Wales! Wales?* a book based on his recent television series, attacks Emyr Humphreys's argument directly. He accuses him of confusing the 'functional role of myths' with a 'deliberate myth-ologising'. The risk is undoubtedly there. To accommodate the evident changes in Welsh life, which as one of its most distinguished modern recorders Emyr Humphreys knows very well, there is a shift within the concept of continuity. This is expressed with reference to one of the themes of the literature: Taliesin the shape-shifter. At a simple level this is merely suggestive, but it is potentially indicative of an observable historical process: at its weakest, the endless fantasies of a subjected people, magnifying past greatness or present uniqueness as forms of disguise not only from others but from hard-pressed selves; at its strongest, however, a capacity for active and flexible survival, in which powers of a certain kind – hope, fidelity, eloquence – are repeatedly distilled from defeat. The test of the strongest sense would then be the welcoming admission of the latest shift: not as the abandonment of 'Welshness', in some singular and unitary form, but as the positive creation of a still distinctively Welsh, English-speaking working-class culture.

It is here, on the ground, that the schools and parties divide, though in adversity they are now speaking with each other in some new ways. An economic analyst said recently that there is no Welsh economy: there are two city regions, Cardiff and Swansea; there is upland pastoral Wales; and there is Greater Liverpool. This is a familiar type of identification of 'regions' within what we call the Yookay. What has then to be asked, though, is why there is such pressure, from many different positions, to hold to some version of a unifying identity, within and across some of the most radical differences of condition that can be found anywhere in Europe. Whether any of its processes are 'functional myths' or 'deliberate mythologising' is being very sharply tested, all the time, in practice. The recent tentative emergence of a new kind of National Left is the most significant current attempt, but then its mood is decidedly not mythical, in either sense. The shift-shape it is attempting is material to the core: the remaking of a land and a people.

One of the most striking facts about the second truth, in industrial South Wales, is that the remarkable school of modern historians of which Gwyn A. Williams is the leading member and to which Dai Smith is a vigorous contributor, had no sooner got their work into print, in what was consciously described as a restoration of memory, than events as dramatic as they had described, and in some cases uncannily of the same kind, began to occur in the very valleys which they had recorded and mapped. The months from spring 1984 have been in many ways like a fast re-run of what was being researched and studied as labour history. In one sense, the repetitions are dislocating, since so much has so clearly changed; the miners themselves, for example, have been pressed back over the years, in apparently endless pit closures, to a small minority. Yet there is another, primary sense of an affirmed location. I have stood with easy and friendly men and women, organising communally donated food for the two hundred babies born in Gwent mining families during the strike, packing their thousand plastic bags a day of basic adult food, and heard the precise words of the histories: the closeness with each other, the intense determination and anger against those who are now so clearly and exultantly their enemies. As so often in Welsh history, there is a special strength in the situation of having been driven down so far that there is at once everything and nothing to lose, and in which all that can be found and affirmed is each other.

It needs only a small shift of position, beyond the crowded closeness of the valleys, to see this communal spiritual energy as tragic. But then this is another paradox of the second prologue. The story of Welsh labour is shot through with suffering, and militant formations are repeatedly on the record. Yet a major strain of the culture of the valleys, well brought out by Dai Smith, is a high-spirited, mocking, even brash style: best exemplified, perhaps, in a literary sense, in the development of that remarkable novelist Gwyn Thomas. His first, unpublished novel was *Sorrow for Thy Sons*, bitter and angry in the suffering of 1935. By the 1950s he was producing those hilarious novels and stories, the most agonisingly funny writing in English in his time, which were not only his but a quite general response to a devastation which had forced many into a hopeless and ironic laughter. The tone is very far from the grave voices of the major Welsh tradition; the alternatives of the prologues are stark in this. Yet his late work is consonant with a quite different kind of energy, in which the industrial Welsh were bypassing the muted tones of English culture for their version of the brash expansiveness of North Americans. Something like this happened also, more generally, in the English working class, as they used cinema and then television, but until recently there was this difference: that these popular and studied-popular styles extended, without break of connection, to some of the most gifted writers and poets. From Welsh-language Wales this was often seen, as earlier in the case of Dylan Thomas's *Under Milk Wood*, as a vulgar, Anglicised betrayal of 'Welshness'. Yet Anglicised, at least, it was not. The work of the English-language writers of industrial South Wales is unmistakably indigenous; its English in tone and rhythm is not an English literary style. There seems good justification, in these writers and in the everyday speech of the valleys, for the recent significant assertion, from within what has been the 'nationalist' tendency, that English is a Welsh language. A distinctive culture is using that diverse and flexible language for its own unmistakably native writing and speech.

There remain problems inside both truths. There are moments in Dai Smith's engagingly exuberant presentation when the gesture towards North America, the intellectually and emotionally sophisticated movement outwards from the confines of a narrow inherited tradition, sits uneasily beside the simple and heartfelt proletarian continuities. This is especially so at a time when many of the same external forces are directly allied, in their presentation of a desirable social world, with the forces which are working to break up not only a restricted working-class culture but all the values which have gathered, under long pressure, around both class and place. Yet again, in the other kind of account, there is the problem of relating Emyr Humphreys's new novel *Jones* to the thesis of *The Taliesin Tradition*. At one level, the smart, empty, fashionable Jones – the Welsh émigré on the make – is precisely caught. It takes one back, though more explicitly, to the experiences of his very fine early novel, *Hear and Forgive*, where the structures of dislocated mobility are more deeply explored than in that later run of English novels of the 'fifties which made the theme fashionable. Yet back where Jones came from, in that hill farm which is so often seen as the homeland of Welshness, there is shown so deep a native failure that quite new questions are raised. Is this, after all, an old way of life which not only from outside pressures but from something in itself could not shape and hold and inform its own people? It is the last bitter question about Wales: the nature of the Welsh who have turned their backs on it, within and outside the country, or who have settled for some portable, export-style facsimile.

It is probable, taking it all in all, that we can as yet engage few English readers in the intricate internal culture and politics of Wales, though its themes, so intensively explored, are close and coming closer to the English condition. It is possible to strike out on a quite different path, as Jan Morris has done in *The Matter of Wales*. The book is engagingly inward with Welsh landscape and history, though whenever it came very close (as in my case on the Black Mountains) I heard a different, informed and sympathetic but observing, voice. In its presentation, however, it is outward: a long open journey through the diversity of Wales, more accessible and I would expect more persuasive than those internal voices of which the interested reader from elsewhere must always wish that he or she had come in at the beginning, to get the shape of the discourse and to understand all the references back. Here, for a certainty, is a book to make other readers want to see and know more of Wales: that interest which has in fact been growing so strongly in England but which in parts of Wales, in ways that can eventually be explained, is treated as a sort of final insult.

This then may be the paradox. The English reader who wants to be better-informed about Wales itself can go to Jan Morris. The same reader who wants to know what, locked in with themselves, the Welsh have contributed and are contributing to European politics and letters can go to Emyr Humphreys and Dai Smith and that whole vigorous school of contemporary Welsh writers and historians.

1985

Review of *The Taliesin Tradition: A Quest for the Welsh Identity* by Emyr Humphreys (1984), *Jones: A Novel* by Emyr Humphreys (1984), *Wales! Wales?* by Dai Smith (1984) and *The Matter of Wales: Epic Views of a Small Country* by Jan Morris (1984)

Wales and England

It can be said that the Welsh people have been oppressed by the English State for some seven centuries. Yet it can then also be said that the English people have been oppressed by the English State for even longer. In any such general statements all the real complications of history are temporarily overridden. Even the names, when they are examined, begin to blur or dissolve. As late as the nineteenth century, radical Englishmen were still identifying oppression as the 'Norman Yoke', which had been clamped on the necks of free Saxons. Down to our own day, some radical Welshmen mutter the comparable curse of the 'English Yoke'. Neither party is mistaken about the facts of oppression and exploitation, but how these are interpreted is a matter for argument. The Norman State; the Anglo-Norman State; the English State; the British State: at different points in this sequence the real complications begin to reveal themselves. Earlier again, how do we understand what the Cymry said of those same free Saxons or English, or what they said and must have said of 'their own' British Princes?

In a period of great tension and of necessary conflict it is especially important to be sure about names. In our own quite exceptional difficulties, it is especially important to be sure of what Welshmen mean by 'English'. I grew up in border country, where the names learned at school were of general and rather vague geographical areas: England to the East, Wales to the West, and where we were, too small for the maps, a village in Monmouthshire, coloured this way or that, or dubiously hatched, by what seemed the mapmaker's fancy. As I learned a little history I saw not border but frontier country: the decaying Norman castles, quite literally overlooking us. Yet one of the worst ravagers of our immediate land had been English Harold, killed by the Normans at Hastings. But then as we used the castles for picnics, and looked up the closer history and statistics, there was a new

64

administrative entity: England-and-Wales. Meanwhile, where we were, we spoke English but recited Welsh poems at anniversaries and sang in English or Welsh at the village eisteddfod. It was a place to find intimations of complexity. As Emyr Humphreys put it, introducing one of my readings: not *Border Country* by Raymond Williams but *Raymond Williams* by Border Country.

It is not now the personal history that matters, but the learned perspective of England. In the politics anxiously watched by a schoolboy in the 'thirties, there was the British Empire, sedulously taught but by me sullenly cursed in our Welsh grammar school, and then somewhere in the pages of the *Daily Herald*, for repulsion more than attraction but in any case for definition, an England which was an amalgam of Neville Chamberlain and Sir Samuel Hoare and Lord Halifax, of Jubilee and Coronation, of London and the Home Counties. (I puzzled for years about those Home Counties: home to whom or for what?) So potent, indeed, was this offensive amalgam that it almost obliterated further questions. Anything that was not it had attractions: the Welsh rugby team, outrucking Chamberlain and Hoare and Halifax and the young toffs they'd persuaded to stand in for them; or Konni Zilliacus and the League of Nations and the Soviet pavilion in Paris, none of these Home Counties; or then, suddenly, Yorkshire people, who were not Home Counties either but who vigorously insisted not only that they were English – I had a go at arguing them out of it – but that they were the real English, not that lot down there.

This was not just a village boy's perspective. Many years later I had a difficult argument with a highly educated Belgian friend, who had just seen the Beatles on television and then, at closer quarters, some visiting Liverpool football fans, and who asked, with some insistence, what on earth had happened to the English, who were well known to be emotionally reserved, quietly behaved, and decently and soberly dressed. When I tried to say that *these* English – with a few Liverpool Irish but then there were to be other football fans, from London and Manchester and Birmingham – had been there all the time but he'd only just seen them, I could feel his world trembling. He *knew*, as we in Wales sometimes *know*, what England is, what the English are. And what was known just happened to exclude both the great majority and most of the diverse minorities of the actual English. England, that for me still awful and sobering name, was for these actual English many quite different things. But for most of the rest of us, England – we can surely see it now – was this dominant English class, these alien figures

65

who ruled us and disposed of us; but there all the time, when we went to visit or live among them, all those other incongruous, incompatible English.

Well, that is their problem though until they solve it there will be not much peace for the rest of us. But it won't help, either side of the border, to mistake the state for the real identity, or the projections for the people. What we can do positively, meanwhile, is explore those regions of habit or argument in which the differentials of Wales, and thus its effective relations with England, are asserted or denied.

We need not stay long in one of the most populated regions, that of race. The ethnic history of what is now Wales is one of extreme complexity, from the earliest times. There seem to be quite basic differences between the Neolithic and Bronze Age settlers and the Iron Age arrivals, though in legend and platitude all tend to be assimilated in terms of the subsequent contrast with 'Saxons' and to be confused as Celts. When this last difficult description is asserted, we have to reply that, on the available evidence, the 'Celts' were the first invading linguistic imperialists. We have also to remember, near the roots of some modern loyalties, that the 'old language' which has been so central to the identity of Wales was the product of an ex-colonial situation in which the native language, British, had been profoundly modified by the imperial language, let in.

Then in terms of people in the implied racial sense, we have to remember not only the premodern immigrations from Ireland and England and even Scotland, but the fact that very large numbers of the Cymry or pre-Cymry went on living in what is now England, and their dependants are among those we now gaze at as the English. Modern movements of population have been even more drastic and they have occurred both ways and in a multitude of directions, to say nothing of the long complexities of intermarriage. Many modern Welshmen must, on the record, be third or fourth generation English and Irish and Scottish immigrants. Sometimes the names tell us this, but often not, since females have lost their family names. Beyond this, of course, that devastation of naming systems imposed by English administration has left us with some of the most radical identity confusions of any modern people. We do not even have wholly to deny some possible genetic correlations with personality and culture, or those observable clusters of some physical features – trends and emphases within a most complex map – to continue to insist that the significant differentials are not in this region at all.

The differentials of culture are altogether more serious. Yet I have spent so much of my working life trying to analyse culture that here too, but now more positively, I have to emphasise great complexity. The central problem is that there are, on the one hand, some very significant continuities and, on the other hand, some unusually drastic changes of direction and periods of effective remaking. The central continuity is of course the language, and this remains critical to cultural identity not only in those who have retained or are re-acquiring it, but even in many of those to whom it is now lost or marginal. The Welsh/English language differential is then quite fundamental, and direct or indirect action by English administration and education against the native language is not only unforgiveable – that is an old score – but must still lead to the most intense and active resistance.

What then needs also to be said, however, is that there is another kind of significant differential – how that majority of the Welsh who have lost their native language now speak and write English. It is true that within Wales this is not greatly noticed, and also that in certain situations, involving relations with the native language, it can even be resented, as the mongrel mark of the 'Anglo-Welsh'. But in relations between Wales and England it is still a most significant differential of a kind which fosters some effective cultural identity. We have only to think of other places where something like this has happened (it is most visible, though not really most important, in literary production – the identifiably Irish writers in English; the English Northern poets and entertainers) to realise that it does indeed matter. It is significant both as a cultural dimension of an otherwise merely geographical or administrative area and, against heavy pressures of standardisation as an unforced and steadily available community.

There is then an area which I find much more intractable. It is clear, to start with, that we can make a significant contrast between the Welsh and English literary traditions. Welsh literature, for quite basic reasons of language and conventions – and even where there has been, as in the later centuries, traceable and important English influence – is in no sense a region of English literature but is at once autonomous and important. What is then difficult, however, is the quite common extrapolation from literary evidence to a more general cultural identity. The idea that the spirit of a people is essentially expressed in its literature obviously speaks to some real situations, but in its ordinary form it speaks to too many, and in the end falsely. Indeed one of the strongest and least noticed English influences on Welsh thought is just this version of cultural nationalism, in which the continuity and inner essence of a people is discovered in a (selective) version of its 'national' literature.

Of course writing in any time and space bears the marks and carries the factors of its time and space. The relative (changing) continuity of a language carries many of these marks and factors into a further perceptible space. But to jump from this complex process, which is in fact always being remade and reinterpreted, to such concepts as continuity and essence is to reproduce that ideology which was forged in the composition of nation-states. It is then not only peculiarly inappropriate to Wales. In its false projections it disguises the more substantial and interesting process of certain autonomies hard won within a subordination.

It is this mixed and uneven process which is the true and complex cultural identity of Wales. The ideology which overrides it, compounding Aneirin and Dafydd ap Gwilym and Daniel Owen and distilling ideal qualities from the forced compound, is not just wrong but hostile. For if there is one thing to insist on in analysing Welsh culture it is the complex of forced and acquired discontinuities: a broken series of radical shifts, within which we have to mark not only certain social and linguistic continuities but many acts of self-definition by negation, by alternation and by contrast. Indeed it is this culture of Wales, profoundly and consciously problematic, which is the real as distinct from the ideological difference from a selective, dominant and hegemonic English culture.

It would take a book to trace this whole process, for which we are only now, in the work of a new generation of committed and critical Welsh historians, getting enough of the detail. One central area would be analysis of the cultural impulses towards democratic community, which have been regularly discussed. Now I do indeed believe that these impulses are stronger in Welsh than in majority English culture, though there can be no simple contrast, and the political effect, which is very complicated, needs to be separately discussed. At the broadest cultural level it is possible to see real relations beween twentieth-century expressions of these impulses, as in Waldo Williams and those influenced by him and the popular cultural initiatives of non-conformism and of the revival centred on the modern *eisteddfod*. But that is not an essence, it is a history.

Moreover it is a complicated history. Nonconformism, with its great cultural values of self-organisation and common literacy, came in over the English border. At one level, indeed, some of the crucial initiations which were specifically English for other reasons, within the general subordination, had a great store of readiness and longing and potential energy, which came to give the movement quite specific passions and intensities. Much the same was to happen, later, with trade unionism. The intensity of the specific Welsh development is a great and continuing modern value. But unless we relate it, at every point, to the long experience of defeat and subordination, we project a quite false essential autonomy. The religious history of Wales is indeed very complicated, and there are some important distinctions to be made between the old Marches, where the interaction with England was most direct, and the old Principality. But we can never exclude from any of its phases the element of seeking an alternative to the current *and changing* forms of English cultural dominance. An earlier Royalist Wales is not easily included in the projection of a radical and democratic Welsh essence, but it makes more sense that Wales was like that when England was going the other way. The cultural forms in which a subordinated people try to express their distinctive identity can be specifically quite discontinuous, and these discontinuities are better related to the realities of subordination than to the idealisations of a submerged essence.

Thus it makes little sense, in my opinion, to connect modern democratic cultural impulses with the customs and beliefs of the old Cymry. It is not that we will fail to find some resemblances, nor that some of the earlier ideals are unavailable, as an idealising and inspiriting mode, to a later and very different world. But the fixed forms of a retrospective essence can be very deceptive. There is an exact analogy in English culture, in the idea of the 'Norman Yoke' and the earlier free Saxon England. The image of a lost communal freedom could sustain and motivate oppressed and otherwise despairing people, but we all know quite well that no English or Welsh radical, from the seventeenth century onwards, could be content for a moment to live within the archaic tribal and early feudal structures of those past English or Welsh centuries. And yet it cannot be a case of merely deriding the idealisation; that, in its turn, would overlook some relevant exemplary communal experiences. The real situation is that in the difficult process of enduring, understanding and then trying to find ways of resisting subordination, there is a very complex creation of images of the past as a way of amending images of the present and of finding images of the future. This very complex creation is surely evident again in the modern national cultural revival.

Thus the experience of England was obviously a leading factor in the revival of forms of Welsh culture. This is so not only in some of the significant sites of the more organised revival, among London exiles or in the border counties. It is so also in the consonance of some of its forms (including the familiar admixture of forgery and fantasy) with contemporary English and European forms of the revival of folk culture and the cult of medievalism. It is still extremely difficult to disentangle these modes – in the forms of the modern Eisteddfod or the Gorsedd, or in attitudes towards early and medieval Welsh literature, and especially the romances – from those elements of continuity and recovery which can properly be seen as, and which undoubtedly eventually became, general impulses towards autonomy and, interacting with the intense nonconformist culture, a genuine popular revival. But in any case this revival is the working through of a history, among now radically dislocated as well as subordinated people, rather than the fortunate re-emergence of a subdued essence.

It is in interpreting this history that the real modern relations between Wales and England begin to come into focus. The history of the period of simple subordination is, in its most general outlines, reasonably clear. English law and political administration were ruthlessly imposed, within an increasingly centralised 'British' state. The Welsh language was made the object of systematic discrimination and, where necessary, repression. Succeeding phases of a dominant Welsh landowning class were successfully Anglicised and either physically or politically drawn away to the English centre. Anglicising institutions, from the boroughs to the grammar schools, were successfully implanted. All these processes can properly be seen as forms of political and cultural colonisation.

But then two major and related economic developments changed the shape of these basic relations. English capital and English management penetrated a relatively underdeveloped economy, inaugurating the major industrial development of iron and coal. At the same time, the rural economy was penetrated in new ways and, even more significantly, was marginalised. Lines of communication, from the turnpike roads to the new railways and canals, were driven through Wales on bearings evidently determined by the shape of the larger economy and trading system (and indeed of the larger political system, in the routes to Ireland). Few of these were ever related to the internal needs of Wales, as a developing country or (as the Rebecca 'rioters' of 1843 recognised) to the customs and needs of the traditional rural economy. The exploitation of Welsh iron and coal for the expanding British industrial and then imperial system went alongside the ruin, from other parts of the same system, of small Welsh rural industries and, even more generally, alongside the increasing marginalisation of Welsh within a marginalised British agriculture.

At many levels, within these complex and devastating processes, Welsh people resisted what was being done to them. Resistance ranged from the Merthyr Rising and militant trade unionism in the industrial areas to Rebecca and the tithe struggles in the rural areas. But, given the complexity of the process as a whole, and especially the radically differential internal responses – of industrial conflict within rapid economic development and of agrarian conflict within impoverishment, depopulation and marginalisation – it was and has remained difficult either to confine or to unify these vigorous and diverse struggles within a national Welsh–English perspective. Indeed, on one count, it is surprising that there was as much national feeling as there was: a common perception of identity, within such diverse situations and conflicts. That this identity was primarily cultural – in language, customs, kinship and community – rather than in any modern sense political is, in this situation, not surprising at all.

It is equally not surprising that over and above this cultural identity large numbers of Welsh people found temporarily effective political identity in wider movements which then in new ways incorporated them: the ideology of Empire, in which there was so much direct (though as between coal and farming contradictory) interest; the ideology and organisation of Liberalism, at once the expression of local radicalism and, in its wider bounds, the means of its containment and displacement; the ideology and organisation of Labourism, at first an expression of local militancy and correctly perceived class conflict but again, in its wider bounds, the eventual means of containment and displacement.

The main point is not that each of these phases was marked by certain specificities of Welshness, as most notably in Liberalism and Labourism where the quality and quantity of Welsh contributions were significantly proportionately high. It is that in each of these phases – and the third is not yet concluded – the complexity of relations between these successive effective incorporations and the continuing (distinguishing or contradictory) self-identification as the Welsh was bound to be extreme. This complexity can be seen both positively and negatively.

Negatively, it has led not only to division but to self-division, as people have found themselves caught in what are ultimately incompatible interests and loyalties, which they yet have urgent and often desperate need to try to unify, so that their conditions might be improved. At its most negative, this has led, on the one hand, to archaic or residual types of nationalism, in which a received, traditional and unproblematic identity has been asserted as overriding all those modern economic and political relations which are in fact inevitable and determining. It has led, on the other hand, to pseudo-modernist rejections of the specificities of Welshness and the Welsh situation, in which the confident imperatives of the incorporation – a transforming Liberalism, a redeeming and transforming Labourism – are repeated long after they have practically failed, both at the centre and in Wales itself. The pseudo-modernist rejections have typically included, also, a particular spitefulness against all or any counter-vailing Welsh specificities; a distinguishing Welsh form of anti-Welshness, finding only partial and insufficient excuse in the excesses of romantic nationalism. It is within these negative forms of the central complexities that much of the surface politics of contemporary Wales is still conducted, and the negative effects have to be reckoned as still predominant (as the 1979 referendum on devolution so damagingly showed).

But the complexity can also be seen positively. As earlier, in certain phases of the culture, the painful recognition of real dislocations, discontinuities, problematic identities has led not only to division and confusion but to new and higher forms of consciousness. It is true that these are very difficult to disentangle from the available forms of description and statement, as is clear in the latest phase of nationalism. But it is, for example, very significant that one tendency in contemporary Welsh nationalism is, so to say, an anti-nationalist nationalism. This has important cultural precedents, in suspicion of any centralised state. But it is also a correct and far-reaching response to certain dominating contemporary political and economic develop-ments, which are outdistancing all earlier forms.

Perception of the relations between Wales and England is then radically affected. New insights are forming beyond the old perspectives of England as the conqueror, the coloniser, the exploiter and even the big neighbour. It is not only a matter of the visible weakening of England, in the aftermath of the weakening and dissolution of the British Imperial order. It is also a matter of the visible weakening of centralised nation-states and economies of just that English size: their inability to maintain political and economic autonomies and sovereignties of the traditional kind; their further inability, as they are themselves increasingly economically and politically penetrated, to maintain their old kinds of singular relation with their peripheral and dependent areas. Many of the things that happened, over centuries, to the Welsh are now happening, in decades, to the English. The consequent confusion and struggle for identity, the search for new modes of effective autonomy within a powerfully extended and profoundly interacting para-national political and economic system, are now in many parts of the world the central issues of social consciousness, struggling to come through against still powerful but residual ideas and institutions.

Of course the surviving power of England – the specific power of its ruling political and economic class – still presses heavily on Wales as on other marginalised communities, including many of the regions of England itself. But at many levels, from the new communal nationalisms and regionalisms to the new militant particularisms of contemporary industrial conflicts, the flow of contemporary politics is going beyond the modes of all the incorporated ideologies and institutions. If only because the Welsh have been inside these cross-pressures for much longer, because we have had to learn if we could not solve the real contradictions between nationality and class, or local wellbeing and the imperatives of a large-scale system, we may be further along the road to a relevant if inevitably painful contemporary social consciousness. But in any case the ideological defences of the old and now disintegrating system are less powerful, though they are still powerful enough to be damaging, in confused and peripheral Wales than in bewildered and ex-central England. What seemed a sectoral problem and impetus, to be dressed or dissolved in mere local colour, is now more and more evidently a focal problem and impetus: not particular to but to a significant extent particularised in Wales.

It is not possible to see any quick or easy way out of the present confusions and complexities. The euphoria of first insights, and of the energy and comradeship they have generated, is likely to have to endure more delay, more quarrelling, more frustration than is ordinarily at all allowed for. Even the authentically differential radicalism of the Welsh, as analysed by Hechter and still residually widely celebrated, will be put to many new tests. For if radicalism is merely the Liberal Establishment and Labour Loyalism – both demonstrably stronger in Wales than in England – it could quickly rot, is indeed already rotting, from the inside. Again the authentically differential communalism of the Welsh, product of a specific history rather than of some racial or cultural essence, could become residual if it does not grow beyond its current elements of false consciousness. The ideological notion, for example, that Wales is classless, because we do indeed have easier immediate ways of speaking to each other, could become a powerful barrier to that practical communalism which requires difficult transformations of political and economic institutions and relations, rather than friendly and informal accommodations to them. The differentials that still matter will have to be taken very much further, and in new and contemporary terms, if they are not to decline into accommodating illusions. Radical and communal Wales, that is to say, will be real to the extent that it develops, in plan and practice, new forms of co-operative work and communal socialism, new kinds of educational and cultural collectives, rather than by what happens to the Labour or even the Nationalist vote.

These are hard things to say, but then the general situation, between Wales and England, has been and remains hard and complex. Indeed the harder we now are, especially with ourselves, the better we shall be, including better, beyond 'England', with the English.

1983

The City and the World

The country and the city are changing historical realities, both in themselves and in their interrelations. Moreover, in our own world, they represent only two kinds of settlement. Our real social experience is not only of the country and the city, in their most singular forms, but of many kinds of intermediate and new kinds of social and physical organisation.

Yet the ideas and the images of country and city retain their great force. This persistence has a significance matched only by the fact of the great actual variation, social and historical, of the ideas themselves. Clearly, the contrast of country and city is one of the major forms in which we become conscious of a central part of our experience and of the crises of our society. But when this is so, the temptation is to reduce the historical variety of the forms of interpretation to what are loosely called symbols or archetypes: to abstract even these most evidently social forms and to give them a primarily psychological or metaphysical status.

This reduction often happens when we find certain major forms and images and ideas persisting through periods of great change. Yet if we can see that the persistence depends on the forms and images and ideas being changed – though often subtly, internally, and at times unconsciously – then we can see also that the persistence indicates some permanent or effectively permanent need, to which the changing interpretations speak.

I believe that there is indeed such a need, and that it is created by the processes of a particular history. But if we do not see these processes, or see them only incidentally, we fall back on modes of thought which seem able to create the permanence without the history. We may find emotional or intellectual satisfaction in this, but we have then dealt with only half the problem, for in all such major interpretations it is the coexistence of persistence and change which is really striking and interesting, and which we have to account for without reducing either fact to a form of the other.

The ideas of the city and the country are among the major cases to which this problem applies. It is clear, for example, that the convention of the country as a settled way of life disturbed by unwanted and external change has been complicated, in our own century, by very similar ideas about towns and cities. The complaints of rural change might come from threatened small proprietors, or from commoners, or even, in the twentieth century, from a class of landlords, but it is fascinating to hear some of the same phrases – destruction of local communities, the driving out of small men, indifference to settled and customary ways – in the innumerable campaigns about the effects of redevelopment, urban planning, and airport and motorway systems in so many twentieth century towns and even, very strongly, in parts of London. I have heard a well argued defence of Covent Garden, against plans for development, which repeated in almost every particular the defence of the commons in the period of parliamentary enclosures.

Clearly, ideas of the country and the city have specific contents and histories; but just as clearly, at times, they are forms of isolation and identification of more general processes. People have often said 'the city' when they meant capitalism or bureaucracy or centralised power, while 'the country' has at times meant everything from independence to deprivation, and from the powers of an active imagination to a form of release from consciousness. At every point we need to put these ideas to the historical realities: at times to be confirmed, at times denied.

But also, as we see the whole process, we need to put the historical realities to the ideas, for at times these express, not only in disguise and displacement, but in effective mediation or in offered and sometimes effective transcendence, human interests and purposes for which there is no other immediately available vocabulary. It is not only an absence or distance of more specific terms and concepts; it is that in country and city, physically present and substantial, the experience finds material which gives body to the thoughts.

I have traced in *The Country and the City* (1973) what I believe to be these major processes, in their major variations, within a single literature and society: a literature, English, which is perhaps richer than any other in the full range of its themes of country and city; and a society which went through a process of historical development, in rural and then industrial and urban economies and communities, very early and very thoroughly – still a particular history but one which has also become, in some central ways, a dominant mode of development in many parts of the world.

Each of the phases of this history can be looked at more deeply in itself, and there are still other ways of describing the sequence, the interaction and the development. But it is not, was not, ever a question of study alone. The very fact that the historical process, in some of its main features, is now effectively international, means that we have more than enough material for interesting comparisons. We are touching, and know that we are touching, forms of a general crisis.

Looking back, for example, on the English history, and especially on its culmination in imperialism, I can see in this process of the altering relations of country and city the driving force of a mode of production which has indeed transformed the world. I am then very willing to see the city as capitalism, as so many now do, if I can also say that this mode of production began, specifically, in the English rural economy and produced there, many of the characteristic effects – increases of production, physical reordering of a totally available world, displacement of customary settlements, a human remnant and force which became a proletariat – which have since been seen, in many extending forms, in cities and colonies and in an international system as a whole.

It then does not surprise me that the complaints in Covent Garden echo the complaints of the commoners, since the forces of improvement and development in those specific forms – an amalgam of financial and political power which is pursuing different ends from those of any local community but which has its own and specific internal rationale – are in a fundamental sense similar, as phases of capitalist enterprise.

What the oil companies do, what the mining companies do, is what landlords did, what plantation owners did and do. And many have gone along with them, seeing the land and its properties as available for profitable exploitation: so clear a profit that the quite different needs of local settlement and community are overridden, often ruthlessly. Difficult and complex as this process is, since the gains in production and the increases in new forms of work and wealth are undoubtedly real, it is usually more necessary to see this kind of contrast – between forms of settlement and forms of exploitation – than to see the more conventional contrast between agricultural and industrial development: between the country as cooperation with nature, and the city and industry as overriding and transforming it.

To be sure, there is a visible qualitative difference between the results of farming and the results of mining; but if we see only this contrast, then we see only some of the results. The effects on human settlements, and on customary or locally self determined ways of life, are often very similar. The land, for its fertility or for its ore, is in both cases abstractly seen. It is used in an enterprise which overrides, for the time being, all other considerations.

Indeed, since the dramatic physical transformations of the industrial revolution we have found it easy to forget how profoundly and still visibly agriculture altered the land. Some of the earliest and most remarkable environmental effects, negative as well as positive, followed from agricultural practice: making land fertile but also, in places, overgrazing it to a desert; clearing good land but also, in places, with the felling of trees, destroying it or creating erosion.

Some of these uses preceded any capitalist order, but the capitalist mode of production is still, in world history, the most effective and powerful agency for all these kinds of physical and social transformation. The city is only one, if now conventional, way of seeing this kind of change; and the country, as almost all of us now know it, is undoubtedly another. Indeed, the change from admiration of cultivated country to the intense attachment to 'unspoiled' places is a precise record of this persistent process and its effects in one of its most active stages.

But we must then also make a distinction between such techniques of production and the *mode* of production which is their particular social form. We call the technical changes 'improvement' and 'progress', welcome some of their effects and deplore others, and can feel either numbed or divided; a state of mind in which, again and again, the most abstract and illusory ideas of a natural rural way of life tempt or at least charm us. Or we can fall back on saying that this is the human condition: the irresolvable choice between a necessary materialism and a necessary humanity.

Often we try to resolve it by dividing work and leisure, or society and the individual, or city and country, not only in our minds but in suburbs and garden cities, town houses and country cottages, the week and the weekend. But we then usually find that the directors of the improvements, the captains of the change, have arrived earlier and settled deeper; have made, in fact, a more successful self-division. The country house was one of the first forms of this temporary resolution, and in the nineteenth century as many were built by the new lords of capitalist production as survived, improved, from the old lords, sometimes their ancestors, of the agrarian change.

It remains remarkable that so much of this settlement has been physically imitated, down to the detail of semi-detached villas and styles of leisure and weekends. An immensely productive capitalism, in all its stages, has extended both the resources and the modes which, however unevenly, provide and contain forms of response to its effects.

It is therefore often difficult, past this continuing process which contains the substance of so much of our lives, to recognise adequately the specific character of the capitalist mode of production, which is not the use of machines or techniques of improvement, but their minority ownership. Indeed, as the persistent concentration of ownership, first of the land and then of all major means of production, was built into a system and a state, with many kinds of political and cultural mediation, it was easy for the perception to diminish though the fact was increasing. Many modern ruralists, many urban conservationists, see 'the state' or 'the planners' as their essential enemy, when it is quite evident that what the state is administering and the planners serving is an economic system which is capitalist in all its main intentions, procedures, and criteria.

The motorway system, the housing clearance, the office block and supermarket replacing streets of homes and shops, may materialise in the form of a social plan, but there is no case in which the priorities of a capitalist system have not, from the beginning, been built in. It may be simple industrial development or mining: the decision will have been made originally and will be finally determined by owners calculating profit. The road system will include their needs and preferences for modes of distribution and transport, and these are given priority, either in the case of lorries against railways or in the more general situation in which the land itself is looked on, abstractly, as a transport network, just as it is looked on elsewhere, again abstractly, as an opportunity for production.

Similarly, housing clearance and housing shortage are alike related to the altered distribution of human settlement which has followed from a set of minority decisions about where work will be made available, by the criteria of profit and internal convenience. What are called regional policies are remedial efforts within these priorities rather than decisively against them. The industrial–agricultural balance, in all its physical forms of town and country relations, is the product, however mediated, of a set of decisions about capital investment made by the minority which controls capital and determines its use by calculations of profit.

When we have lived long enough with such a system, it is difficult not to mistake it for a necessary and practical reality, whatever elements of its process we may find objectionable. But it is not only that the specific histories of country and city, and of their immediate interrelations, have been determined, in Britain, by capitalism. It is that the total character of what we know as modern society has been similarly determined. The competitive indifference or the sense of isolation in cities can be seen as bearing a profound relation to the kinds of social competition and alienation which just such a system promotes. These experiences are never exclusive, since within the pressures and limits people make other settlements and attachments, and try to live by other values. But the central drive is still there.

Wordsworth saw that when we become uncertain in a world of apparent strangers who yet, decisively, have a common effect on us, and when forces that will alter our lives are moving all around us in apparently external and unrecognisable forms, we can retreat for security into deep subjectivity, or we can look around us for social pictures, social signs, social messages to which, characteristically, we try to relate as individuals but so as to discover, in some form, community. Much of the content of modern communications is this kind of substitute for directly discoverable and transitive relations to the world, and can be properly related to the scale and complexity of modern society, of which the city is always the most evident example. But it has become general, reaching to the most remote rural regions. It is a form of shared consciousness rather than merely a set of techniques.

As a form of consciousness, moreover, it is not to be understood by rhetorical analogies like the 'global village'. Nothing could be less like the experience of any kind of village or settled active community. For in its main uses it is a form of unevenly shared consciousness of persistently external events. It is what appears to happen, in these powerfully transmitted and mediated ways, in a world with which we have no other perceptible connections but which we feel is at once central and marginal to our lives. This paradoxical set of one way relationships, in itself determining what we take to be relevant information and news, is then a specific form of consciousness which is inherent in the dominant mode of production, in which, in remarkably similar ways, our skills, our energies, our daily ordering of our lives, our perceptions of the shape of a lifetime, are to a critical extent defined and determined by external formulations of a necessary reality: that external willed reality – external because its means are in minority hands – from which, in so much of our lives, we seem to have no option but to learn.

Underlying social relations often manifest themselves in these habitual and conventional ways. The communications system is not only the information network but also the transport network. The city, obviously, has always been associated with concentration of traffic. Notoriously, in modern transport systems, this is still the case, and the problem often seems insoluble. But traffic is not only a technique; it is a form of consciousness and a form of social relations. I do not mean only the obvious derivation of so many problems of traffic from a series of decisions about the location of work and the centralisation of political power; decisions which were never, in any real sense, socially made, but which were imposed by the priorities of a mode of production. I mean also the forms of modern traffic.

It is impossible, for example, to read the early descriptions of crowded metropolitan streets – the people as isolated atoms, flowing this way and that, a common stream of separated identities and directions – without seeing, past them, this mode of relationship embodied in the modern car: private, enclosed, an individual vehicle in a pressing and merely aggregated common flow; certain underlying conventions of external control but within them the passing of rapid signals of warning, avoidance, concession, or irritation, as we pursue our ultimately separate ways but in a common mode. And this is no longer only a feature of the city, though it is most evident there. Over a whole network of the land this is how, at one level, we relate; indeed, it is one form of settlement, intersecting and often deeply affecting what we think of as settlements – cities, towns, and villages – in an older mode.

In all these actual social relations and forms of consciousness, ideas of the country and the city, often of an older kind, continue to act as partial interpreters. But we do not always see that in their main bearings they are forms of response to a social system as a whole. Most obviously since the industrial revolution, but in my view also since the beginning of the capitalist agrarian mode of production, our powerful images of country and city have been ways of responding to a whole social development. That is why, in the end, we must not limit ourselves to their contrast but go on to see their interrelations, and through these the real shape of the underlying crisis.

It is significant, for example, that the common image of the country is now an image of the past, and the common image of the city an image of the future. That leaves, if we isolate them, an undefined present. The pull of the idea of the country is toward old ways, human ways, natural ways. The pull of the idea of the city is toward progress, modernisation, development. In what is then a tension, a present experienced as tension, we use the contrast of country and city to ratify an unresolved division and conflict of impulses, which it might be better to face in their own terms.

If we take only the images, we can swing from one to the other, but without illumination. For we have really to look, in country and city alike, at the real social processes of alienation, separation, externality, and abstraction. And we have to do this not only critically, in the necessary history of rural and urban capitalism, but substantially, by affirming the experiences which in many millions of lives are discovered and rediscovered, very often under pressure: experiences of directness, connection, mutuality, and sharing, which alone can define, in the end, what the real social deformation may be.

In the late 1940s, I knew that I was separated from the village in which I had grown up. I began to write what I thought this experience was, in the seven versions that eventually became the novel *Border Country*. It wasn't only, through those versions, that I found myself connecting the experience to a more general history of physical and social mobility, and beyond that to a crisis of education and class which, when I had worked it through, I went back and read, as if for the first time, in George Eliot and Hardy and Lawrence. It was also that I had to look at the village again and to set up some tension between my childhood memories and the adult working experience of my father's generation.

But even that was not enough. Many people have assumed that Harry Price, the signalman with his garden, was a portrait of my father; but this is not really so. I found that, to get the real movement, I had to divide and contrast what I had seen in my father as conflicting impulses and modes. I had to imagine another character, Morgan Rosser, the politician and dealer, who in his relation to Harry Price could express and work through what I believed I had seen as an internal conflict. The modes of contemplation and of action, of absorbed work and of mobile and critical change, had to be expressed in a relationship if the complicated development of the life of the village was to be fully expressed. Beyond this again was the son, the observer, more specifically removed; bound to these two modes, these two figures of a father, and taking that continuing action into his work in the city.

But at one time, while writing *Border Country*, I felt a sudden sadness, apparently separate from my theme. I felt, because I think I had been told, that the rural experience, the working country, had gone; that in Britain it was only a marginal thing, and that as time went by this would be so everywhere. I accepted this, at one level, for much longer than now seems possible. It was one of the impulses, I can see now, that kept sending me back to old rural literature and history. And I cannot clearly remember when I suddenly realised that it was not really true at all. Even while I was showing, in the novel, a different and persistent experience, this idea had stuck.

When at last I saw that it was false, I knew that I had to look for its sources. These were not only, as might be supposed, the sentimental ruralists, though just because of my experience I had to face them. They were also, and more critically, the brisk metropolitan progressives, many of them supposedly internationalists and socialists, whose contempt for rural societies was matched only by their confidence in an urban industrial future which, in one way or another – by modernisation, the white heat of technology, or revolution – they were about to convert into socialism. There are enough writers and thinkers, still, of each of these kinds, that it takes a long time, a long effort, to look round and say that their common idea of a lost rural economy is false.

Is it then not false? Is it not obvious that in Britain a working agriculture is marginal? That was the first mode of error I learned to perceive: an unnoticed persistence, in the old imperialist countries, of a kind of abstract chauvinism: that what happened to them was what was happening or would happen to everyone. Most countries in the world were still predominantly rural, but within the imperialist division of the world they did not really count, were not in important ways 'there'. Even those who saw that they were exploited, within the imperialist division of the world, did not necessarily go on to see that in and through this condition and its struggles a working agriculture, a rural economy in any of its possible forms, simply had to persist: in the exploited countries themselves, and if some elements of the exploitation were to be diminished, in what had been abstractly thought of as the developed metropolitan countries.

Perhaps more of us now know this. The facts of the food and population crisis have been widely and properly publicised. If we are to survive at all, we shall have to develop and extend our working agricultures. The common idea of a lost rural world is then not only an abstraction of this or that stage in a continuing history (and many of the stages we can be glad have gone or are going). It is in direct contradiction to any effective shape of our future, in which work on the land will have to become more rather than less important and central. It is one of the most striking deformations of industrial capitalism that one of our most central and urgent and necessary activities should have been so displaced, in space or in time or in both, that it can be plausibly associated only with the past or with distant lands. Some of this is now changing, even within old imperialist Europe. But it is still the case that the future of agriculture is seen, here and in the third world, in mainly capitalist forms, and especially as involving massive social displacement. It could be done in quite different ways. And the urgency of its doing, in ways that break with capitalism, is linked with that other complementary aspect of the crisis: the condition and the future of the cities and of industry.

One of the real merits of some rural writers, often not seen because other elements are present, is an insistence on the complexity of the living natural environment. Now that the dangers to this environment have come more clearly into view, our ideas, once again, have to shift. Some of the darkest images of the city have to be faced as quite literal futures. An insane overconfidence in the specialised powers of metropolitan industrialism has brought us to the point where, however we precisely assess it, the risk to human survival is becoming evident; or if we survive, as I think we shall, then there is the clear impossibility of continuing as we are, or with that more of the same which is still a dominant political programme.

It is necessary to say this, in the deepening crisis of modern metropolitan and industrial living, and in the more serious crisis of persistent and impracticable poverty in the rest of the world, even while we know it can easily be diverted into yet another rural threnody, or into a cynical fatalism. It is important to remember how much damage to the environment was and is being done by the capitalist mode of progressive agriculture; this is not a crisis of manufacturing industry alone.

Similarly, we need to acknowledge that recognition of the crisis, and almost all possible ways of resolving it, are functions of consciousness, of a flexible and highly mobile capacity to observe and intervene: in techniques and modes of planning and conservation, but even more critically in the area which will really decide our future – the area of decision itself. As we perceive a total environment, and as we register the consequences of so many abstracted and separated activities, we begin to see that all the real decisions are about modes of social interest and control. We begin to see, in fact, that the active powers of minority capital, in all its possible forms, are our most active enemies, and that they will have to be not just persuaded but defeated and superseded.

The scale and connection of the necessary decisions require social powers and social resources which capitalism in any of its forms denies, opposes, and alienates. The different social consciousness of the dispossessed labourers and of the urban workers, born in protest and despair, has to come through in new ways as a collectively responsible society. Neither the city will save the country nor the country the city. Rather, the long struggle within both will become a general struggle, as in a sense it has always been.

We have more to work with than we ordinarily acknowledge. Rural

England is said to be a thing of the past, and of course the changes are evident. But if we look up from the idea and back at the country, we see how much is still present, even in this exceptionally industrialised and urbanised nation. Four fifths of our land surface: the cultivated land, much of it better kept than it has ever been; the wild land, made more accessible, in a complicated process of pressure and openness. Most of the natural and working experiences which have been so powerfully celebrated in our rural literature are still directly available today.

This is still in so many places a beautiful country, and many of us can work, in different ways, to keep and enhance it. I have had the luck to thin a wood and watch the cowslips and bluebells and foxgloves come back; to repair and rebuild old drystone walls; to hedge and ditch, after long neglect, and to see from skilled men how the jobs should be done. And if we look up from the idea of the city, we find in and through the extraordinary pressures a good deal of caring and intelligent work to make the cities cleaner and finer, to bring out and build their best qualities.

To know any of this directly is to know also, very closely, the constant threat of deliberate and indifferent destruction. But each process is a fact; in the best and in the worst there is neither a lost nor a won cause; it is an active, immediate, and persistent struggle. It is also, as we shall see, a very complicated struggle, reaching into every part of our lives.

I have been arguing that capitalism, as a mode of production, is the basic process of most of what we know as the history of country and city. Its abstracted economic drives, its fundamental priorities in social relations, its criteria of growth and of profit and loss, have over several centuries altered our country and created our kinds of city. And, in its final form of imperialism, it has altered our whole world.

Seeing the history in this way, I am then of course convinced that resistance to capitalism is the decisive form of the necessary human defence. Many particular defences stop short of seeing this decisive process, and need to be challenged to take the ideas and the feelings right through. Many others, however, get through as defences, as forms of opposition to what is called the modern world, in which capitalism or technology may well be included, but with no specificity: the reflex indeed being fundamentally defensive, with no available confidence in any different way of life, or with such confidence replaced by utopian or apocalyptic visions, none of which can connect with any immediate social practice or political movement.

And what serious movement, it is asked, could there be? Look at socialism or communism: historically the enemies of capitalism, but in detail and often in principle, in matters of the country and the city, continuing and even intensifying some of the same fundamental processes.

This is a genuine historical and political difficulty. Trotsky said that the history of capitalism was the history of the victory of town over country. He then proceeded, in the critical first years of the Russian revolution, to outline a programme for just such a victory, on a massive scale, as a way of defeating capitalism and preserving socialism. Stalin carried through very much that programme, on a scale and with a brutality which made that 'victory' over the peasants one of the most terrible phases in the whole history of rural society.

To be sure, the local needs and priorities in Russia were desperate: a shattered economy and an appalling food shortage; rural capitalism, in new forms, undoubtedly spreading. But the way it was done, and the spirit in which it was done, were not only brutal; they drew on one element of an ambiguity in marxism which in its turn had massive consequences on the character of the society as a whole.

Engels was among the first to see the modern city as a social and physical consequence of capitalism: built and living in its modes. He added, later, the decisive idea that the very processes of disturbance and exposure, in those particular forms, had created a proletarian and a socialist movement which could end capitalism and create different social relations and different kinds of human settlement. In the *Communist Manifesto*, Marx and Engels agreed that 'the bourgeoisie has subjected the country to the rule of the towns, has created enormous cities, has made barbarian and semi-barbarian countries dependent on the civilised ones': the familiar history of capitalism and imperialism. They argued that these relations of centralisation and dependence had created the conditions for revolution, and in one sense they were right.

But there was an ambiguity at the core of the argument. They denounced what was being done in the tearing progress of capitalism and imperialism; they insisted that men must struggle to supersede it, and they showed us some ways. But implicit in the denunciation was another set of value judgements: the bourgeoisie had 'rescued a considerable part of the population from the idiocy of rural life'; the subjected nations were 'barbarian and semi-barbarian', the dominating powers 'civilised'. It was on this kind of confidence in the singular values of modernisation and civilisation that a major distortion in the history of communism was erected.

The exposed urban proletariat would learn and create new and higher forms of society: if that was all that had been said, it would have been very different. But if the forms of bourgeois development contained, with whatever contradiction, values higher than 'rural idiocy' or 'barbarism', then almost any programme, in the name of the urban proletariat, could be justified and imposed. The terrible irony has been that the real processes of absolute urban and industrial priority, and of the related priority of the advanced and civilised nations, worked through not only to damage the 'rural idiots' and the colonial 'barbarians and semi-barbarians', but to damage, at the heart, the urban proletarians themselves, and the advanced and civilised societies: over whom, in their turn, the priorities exercised their domination, in a strange dialectical twist. To see exposure creating revolution was one thing; to see more of the same producing more of something quite different was at best an apocalyptic hope.

This difficulty worked itself through, in a surprising way, in our own century. Revolutions came not in the 'developed' but in the 'undeveloped' countries. The Chinese revolution, defeated in the cities, went to the country and gained its ultimate strength. The Cuban revolution went from the city to the country, where its force was formed. In a whole epoch of national and social liberation struggles, the exploited rural and colonial populations became the main sources of continued revolt. In the famous Chinese phrase about world revolution, the 'countryside' was surrounding the 'cities'. Thus the 'rural idiots' and the 'barbarians and semi-barbarians' have been, for the last forty years, the main revolutionary force in the world.

We can look back, from this real historical experience, to one of the underlying forms of the idea of revolution. In some of the fundamental thinking of the socialist tradition, including that of Marx and Engels, there is a formulation which is at once the most exciting, the most relevant, and yet the most undeveloped in the whole revolutionary argument. Engels wrote of socialism as 'abolishing the contrast between town and country, which has been brought to its extreme point by present day capitalist society'. Marx and Engels wrote that the housing question could never be solved while 'modern big cities' were maintained, and that only with socialism could we restore 'the intimate connection between industrial and agricultural production'.

The utopian socialists had also made many proposals for new kinds of balanced communities and societies; William Morris continued to think in this way. But under many pressures, in the twentieth century, from the sheer physical drive of developing capitalism and imperialism to the class habits of thought of metropolitan socialist intellectuals, this extraordinary emphasis was virtually lost. Its phrases were remembered, but as an old, impractical, childish dream. Yet it is an emphasis that is now being revived. It has been stated as a direction of policy in the Chinese revolution. And it has been significantly revived, among western revolutionary socialists, as a response to the crisis of industrial civilisation and what is seen as megalopolis.

The division and opposition of city and country, industry and agriculture, in their modern forms, are the critical culmination of the division and specialisation of labour which, though it did not begin with capitalism, was developed under it to an extraordinary and trans-forming degree. Other forms of the same fundamental division are the separation between mental and manual labour, between administration and operation, between politics and social life. The symptoms of this division can be found at every point in what is now our common life: in the idea and practice of social classes; in conventional definitions of work and education; in the physical distribution of settlements; and in the temporal organisation of the day, the week, the year, the lifetime.

Much of the creative thinking of our time is an attempt to reexamine each of these concepts and practices. It is based on the conviction that the system which generates and is composed by them is intolerable and will not survive. In many areas of this thinking there are not only analytic but programmatic responses: on new forms of decision making, new kinds of education, new definitions and practices of work, new kinds of settlement and land use.

I can now look back a generation, to the immediate postwar years, and remember my feeling that, except for certain simple kinds of idealising retrospect, there was no main current of thought in the world which had not been incorporated within the fundamental forms of the capitalist and imperialist system. Orthodox communism and orthodox social democracy – its traditional opponents – indeed showed many features of this system in their most powerful forms, all the more dangerously because they had been fused with continuing aspirations to social liberation and development. But to feel this was to be pressed back toward the extreme subjectivism and fatalism which then, and for a generation, dominated our thought. Many descriptions of our current crisis were and still are cast within these subjectivist and fatalist forms.

Yet a deeper change has now become quite evident. All the conventional priorities are again being questioned. Other kinds of social response and social analysis have worked their way through, until in often confused and still unfinished forms they hold a certain initiative.

The theoretical if not practical confidence of defenders of the existing system has gone. The position in ideas is again quite open, ironically at the very time when the practical pressures are almost overwhelming.

This change of basic ideas and questions, especially in the socialist and revolutionary movements, has been for me the connection which I have been seeking for so long, through the local forms of a particular and personal crisis, and through the extended inquiry which has taken many forms but which has come through as this inquiry into the country and the city. They are the many questions that were a single question, that once moved like light: a personal experience, for the reasons I described, but now also a social experience, which connects me, increasingly, with so many others. This is the position, the sense of shape, for which I have worked. Yet it is still, even now, only beginning to form. It is what is being done and what is to be done, rather than anything that has been finally done.

For there is nothing now more urgent than to put the fundamental idea – the problem of overcoming the division of labour – to the tests of rigorous analysis, rigorous proposal, and rigorous practice. It can be done only in new forms of cooperative effort. If what is visible already as the outlines of a movement is to come through with the necessary understanding and strength, we shall have to say what in detail can be practically done, over a vast range from regional and investment planning to a thousand processes in work, education, and community.

The negative effects will, of course, continue to show themselves, in a powerful and apparently irresistible pressure: physical effects on the environment; a simultaneous crisis of overcrowded cities and a depopulating countryside, not only within but between nations; physical and nervous stresses of certain characteristic kinds of work and characteristic kinds of career; the widening gap betwen the rich and poor of the world, within the threatening crisis of population and resources; the similarly widening gap between concern and decision, in a world in which all the fallout – military, technical, and social – is in the end inescapable. And to see the negative effects, with whatever urgency, can be to paralyse the will.

The last recess of the division of labour is this recess within ourselves, where what we want and what we believe we can do seem impassably divided. We can overcome division only by refusing to be divided. That is a personal decision – but then a social action.

1973

II

A Kind of Gresham's Law

Some of the most radical questions about our present society are questions about its culture. Yet, for a number of reasons, these are still largely open questions: we have a long way to go not only in practical enquiry but also in theory. This work can be done; some of it is already in progress. But the field is made difficult, not only by its actual problems, but also by the existence of certain formulas of interpretation, that never had much evidence behind them, but that are nevertheless, for other reasons, repeated and apparently relied on. I shall briefly examine one of these formulas, which I think is particularly misleading: what is known, in discussions of culture, as 'a kind of Gresham's law'.

Gresham's Law is a proposition in economics, and the name attached to it is that of Sir Thomas Gresham (1519?–79), a financier who founded the Royal Exchange. We can read with interest of his energetic and not always scrupulous transactions in the service of several English courts, but unfortunately he did not make his Law. We first hear of Gresham's Law, in fact, in 1858, in a book called *Elements of Political Economy*, by Henry Dunning MacLeod (1821–1902). The ascription to Gresham is a mistake by MacLeod: the proposition in question had been well understood long before Gresham, and had appeared in print in Oresme and Copernicus. The law is, in its popular form, that bad money drives out good, but it will be convenient to take one or two more exact definitions:

(i) 'Where two media come into circulation at the same time, the more valuable will tend to disappear.'
(ii) 'The worst form of currency in circulation regulates the value of the whole currency, and drives all other forms of currency out of circulation.'

These, of course, do not say the same thing, but in the present context the difference is not relevant, since the application of the law to culture was in the most general terms. The application is an analogy: just as bad money drives out good, so bad culture drives out good. The terms of the definitions quoted will show how tempting the analogy was, especially as we use terms like 'currency' and 'circulation' quite ordinarily in relation to ideas.

The analogy was first made, so far as I know, by Sir Norman Angell, in the late 'twenties, in his book *The Press and the Organization of Society*. He was concerned with the effect of bad newspapers, and drew attention to

> a psychological Gresham Law; just as in commerce, debased coin, if there be enough of it, must drive out the sterling, so in the contest of motives, action which corresponds to the most primitive feelings and impulses, to first thoughts and established prejudices, can be stimulated by the modern newspaper far more easily than that prompted by rationalized second thoughts.

This is confused, but from the general argument we know what is in question: the fear that irrational thinking, and opinion masquerading as facts, will, in their widespread dissemination by bad newspapers, make rational thought and informed judgment more difficult; may even indeed, if the dissemination is wide enough, make them practically disappear. This is a fear that had often been expressed since the new journalism began in the 1850s.

But the analogy was not to rest there. The phrase, Gresham's Law, was taken up by F.R. Leavis and others, and has since been widely repeated as Leavis's influence has grown. I see it now quite often in newspapers, in magazines, and in reports of speeches. When it reached a speech in the House of Lords, it seemed that it had been finally taken into the establishment. In its repetition, its scope has been expanded. 'A kind of Gresham's Law' is now a very usual way of expressing disquiet at the amount of bad art, bad entertainment, bad writing, and bad argument in our culture, and of fearing that this flood will sweep away the kind of traditional culture that we value. The facts are serious enough, but it is a mark of our theoretical poverty that 'a kind of Gresham's Law' has been grasped so eagerly. In a field that is in fact chaotic, it sounds reassuringly scientific and authoritative.

Is There Any Real Analogy?

We should look first, not at the analogy itself, but at the facts which it offers to interpret. There is, undoubtedly, a great deal of bad art in wide circulation. There are very bad newspapers, and these the most widely bought. The public level of thinking and writing is often, for a democracy, dangerously low. There is, further, a powerful body of opinion, affecting these matters, which can be best expressed by adapting Pope:

> For ways of valuing let fools contest:
> Whate'er is best distributed is best.

I will not, in questioning the analogy, join in any apologia for these facts.

Yet is there any evidence, we must now ask, that this bad culture is driving out, or tending to drive out, the good? We should need a very detailed enquiry to answer this question adequately, and this is where 'a kind of Gresham's Law' is in practice so dangerous, for it assumes an answer which is not based on evidence, but on an analogy from another field, and the assumption leads to very questionable social attitudes. My own view in these matters is that there has been an increase in the distribution of both good and bad cultural products, in a notably expanding culture, and that this increase, both of good and bad, may be expected to continue. More people than a hundred years ago now listen to bad music, read bad novels, see bad dramatic works, and look at bad visual art, because all of these things have become technically easier to distribute, and leisure to receive them has greatly increased. Yet, also, more people than a hundred years ago now listen to good music, read good novels, see good dramatic works, and look at good visual art. These facts can be easily checked by comparing attendances at concerts, galleries and theatres of all kinds, or the sizes of publishers' editions. I know of no case in which the audience for good work has declined, or indeed failed notably to increase. It is true also, of course, that the audiences for bad work have increased in a spectacular way, over the same period, and that many hopes, based on a simple formula of extending the good life, have been falsified or not yet realised. This does not mean, however, that the experiment in universal literacy, or in making a popular culture, has failed. It is just this conclusion of failure with the consequent adoption of other social allegiances, which is the really damaging product of 'a kind of Gresham's Law'.

I will take one example: from the Press, since it was there the analogy started. In 1851, when *The Times* was at the height of its virtual monopoly of the Press, it sold 40,000 copies in a population (England, Wales and Scotland) of some twenty millions: a ratio of 1 to 500. In 1870, when the monopoly had been broken, and not only a serious provincial daily press but also a cheap metropolitan press had been established, this ratio had improved to 1 to 390. Today, with a vast popular press, and other good newspapers as competitors, the ratio has further improved to about 1 to 165 (on the latest available figures). Not only has the mid-twentieth century *Times* more than seven times as many readers as that of the mid-nineteeth century, but, when the rise in population has been allowed for, the rise in circulation is about threefold. This hardly suggests any direct working of 'a kind of Gresham's Law'. Indeed, one may be tempted to what may be called the John Walter III Law (as expressed in *The Times* of 1847):

> It is commonly said that cheap things do not interfere with the sale of good things, but that they rather diffuse a taste for the article, and in that way ultimately enlarge the class of consumers. We believe it to be so in our case.

It has been so, with *The Times*, but we must add the next sentence:

> They who start with a twopence halfpenny, or threepenny, or fourpenny journal, will soon not be satisfied with anything under a fivepenny journal.

With the ratio of the *Daily Mirror* or *Daily Express* at about 1 to 12, and still rising, we can hardly share the optimism of that 'soon'.

The fact is, surely, that we are faced with two versions of cultural change, the Utopian and the Apocalyptic, and that, on the evidence, we can accept neither. It was expected, by reformers, that cultural expansion would quite quickly produce the results *The Times* had predicted, and, when these hopes were disappointed, there was a relapse into the despair of 'a kind of Gresham's Law'. Yet the necessary theoretical revision is in fact something quite different. It would seem that in our kind of expanding culture we must expect increases in the rate of distribution of both good and bad work, and that, in the early stages of the expansion, the rate of the latter will be much higher than that of the former. Historically, it still seems to me that we are in the early stages of this cultural expansion. In the case of the cheap press, for example, the penny *Daily Telegraph* was the first wave of expansion into new sections of the middle class (242,000 in 1875), and the halfpenny *Daily Mail* the next wave (400,000 in 1898, 1,000,000 in 1915, 1,845,000 in 1930). It is only with the figures from 1915 on that we find large-scale expansion into the working class, and this did not reach its peak until the 1939–45 war and the subsequent years.

It is understandable to be impatient with what is happening, especially since in a narrow sector there has been very rapid cultural mobility and advance, in direct relation to exceptional educational opportunities. But, through the impatience, we must keep our eyes on the whole process, and refuse to surrender to an apocalyptic formula. Of course the wide distribution of bad work is affecting the good, in particular in relation to rates of profit, as the necessary capital in an expanded culture rises, and the system of production and distribution is still largely capitalist in nature. We are faced with important social decisions, as the effects of the cultural expansion become clear. But nothing, finally, is to be gained by the Gresham analogy. Bad cultural products are not really like bad money: the complex of values to which they refer is inexpressible in a single standard. There is, in fact, no simple opposition of bad and good, but a great variety of levels, the majority of which are accepted as good at the cultural level at which they are received. All criticism now is social criticism, and it is vitally important which way criticism goes: either to the assertion of cultural class distinctions, or to the direction of an expanding common culture. The key critics are those who have experienced cultural mobility, in their own persons. It is easy, in the tension which mobility causes, to go wrong in either of two opposite ways: to adopt Gresham's Law, which leads to the rejection of a 'mass culture' and confuses the democratic allegiance; or to resign, in a latter-day Utopism, pretending that bad work is not so bad because it is enjoyed by good people. The necessary balance is difficult, but it is not impossible. Values are not a kind of gold standard, but living affirmations and conclusions. If we look at our culture as it is, we may come to understand, in affirmed detail, the process and problems of cultural expansion, and to find an adequate theory in our work to enrich the change.

1958

Middlemen: The Arts Council

One of the more entertaining delusions of English public life is the belief that the man in the middle is always right. Thus if the Arts Council is under attack from both Right and Left it can conclude, falsely, that its policies are likely to be broadly correct. If the Right alleges that the Council squanders money on subversive, obscene or trivial 'art', and the Left alleges that the Council is élitist, undemocratic and unaccountable, it seems natural, under the spell of the delusion, to look comfortably down at one's feet and see the always virtuous middle ground. Yet it should be obvious that there is no middle ground between complaints and allegations of these radically different kinds. English public life is similarly misled by the metaphor of the pendulum, swinging to left and to right but always returning to the centre. We should perhaps remember that when a pendulum stays in dead centre, the clock stops.

The idea of a virtuous middle ground, proved to be virtuous because it is attacked from opposite directions, conceals one crucial assumption: that what is being attacked is itself simple and coherent. Otherwise nothing is proved, since one variation may be attacked from one position, and a quite different variation from another. Looking at the Arts Council, I find this kind of case: deep-rooted inconsistencies; incompatible variations; indeed, for all its notable efficiency in its day-to-day business, a radical incoherence. We are dealing not with a negatively defined middle ground but with a whole series of contradictions, themselves the result of many shifting and diverse intentions and pressures.

The Arts Council, historically, is a Keynesian body. That in itself goes some way to explaining its current problems. But what is really interesting is that, as in so many other institutions and policies in which Keynes had a big guiding hand, there were from the beginning uncertainties and confusions of definition and intention. These are significant both in themselves and in their continuing, often muddling effects on general policy. I will briefly recall the history because we are still under its contradictory pressures.

Keynes saw much further than most of his contemporaries, and had a much broader humanity. To recognise his distinction we have only to look at the founding meeting of CEMA (the Council for the Encouragement of Music and the Arts), the immediate predecessor of the Arts Council, before Keynes was involved. The President of the Board of Education, de la Warr, who was being asked for the money,

> was enthusiastic. He had Venetian visions of a post-war Lord Mayor's show on the Thames in which the Board of Education led the arts in triumph from Whitehall to Greenwich in magnificent barges and gorgeous gondolas; orchestras, madrigal singers, Shakespeare from the Old Vic, ballet from Sadler's Wells, shining canvases from the Royal Academy, folk dancers from village greens – in fact Merrie England.[1]

It seems fair to say that this is about as far as the English ruling class would have got on its own. Perhaps not even that far, as the dancers tried to manoeuvre in the barges or the actors shouted and the canvases shone from the gondolas. Yet this simple appropriation of the arts for a State spectacle is still their ruling perspective. From a Lord Mayor's show to a Royal Wedding, versions of the arts are selected and hired to embellish what Bagehot accurately called the theatrical apparatus of the State.

Keynes is very far beyond that. But, looking back, we can distinguish four different definitions of what a new kind of institution should do.

First, and best known, is the idea of State patronage of the fine arts. As Keynes said in a broadcast talk in 1945:

> I do not believe it is yet realised what an important thing has happened. State patronage of the arts has crept in. It has happened in a very English, informal, unostentatious way – half-baked if you like. A semi-independent body is provided with modest funds to stimulate, comfort and support any societies or bodies brought together on private or local initiative which are striving with serious purpose and a reasonable prospect of success to present for public enjoyment the arts of drama, music and painting.[2]

Second, however, and less well known – indeed now whimsical to recall – is an idea of what is in effect pump-priming. Keynes believed that in the long run the fine arts should be self supporting. As his biographer Harrod records:

> His ideal for CEMA was that at the final stage, no doubt not to be reached for a long time, it should have no disbursements except the cost of administration.[3]

Yet, third, Keynes characteristically saw such an initiative as an intervention to modify the market economy, or, perhaps more strictly, as an intervention to take the arts out of the market economy. As he had put it in 1936:

> The exploitation and incidental destruction of the divine gift of the public entertainer by prostituting it to the purposes of financial gain is one of the worser crimes of present-day capitalism. How the State could best play its proper part it is hard to say. We must learn by trial and error. But anything would be better than the present system. The position today of artists of all sorts is disastrous.[4]

Meanwhile, fourth, there is a different perspective. The public and potential public for the arts is very much larger than commonly supposed. The wartime success of CEMA, the successes of the BBC, already showed this. Earlier successful efforts to take the arts to people who had been deprived of access to them were recalled in this emerging (and temporary) consensus of belief in an expanding, serious and popular culture. As Keynes put it in 1945:

> The task of an official body is not to teach or to censor, but to give courage, confidence and opportunity. Artists depend on the world they live in and spirit of the age. There is no reason to suppose that less native genius is born into the world in the ages empty of achievement than in those brief periods when nearly all we most value has been brought to birth. New work will spring up more abundantly in unexpected quarters and in unforeseen shapes when there is a universal opportunity for contact with traditional and contemporary arts in their noblest forms.[5]

These, then, are the four definitions and intentions: State patronage of fine arts; pump-priming; an intervention in the market; an expanding and changing popular culture. It is evidently possible to hold them all within a single mind, indeed within a notably clean single mind. But as they pass from the level of public remarks and declarations to the level of actual policies, first differences of emphasis and problems of priority, then actual contradictions, soon emerge.

Let us take the four definitions in turn. The first has probably been dominant in the Arts Council's work. It doesn't often talk of State patronage; it talks of public money and what it primly calls its 'clients'. The effect is much the same, except that there is an immediate practical problem about that phrase 'the arts'. Keynes said 'the arts of drama, music and painting'. The Council's 1946 Charter said 'the fine arts exclusively'. This was changed in the 1967 Charter to 'the arts', which of course returns us to the problem. Keynes, when specifying, had left out literature, where the situation of writers was and is as difficult as that of any other practitioners, but where the problem could be masked and rationalised by the fact of the provision of public libraries. But public libraries are an initiative under the third or fourth definitions, and the exclusion of literature from the first had serious effects, which persist in the Council's failure to find an equitable policy for literature, even after it has marginally reincluded it in 'the arts.'

That other phrase, 'fine arts', has even more problems; traditionally understood as painting and sculpture it now offered to include music and, very surprisingly, theatre. On the other hand, with its (deliberately?) antique air, it could plausibly exclude film, photography, radio and television ('new work... in unforeseen shapes').

Yet the problem is deeper than this. Keynes sometimes spoke interchangeably, as we have seen, of 'the artist' and 'the public entertainer'. Yet this confused and inherited cultural division was in new ways being rationalised and fixed during the war: as well as CEMA there was ENSA; on the one hand 'art', on the other 'entertainment'. As we approach the problems of that division, in a context of spending public money, we can almost understand that draftsman's evasive 'fine arts'. This is the area of contradiction. On one interpretation, the Arts Council's task is to dispense money to support the older, traditional 'fine' arts, 'exclusively' as the 1946 Charter said. On another interpretation, since it is not actually the State but the general public which is providing the money for what is not then 'patronage' (the rich and powerful with their clients) but a form of public service, can 'the arts' be limited to those received forms already recognised by existing minority publics, or must the scope be widened to the range of the actual artistic work of the time?

Clearing this confusion, which in practice leads to every kind of resentment, from very variable positions, is not helped, is indeed made virtually impossible, by the crazy division of what we can charitably call 'responsibility' between different government departments: the arts at Education, then through Keynes at the Treasury, then back in 1964 to Education; the press and publishing and cinema at Trade and Industry; broadcasting at, of all places, the Home Office. We can see even from this level that there has never been a coherent public cultural policy, and moreover that there are powerful groups who are determined that there will never be one; we should not always flatter such people by calling them stupid and muddled. And it is in this crazy structure that the Arts Council, already carrying its own unresolved definitions of 'patronage' and 'the arts', has in practice to operate.

The second definition, as pump-priming, may now induce only a certain wistfulness. Even before the worst phases of inflation, it was obvious that neither 'the arts' nor 'the fine arts' would be, in the ordinary sense, 'self-supporting'. The sums of money now required, not only for pump-priming but for the whole waterworks, are very different from CEMA's initial £25,000 a year, or from the 1938–39 expenditure of some £920,000 on the still separated area of museums, galleries, historic buildings and ancient monuments (the received, traditional and residual works which, in yet another division of 'the arts', the State spent public money on, for the mixed purposes of 'heritage' and public education).

Yet two points have still to be made. First, that it is not only 'the arts' but a very much broader area of cultural activity that has proved to be not self-supporting, under the conditions of corporate capitalism. It is not only orchestras and dance and theatre companies and poets who work 'at a loss'; it is also, in direct revenue, most of the British press, the British cinema, most sports, and in their different ways radio and television. To specialise the problem of deficit, in capitalist terms, to 'the arts', is absurd. There is a whole general and pervasive crisis of the cultural economy, made worse by, but still quite distinguishable from, the crisis of the economy as a whole.

But then, second, it has also to be said that the whole problem of revenue from the arts is confused by a familiar kind of false accounting. In fact a significant part of the real and enduring wealth of our societies – and I mean here negotiable wealth, cash-value, rather than the important but in this context evasive 'human richness' – is in works of art. Openly and even notoriously the art works of other periods enter this world of monetary exchange, often as some of its most durable and reliable forms. Orthodox accounting excludes this whole area from the field of profit and loss in art. Yet if we were to institute two new practices – an Art Sales Levy, taking a substantial percentage of the profits of this dealing and speculation in other people's work; a National Copyright Fund in which after the interest of the author and his estate had expired (at the present fifty years after death) the copyright proceeds of some then heavily exploited work could continue to be collected – we could see the whole question of 'pump-priming' in a new and practical light. It could then be clearly seen that to say that art never makes money is a bloody lie. It could also be seen that, on one level at least, the problem of financing art is to cover or diminish short-term losses with the reasonable expectation of some very important long-term gains. And this is to speak only in money terms. The wider case for such early encouragement and support, while work has time to be done and to make its way, comes of course under a different definition.

Yet it is in the area of the third definition that the sharpest contemporary engagement must be sought. It is hardly surprising that the Keynesian idea of taking art out of the general market should get short shrift in a period in which more widespread advances – in health care, in education, in utilities – are in the process of being temporarily rolled back. Instead, in art as in these other areas, the arts are under pressure to be reinserted in a new kind of market, based not on costs and revenue but on the new major forms of advertising and sponsorship.

I cannot, on this occasion, make the whole general case against advertising and sponsorship, in their contemporary forms, as major distortions of the economy and indeed of the market itself in its earlier workings: distortions which have already wrenched our culture from its bearings, to the point where advertising itself is virtually the only profitable contemporary art.

But there are two more immediate points. First, that Keynes himself was confused in this matter. The idea of State intervention in a few selected areas, so that they will be no longer 'prostitut(ed)... to the purposes of financial gain', is generous but in the end impractical. An economy is determined by its major dominant structure and what has been hopefully taken out to work on different principles is eventually drawn back into the major orbit, or is at best made marginal and, in its explicit funding, vulnerable. We have seen this, since the 'sixties, in case after case, where commercial standards and priorities have been steadily reimposed. Moreover the social relations and ideas of the dominant economy continually replenish crude ideas of isolated profit and loss, from which resentment against the selected areas both grows and is nourished. The Arts Council has not been the only sufferer from this, but that it has suffered – in tendentious and often malevolent scrutiny of its expenditures, of a kind which is only rarely applied to commercial enterprises themselves benefitting from more hidden forms of public support – is clear.

Moreover, second, the dominant economy has its own ways of using the selected areas. This has been seen most grossly in the case of transport and of utilities, but it has also been the case in the small area of the funded arts. The prestige arts institutions, already taking so large a share of Arts Council money, are used not only as art but as tourist attractions and for business entertaining, themselves directly commercial in purpose. Again, many kinds of artistic production, but especially those in the metropolis, are basically funded by the Arts Council and could indeed not carry on without it, yet can be topped up, at relatively small cost, by commercial institutions which are represented as 'sponsoring' the work, and which gain prestige by association with the quality of other people's efforts – the oldest public-relations technique of them all.

The current drive to make the arts more dependent on such 'sponsorship' has to be resolutely opposed, for two reasons. First, because at any stage yet foreseen, such commercial sponsorship is getting a low-cost ride on the back of a system of public funding which at the same time, when it suits it, it can deride. We shall be able to see how serious they are about the arts when they offer to fund anything like full cost. But, second, because the deformation of the arts, by what will inevitably be a commercially selective sponsoring, for prestige or public relations, is something that ought to be resisted while it is still at a relatively early and apparently innocuous stage. If we let in that principle, that the arts which get funded, and where they get funded, are subject to commercial and public-relations calculations, we shall have lost a half-century of effort, of achievement and of dignity.

The irony is, of course, that 'the fine arts exclusively', or shall we say 'the metropolitan fine arts exclusively', might, in certain very limited and conventional forms, be funded by a mixture of State and commercial sponsorship. That is indeed one future now foreseen for the Arts Council. It is often backed, voluntarily or involuntarily, by the plausible argument that only the 'high culture' should be supported, at the highest professional levels. Of course there are variations in this position, but at its crudest it means dropping the non-traditional arts, dropping the roadshow and small touring companies, dropping or 'devolving' arts centres and community arts and various kinds of low-cost experimental works. The regions and interests which are then not supported will have the pleasure of being told, not only that they must continue to contribute, through taxes and prices, to this amalgam of high-level State and commercial Art, but that they are themselves being excluded by that most potent criterion: Standards!

There is a genuine difficulty here. I would support Keynes in his early definition of 'striving with serious purpose and a reasonable prospect of success'. I would agree that this involves professional judgments, preferably by fellow-practitioners. But it also involves genuine consideration of 'purpose', and a recognition that not all purposes in art are identical. The changes of purpose – that is of artistic intention and of foreseen relations with possible audiences which the historian knows in the transition to the great Elizabethan drama (denounced, early, on traditional standards, by Sidney), or in the awkward and prolonged transition to the bourgeois drama which now fills our serious theatres, or in the contested transition from Academy art to the independent groups and exhibitions of the painters who now take pride of place in our galleries – these changes of purpose are the real history of art. They are easy to read retrospectively, and the narrowest proponent of the idea of 'high culture' can, with these successful instances (for there were and always will be some failures), be as sharp a retrospective radical as may be wished. Yet it is in our own time that the questions are not only harder but much more real. They cannot be pre-empted by custom. What Keynes said about 'unexpected quarters' and 'unforeseen shapes' is not only relevant and true; it is also evidence that he belonged to high culture in its only important sense, beyond prejudice and habit, and with its characteristic and essential quality of openness. These real values must not be allowed to be appropriated or suppressed by the always confident executors of a pillared and patented Art.

It is here that all the problems of the fourth definition come to a practical centre. If you are indeed that kind of pillared and patented executor who *knows* – of course in advance, but afterwards will make no difference – that any ballet at Covent Garden, any play in the National Theatre, any picture in the National Gallery, is much more likely to be high art than a new play in a local theatre or in a roadshow hall, or than the experimental dance of a small touring company or than the odd canvas of an isolated man who still has paint on his hands – if you know all this, will you be an obvious candidate for appointment to the Arts Council or to the Business Sponsorship Panel?

It is in the nature of the fourth definition – that of encouraging a serious, expanding and changing popular culture – that the whole question of the nature and purposes of art is being redefined, and that the key element of this redefinition is openness. In any serious view, it is a long and complex process. Traditional art in its traditional institution has of course to be given its reasonable place. Moreover, as we have seen new work will then appear within the sustained traditional institutions. But what is hardest to realise is that even traditional art changes when its audiences change, and that in the making of new art changing audiences are always a significant factor – not only sociologically but, as we can see in thousands of cases, formally. Thus it is never only a quantitative extension or expansion of a culture. If we take seriously the idea of making art, as practice and as works, more accessible to more people, we have to accept and indeed welcome the fact that as part of these changes there will also be changes in the arts themselves. Nobody who knows the history of the arts need fear these changes. Indeed there is much more, from the record, to fear when art is locked in to courts and academies, or when, at the opposite extreme, artists are pushed by neglect into isolation and there is no flow between them and a wide and divers public.

I am then, on strictly artistic and cultural grounds, a proponent of the fourth definition. But I am also its proponent on the plainest and political and economic grounds. Any of the first three definitions might attract some limited public support, but it is really only from the fourth definition that we can, in good conscience, raise money for the arts from the general revenue. The struggle for this idea has important cultural intentions, but it is also the only safe way of meeting the more limited and at their best valid needs of the alternative definitions of policy. Thus instead of apologising for the principle of public funding of the arts, or nervously excluding or reducing those aspects of policy which either the pillared and patented or the political and commercial hangers-on disapprove of, we should get together, in such numbers as we can, and fight the real battles.

Will the Arts Council do this? I began by saying that it was formed by and has inherited not only different but at times incompatible and even contradictory principles. With its 'semi-independent' status, with its members nominated by Ministers of the day, with its dependence on tight departmental negotiation and funding, it is not, indeed, in a good position for a fight. Yet because it is there it is where the argument has to start. The Council are trustees not only for public money but for public policy in the arts. I say 'trustees', but the accent has only to be shifted a little, to 'trusties', to name the most obvious danger. Imprisoned by the most convenient but weakest definitions, locked in by their departmental sponsors and bankers, glancing nervously at the barons of the system who can make their term more comfortable, in any case pressed and hardworked and seeing trees much more often than the wood, they can indeed function as trusties, those other men in the middle, whom neither side respects.

I have argued before, on the Council and off it, for a process of election rather than Ministerial nomination of members. The details and practicalities of that belong to another occasion, and I have already put forward my own suggestions. But in the present context I want to say that the necessary public argument about these four definitions of policy (and perhaps there will be others) should be initiated by and openly centred in the Arts Council itself. Indeed that is centrally now what it is for, and what in the last few years, under pressure, it has begun in small ways to attempt. But then, if it is to be a real public argument, with all our diverse positions represented, the Council needs the range and diversity, the specific responsibility and accountability, which in my view only open public election can assure.

I have criticised Keynes, but in the present social climate I look across to him, and to the adult educator* in whose name this lecture was founded, in an open and recognising spirit. For the task, as Keynes said, is still to give courage, confidence and opportunity.

1981

Notes

1. *The First Ten Years:* Eleventh Annual Report of the Arts Council of Great Britain, 1955-56, p.6.
2. *The Listener*, 12 July 1945, p.31.
3. *The Life of John Maynard Keynes,* R.F. Harrod, New York, 1951, p.401.
4. *The Listener*, 12 July 1945, p.31.
5. *Ibid.*

* W.E. Williams

Gravity's Python

What is the difference between a satirist and an impressionist? I don't know – what is the difference between a satirist and an impressionist?

The sad little question is properly cast in the form of a comic routine. There must be some people, perhaps most of us some of the time, who can look back on the wit of the last twenty years and simply revive old laughter. Any book of quotations from *Beyond the Fringe* to *Monty Python's Flying Circus* offers enough occasions, and there is still *Not the Nine O'Clock News*. But then other memories intrude. The early impersonations of Harold Macmillan seemed at the time to have some political content. But go across from that memory to, say, Mike Yarwood, doing the whole run of political leaders. We still laugh, but with other questions. Isn't there a certain air of obeisance in this whole exercise with celebrities? Isn't being impersonated now a mark on the scale of effective image-building? Is it true that all celebrities ask even the hardest cartoonist for their originals?

That may only mean that the bite has gone out of it all. Yet Peter Cook, one of the early impersonators, is quoted here as saying: 'My impersonation of Macmillan was in fact extremely affectionate – I was a great Macmillan fan.' On the printed evidence, he could have fooled us. Did he fool us?

It is useful to have even this broadly adulatory record of the last twenty years of – what? It seems that Kenneth Tynan first called it satire. Others have called 'it' almost everything, but the only reasonably constant factor, of any importance, is a specific conjunction of university revue with popular television. Yet that can then override the obvious differences of content. There is really hardly anything in common between, say, *That Was the Week that Was, Monty Python's Flying Circus* and *The Goodies*, except this very general fact of formation. Should we then set it aside, as a matter of mere biographical or vulgar sociological interest? Glad of the laughs, I can usually agree to this until I notice a fair number of these performers turning up between the acts, doing their funny commercials. With the commercials still running we remember how often and how brilliantly the commercial mode has been guved. Take the point across to politicians and official spokesmen, and it begins to seem a problem that after twenty years of mocking impersonation we are stuck with public figures even more ludicrous than any of the original targets.

So satire can't change the world? But then how much of it was satire anyway? There is one old sense of satire as medley, supposedly derived from a dish of various fruits offered to the gods. That is getting more like it. The range has been very wide, from social and political comment through traditional comic sketches and monologues to prolonged verbal jokes and a kind of late Dadaism. In some of the contributors, it has edged towards a kind of drama, full of intricate subjectivities. In others, it has moved happily towards commercial farce. There has been a general supposition that it was broadly progressive, but it has included its share of racial and foreigner jokes and a persistent proportion of mockery of the English working class. In the early days it included several internal parodies of theatre; lately it has sometimes seemed that its whole content is internal parody of television.

With this range of content it is reasonable to ask why it is still distinguished from the general run of comic entertainment. Certainly the range can be wider, including kinds of educated joke (the persistence of Proust) and more black comedy. There has been wider use of comedy drawn from the mechanics of the show itself: internal mix-ups; self-conscious reference to the sketch while it is playing; the use of devices to undermine the device. It could be said that this is the world of late Modernism and Brechtian influence, but there is no need to say this: the Marx Brothers and the Goons were already in place. What may be distinct, in the use of some of these methods, is a kind of amateurism. It is often difficult to distinguish between deliberate amateurism as a joke on professional routines and the amateurism which has simply run out of writing and rehearsal time. Either is compatible with the brilliance of some of the performers and the high spirits of each new wave.

Without radio and especially television, many of these performers would have passed through comedy in their student and training years, and then dropped it. Some of them have indeed dropped it, but with a popular reputation to launch other projects. Others, in larger numbers than in earlier generations, have stayed with the shows. I don't know whether this is loss or gain. I have met former student performers in such surprising places that I don't know how there could be any rule of advantage. But this fact of persistence, beyond the generation of student comedy, gives us an unusual opportunity to watch what happens when that frisky irreverence becomes successful, professional, stabilised.

This broadens into the question of the sheer amount of comedy on television. The amounts of drama and of news are equally striking. Many of us can spend more time watching any of these than in, say, preparing and eating food. That is why it is difficult to go along with the opening paragraph of Mr Wilmut's 'Prologue', with its references to the jester in the baronial hall and the 'continuing and changing tapestry of laughter'. The quantities alter any simple notion of a historical mode. Whether or not the appetite grows on feeding, the slots are still there, in hitherto unimaginable numbers.

This has required exceptional invention. Without this new range of writers and performers, the traditional comedian could hardly have coped. The Oxbridge network, so important in British broadcasting, made opportunities easier to come by than in most cultures. The formation moved through.

Yet it can't, in some of the cases, be only a matter of quantity. The quality of some of the modes found a ready or almost ready audience. The grim reproductive character of official English culture went on providing occasions for anything from the most studied parody to a kind of helpless, hysterical flatulence. Thus, long after the public-school jokes had faded, the world created and managed by the sober face of the same institutions provoked the same ribaldry. The dissident comic fraction of the governing and administrative class joined the rest of us in our amazement, and because they were much nearer to it could be much funnier about it.

That process happened, but though it's often told as the whole story, it is, in fact, only part of it, perhaps a small part. For with that specific dissidence came the other attitudes that had not been shed; the funny foreigners, the funny regional accents, the funny housewives and working men. In a period of anxious mobility and of national decline, the familiar repertory had a new edge. If there was one thing English culture could agree on, at least in off-business moments, it was that it was all bloody ridiculous.

It? We? Of course comedy at its best takes everything on. It can at times be very ridiculous to ask it for a consistent point of view. But there are usually specific forms under any apparent universality, and this period is not an exception. Beyond the general medley, beyond the specific class characteristics, beyond the hurried improvisations to capitalise on success, there are some specific features which invite reflection from the point of view of the 'eighties. They are difficult to describe, for they are the most genuinely contemporary elements. Much more than the topical references and allusions, they situate some of this work in a period. I think they can be seen now as a very specific problem about seriousness, which was comically discharged.

There are different levels in this. One obvious effect of some of the best work – for example, in *Monty Python* – is to create a residual mood in which virtually nothing can be said or done without becoming absurd. Perhaps I am too preoccupied with problems of sequence and flow on television, but I keep noticing a sense of devastation of others kinds of work and statement around this kind of comedy. It often needs a sleep to get back, with any kind of attention, to the straight-faced or poker-faced statements of the dominant programming. Considering what much of that is like, the effect is salutary.

It is interesting that some of the best sketches seem to be centred on this problem of how to take anything seriously. Of course, these vary. How much of the comedy in the Dud and Pete sketches (the *Dagenham Dialogues*) comes from a shared sense of helpless philosophical rumination, and how much from the fact of helplessness in those precise accents: the absurdity of the thinking working-class man, the autodidact, and his errors in university-style vocabulary? The sketches can be reduced to this latter component, which is often heavy, but at other times behind them there is indeed a shared helplessness. It is in some of *Monty Python*, and perhaps at its best in *The Life of Brian*, that this note is most often struck. Somebody is trying to say something, or to think something through, and every kind of interruption and disability not only intrudes and prevents him, but seems marshalled, systematically, to prevent him. At its best, this has much in common with the more officially recognised art of what is called 'non-communication'. Indeed often, in its exuberance, it is less decadent than these more prestigious currencies of the official art and theatre world. But still, less *decadent*.

English philistinism has always comforted itself with the half-memory of the man who tried to be a philosopher but found that cheerfulness kept breaking through. What we have in some of this comedy is the opposite and probably now more relevant situation: of the man who tries to be cheerful and amusing, but finds sadness, loss, a sense of arbitrary insignificance, welling up and needing to be hit sharply over the head.

But then the decadence, if it is there, is quite general. It has very little to do with what is officially complained about: the irreverence, the rudery, the cruel jokes and joking cruelty. Those fit the culture like a glove: the comic version of alienation and of hang-up and of overtight nerves. What underlies all this is a determining sense of loss. Most of the old serious statements have moved to at least the edge of absurdity, when at all carefully listened to in this actual world. But there is then a long gap before any new serious statements can be made and really listened to. It has seemed for perhaps two generations to require the thickest hides and the most rooted or protected of situations even to attempt them, in any sustained way. The laughter of instant parody is at the shoulder of every gravity. An awareness of lightness, of darting and laughing mobility, accompanies most consciousness of weight. Suddenly, and perhaps against our will, the snigger and the belly-laugh rule. And all the time that grim old culture keeps providing their occasions, while directing, at a different level, a cruel danger and misery.

There is no point then in blaming the boys, even when they have become men. They have filled, are still filling, that long gap, at most of the levels from distraction through caricature to wild bursts of anarchic energy. When they got to the BBC, from the early 'sixties, their chief patron used to refer back to the Berlin revues of the 'twenties, and, characteristically, they both accepted this patronage and laughed about the boring historical reference. It seems less boring now, and not only because of what came after it, in Germany, which was usually left out of the flattering retrospect. What is really in question is how we get through, get out of, a state of disbelief and helplessness which is bound, in all its early stages, to seem comic and edgy: demanding the funny face and the paranoiac prance.

Those at least we have had, brilliantly, in a sketch which hopes it will never have to hear the probable punch line.

1982

Review of *From Fringe to Flying Circus* by Roger Wilmut (1980)

112

Isn't the News Terrible?

'I see the news is bad again.' The banal phrase punctuates my memories of the late 1930s. I remember an adolescent anger that people would not name the things that were happening: the invasion of Austria; the cession of the Sudetenland; the invasions of Czechoslovakia and Albania – all packaged as 'the news'. While in London it no doubt seemed ridiculous that Chamberlain referred to Czechoslovakia as a far-off country of which we knew little or nothing, I could see, there in Wales, that what he said was true for these railwaymen and farmers, whose gravity and abstraction, at this level of affairs, at once puzzled and irritated me.

This situation is still, in general, too little understood. The banal phrase of our current years is a rhetorical question: 'Isn't the news terrible?' I still sometimes make the mistake of trying to answer it, since when I have taken off the packaging some of it is not at all terrible to me; indeed, some of the most officially outraging events are positively welcome. Yet the structural problem persists, and has become more acute. In the late 'thirties, after all, the wireless news of these European convulsions came only after a steady reading of the fat-stock prices. Now the bumptious arresting music, the spinning image of the world, the celebrity reader, induce forms of attention and of stress which are often justified, though the signals occur whether there is anything of substance to follow them or not. And then what we can observe, past the apparent sophistications, is a lack of human fit between exposure to reports of world-wide events and either effective knowledge, through which to try to assess them, or any effective possibility of response – some action even if it is as occasional as a vote: anything practicable, that is, beyond either spectacle or worry.

The official answer to this problem is at once easy and beside the point. It is factually true that some of these reported events could signal, through a chain of relationships, the most immediate effects, from a nuclear war through the more imaginable scales of disaster, disturbance and nuisance. Thus the public must be informed. If they do not know these connections, they must be made aware of them, or have them pointed out by our diplomatic, defence or industrial correspondents.

But this is an abstraction less forgivable than the more mundane blocking of all events as 'the news'. Those railwaymen and farmers did not need to be told that distant events could end in their own bodies. Some of them, including my father, still carried in their flesh the wounds of the wanton metal that had attended the last demonstration of relationships and consequences. It was not, then as now, the gravity of generalised attention that was lacking. Instead, now as then, the news was received, accurately if too simply, as alien: not just because it was coming from places and peoples of which there was no direct knowledge, beyond these isolated reports, but also because its mode of communication was not that of people talking, questioning, moving across to talk or listen to others, as in everyday practice and knowledge, but was this authoritative transmission – an authority without rivals and beyond effective challenge, imposing itself professionally, in every signal, accent and tone, upon the near and the far.

Let us face it then: the news has been very bad lately. But it is very difficult to be sure how much of this badness has been in the events themselves, and how much in their intense and relentless interpretation by the authorities: a one-sided polemic which I cannot remember being at this pitch since the late Forties. Some of us, at least, must be ready to appreciate the verbal joke by the Glasgow University Media Group, whose *Bad News* and now *More Bad News* indicate the faults of news presentation rather than the import of the actual events.

To be sure, we cannot draw any firm line between events and their presentation. A very large number of the events now presented are in fact interpretations, by a small group of highly privileged voices, directly transmitted or read out by the hired celebrities. The privilege of such voices would matter less if it were not also, in the leading cases, the privilege of command of men and resources. Such privilege, now quaintly known as a 'mandate', even where it refers to unforeseen events on which no wider opinions have been canvassed, has to be distinguished, of course, from that of the voice alone. But then it is a very long time, in British broadcasting especially, since we heard any voice of this kind that sounded as if it were speaking quite for itself, from its own knowledge and experience. An institutional definition encloses this absence. Discussion and argument occur elsewhere, but meanwhile, here is the news.

It is, then, a major intellectual gain, in recent years, to have found ways of seeing the news as a cultural product. There is still a central difficulty. On the one hand, it is true that in some respects we have to read the news as if we were reading a novel. Until the early eighteenth century the word 'novel' carried two senses – of a tale and of what we now call the news. Spenser had written, in a sense that we might now echo, observing the arranged features of a news-reader: 'You promise in your clear aspect, some novel.' 'Novelist', in the eighteenth century, meant a newsmonger as well as a writer of prose fiction. But a distinction was forming between 'fiction' and 'fact', and this had serious effects, both ways, on what appear at first sight two distinct kinds of narrative. At its most confident, this assigned all novels to 'fiction' in the sense that the events had not occurred, but had been imagined or created: a definition that not only makes for many difficulties with the reading of certain novels of the past, from *Romola* to *War and Peace*, but is now in trouble with the arrival of the important contemporary form of the 'novel based on a real-life event', or 'faction'.

Yet the worst effects were at the other end of the scale. The fact that certain events have undoubtedly occurred – have happened to people, have been observed, have been reliably reported, have been tested from the evidence of participants and witnesses – has been used to conceal or to override the equally evident fact that as they move from events to news they are being narrated, and that certain long-standing problems of narration – the identity of the narrator, his authority, his point of view, his assumed relationship to his readers or hearers, his possible wider purposes in selecting and narrating these events in this way – come inevitably into question. Most experienced adults get used to having to ask these questions, however politely or tacitly, when they hear stories and reports in everyday talk. Yet it seems that we have only to ask them about a broadcasting service or a newspaper to produce outraged cries about an assault on professional competence and independence, or to provoke dark hints, which at least sometimes are surely projections, about a conspiracy to interfere with freedom of news and indeed to manipulate or censor it.

Thus it would be reassuring to know that the minute of a high-level discussion in the BBC (quoted in the *Leveller* of January 1978) was inaccurate: the Director-General 'said there would be no sense in attacking *Bad News* in detail... he thought however that the ideology of sociologists was a subject which would repay a little study and hoped that it would be possible for a programme like *Analysis* to tackle it.' What *Analysis* or some other programme might equally have tackled, down to that level of detail which is one of the surest means of testing accuracy, was the body of evidence about actual news presentations which *Bad News* had presented. The 'ideology' (ideologies) of sociologists would have been a wholly proper matter to include, not least because it would have helped to promote a genuinely critical attitude to sociological 'findings', which in other, happier cases – this or that poll or survey – make their unproblematic way into the news. Moreover, once discussion had begun, the problem of the 'facts', and the related problems of selection and interpretation, could have been rationally addressed over the whole range, in and out of university and newsroom.

There are at least two reasons why this has not happened. The first, undoubtedly, is that this kind of independent criticism is taken, almost instinctively, as a challenge to authority, of a piece with all those other challenges to authority which sociologists (by those who do not know them, but have heard the ugly word) are supposed in recent years to have been making and inciting. Yet I do not find this response, however hasty or muddled, unreasonable. What is at stake is indeed authority at its deepest level: that deep sense of propriety and legitimacy which has assigned both authority and responsibility to certain public sources of news and interpretation. These qualities are tested over the years, and over a range of events are proved to have certain reliabilities. It is then easy to move from that kind of public record to an assumption of more general authority, in which the institution comes to see itself, and to be widely seen, as an organ of the 'national interest', a warrant of independence and fairness, standing above the mere ideologies which this or that minority might indulge. Anyone questioning this identity, backed as it is by a centralised and very powerful technology, and by the symbols, rhythms and timed regular occasions of public address, can rather readily be seen as a small boy throwing stones. And if he has written a fat book, full of tables and referenced details, he does not cease to be an unruly small boy: it is only that he has provided himself, for his own questionable purposes, with even more stones.

The second reason, an outraged professionalism, needs to be carefully considered. It is true that the same kind of defence is rather often rejected, by news-gatherers, when it is made by other professions. 'What evidence do you have for saying that?' 'Don't other experts disagree with you?' 'Doesn't this go against what most of us believe?' These are the regular and admirable questions of the most persistent reporters, and at their best they are asked of the most as well as the least privileged. It seems then reasonable that they should be asked, with the same persistence, of reporters, correspondents and editors themselves. And indeed it is noticeable that when a reporter has delivered a certain kind of story – when he has, say, interviewed a representative of the IRA, or a Welsh republican, or has what he takes to be secret or confidential information about some national body – he is often quite sharply interrogated, within his profession and in other ways. These are indicators of situations in which reporters have broken the consensus of 'responsible' news-gathering. The professional defence, of the right to establish and publish the facts, is then qualified or overridden by other criteria.

Yet what this situation most illuminates is the underlying structure of communicative relationships, within a particular social order. For there is no normal space in which news reports can be examined and interrogated, unless the consensus has been broken and other social forces move through and take it into a public, administrative or legal domain. In the ordinary rush of news reports, within the consensus, this does not often happen, though the need is as great for events within the consensus as outside it.

It is at this point that the 'sociologists' announce themselves. The growth in media studies and cultural studies has been remarkable, in the last twenty years. A space which does not exist, to any effect, within the major news-and-opinion institutions is carved out in other institutions, mainly educational. Hence books like *Bad News* and *More Bad News*. But it is then obvious that the conditions under which such work is done are radically different from those in which the work being studied is and in most cases has to be done. It is understandable that reporters and editors, who work under considerable pressure, especially of time, are impatient when confronted by analyses of their work made by researchers who seem to have all the time in the world. I remember a related exchange between a gifted analyst of television and a gifted producer. The analyst had indicated a particular effect through a particular use of shot. 'Tell me that,' said the producer, 'next time I'm filming in the rain on Liverpool Docks at five in the morning.' But then neither position, as it stands, can be quite accepted. The effect, after all, was there, and so were the real and difficult conditions of practice. When Annan found that editors and reporters were 'bewildered' by the findings of *Bad News*, it should not have been the end of the matter. The point is to investigate the social conditions of such bewilderment.

It is just because of the immediate pressures, the difficult moment on Liverpool Docks, that a detached analysis of methods and conventions is necessary. What we do, under pressure, and especially what we do as professionals, is what we have been trained to do, what we have got used to doing, what at deep levels we can take for granted so that we can get on with an immediate job. And there is no profession which can fail to learn from someone making explicit just the training, the usage, the taking for granted, that underlie all practice. These can then be consciously affirmed, or consciously amended. This is how all rigorous professions work.

The special problem of communications is not only the relative absence of fundamental as distinct from on-the-job training. It is also that the fundamental analyses of method – for example, the quite new problems of *visual* presentation – are being carried out in one place, and the practice in another. Yet nothing can be understood if it is not recognised that both these real levels exist. I do not see what more the *Bad News* group could have done to show the intricate practical problems (highlighted, of course, by the many practical failures) of the 'objectivity' and 'balance' which the professional broadcasters claim. The greater relative monopoly of broadcast news has at least this advantage: that the greater relative diversity of the press (for all its own tendencies to monopoly and shrinkage) provides accessible evidence to test 'objectivity'. This is well demonstrated in the reporting of the Price Commission's calculations of the contribution of wage rises to inflation (*More Bad News*, pp. 19-22), where, in complicated ways (professionally traced by the *Financial Times*), an estimated 20 per cent contribution became, through various hands, a 'between 60 and 75 pence in the pound' contribution in a BBC news item. Given the importance of such issues, and the genuine difficulties of interpreting such statistics, within different theoretical frameworks, there is really no case at all for saying that the exigencies of practice must override fundamental questions of method. Thus, on so contentious and professional an issue, there is no defensible practical reason for leaving interpretation to the single voice of 'our correspondent' or to the demotic skills of a particular news-writer. Why could there not be two 'correspondents', deliberately chosen for their theoretical differences? Because that would be discussion? But the whole problem is the selection of one interpretation as *news*.

Are we then asking for the impossible, a neutral news service? The *Bad News* team argue that neutrality is impossible and undesirable; indeed, that it is the claim of the existing organisations that what they offer is 'neutral, unbiased, impartial and balanced' which is at the heart of the problem, since what happens in practice is a demonstrably ideological presentation, at many levels, which at once presumes and helps to form an effective consensus of news and other values. There can be little doubt that they have, in general, made out their case, yet where, theoretically and practically, do we go from there?

It is a further effect of the institutional division of labour that professional researchers follow the rules of their own profession, presenting and commenting on evidence, but not otherwise, except implicitly, declaring themselves. I do not blame the *Bad News* team for this, but I notice the contrast with, say, Todd Gitlin's *The Whole World is Watching*, where a comparable but more committed analysis is made of the American media on a specific set of issues. There the focus is on the definition and characterisation of the American New Left, and the fact that it is written by one who actively participated in the events reported, and saw not only their slanting by the media but the complex results within the movement itself, adds a welcome sharpness. I think we do have ultimately to say that the practices in question are matters of fundamental social and political conflict, though this should not prevent us from also saying that it has been an achievement of certain kinds of society, and of certain institutions and professionals, to create *some* space in which, over and above the conflict, the integrity of information and the actual diversity of opinion can be reasonably assured, and that we should all be looking for ways to enlarge that space to its still distant limits.

One notable opportunity for such enlargement now exists in the new communications technology, especially in the common-carrier and interactive versions of teletext. It may well not be taken, given the pressure to adapt the technology to current forms of news and marketing. But there would be immediate gain if broadcast news could be, in effect, footnoted, given the developing teletext services which can both handle and recall complicated information and necessary context. Moreover, here as more generally, an enlarged space requires that diversity of channels and voices which all existing systems and their ideologies seem determined to limit, in the name of their own irreplaceable excellence. This looks like being a very long struggle, but it is worth saying, finally, that a considerable amount of that 'terrible news' – the events, not the reports – occurs and will continue to occur because too few people are speaking to and for too many, in conditions in which, increasingly, they nevertheless cannot prevent others from acting and failing to act. That, more than anything, is now the welcome and terrible news.

1980

Review of *More Bad News* by Glasgow University Media Group (1980) and *The Whole World is Watching* by Todd Gitlin (1980)

The Press and Popular Culture:
An Historical Perspective

It is still difficult to write the history of any element of the new urban industrial culture of the English nineteenth century. It is correspondingly much more difficult to give any general account, even in outline, of that culture as a whole, in its specifying historical features and in its internal and external connections. The emergence of a popular press, in the first half of the nineteenth century, can be fairly taken as a leading element. Yet, if the history of the press is isolated, not only from the cognate forms of other writing, publishing and reading, but, as usually happens, from other kinds of political and cultural formation and organisation – from political movements, new industrial organisations, educational developments, changes in the theatre – it can be seen as a mere phase in newspaper history from the seventeenth to the twentieth centuries, itself retrospectively determined by definitions of what the newspaper *became*. In the case of the early nineteenth-century popular press, any such procedure is especially disabling because it conceals what are probably its two most important features: first, the decisive history of the institution and then the incorporation and eventual transformation of a radical popular press; second, the problem of content, which can indeed only be approached by comparison with other forms of popular publishing and with the popular theatre.

The most significant standard error, in accounts of the nineteeenth-century press, is an emphasis on the history of the popular *daily* newspaper, based on a correlation between the board-schools of the last third of the nineteenth century and the new popular readership of the cheap papers of Northcliffe and his contemporaries. But the real history of the nineteenth-century popular press has to be centred in the development of the *Sunday* paper, which even in the twentieth century has significant cultural differences. And then it is not only that in the history of popular journalism the Sunday paper came first, by some 60 years; it is also that, to understand the Sunday paper as a cultural form, with its specific and influential selection of content, it is necessary to understand certain general features of urban popular culture as a whole. I shall discuss what seem to me the most significant of these features – literacy, popular publishing, the theatre, the lecture – before returning to the specific development of the popular press.

The precise extent of literacy in the early nineteenth century is virtually impossible to quantify. One kind of evidence is from school attendance, and it was calculated that in 1816 some 875,000 children – out of a potential 1,500,000 – attended a school of some kind for some period, and in 1835 some 1,450,000, out of a potential 1,750,000. It was also calculated that at the second date the average duration of school attendance was one year. By 1851 the average duration was reckoned to be two years, and the proportion attending any school had again risen. It was not until the very end of the century that virtually all children attended school until the age of twelve.[1]

Another kind of evidence is the well-known record of ability to sign the marriage register, for which there are national figures from 1837. A sample shows:

	Men	Women	Total
Able to sign	%	%	%
1839	66.3	50.5	58.4
1873	81.2	74.6	77.9
1893	95.0	94.3	94.65

Here both the general steady trend, and the equalisation between men and women, are significant. Yet, as also in the case of the figures for school attendance, it cannot be assumed that the development of the popular press was a simple consequence of extending literacy. Indeed, throughout the nineteenth century the numbers of people who either bought or read newspapers were far below the lowest possible estimates of the numbers of people who were able to read. By my own calculations, the newspaper-reading public in 1820 was about 1 per cent of the adult population; in 1860 the daily public 3 per cent and the Sunday public 12 per cent.[2] These are, necessarily, rough estimates, but it is clear that general literacy was always far ahead of newspaper reading, and can in no way be seen as casual.

The development of general publishing, other than newspapers, is very marked in the period of the Industrial Revolution. The figures for annual titles are significant. In the 1750s these were still at around 100 titles: a figure which had been exceeded in the first half of the seventeenth century but which had declined and settled after the Restoration. By the 1790s the annual average had risen sharply to about 370 and by the 1820s to over 500 – and to more than 2,600 by the 1850s. It was to rise to over 6,000 by 1900, to more than 17,000 by the late 1930s and to more than 20,000 by the late 1950s.

Within the striking general development at the end of the eighteenth century and in the first half of the nineteenth century, when the general characteristics of the new urban industrial culture were being defined, there are distinct and in some respects contradictory tendencies. In traditional forms of publishing there was a marked tendency towards small editions at high prices, but at the other end of the scale there were the first series of regular cheap reprints, with poetry and drama selling in quite large editions at sixpence a copy. From the 1780s the publication of fiction increased rapidly, though most editions were still small and prices high. There was then a virtual invasion of orthodox publishing by pirates, undercutters and reprint houses which decisively expanded the book-buying public. Meanwhile the older circulating libraries were joined by many new kinds of library and collective buying. There was also the crucial extension of number-publication and serialisation, which by mid-century were to expand the reading public for fiction significantly. Leading fiction sales at the beginning of the century only occasionally reached 10,000 copies; by mid-century the comparable figure was 100,000.[3]

In a period of intense political struggle, an exception must be made for certain notable political books. Paine's *Rights of Man,* at three shillings, sold 50,000 copies within a few weeks in 1791, Cobbett's *Address to the Journeymen and Labourers* sold 200,000 in 1826. The existence of a radical reading public, forming at the edges of and beyond the expanding middle-class public, is evident, and is crucial in diagnosis of the development of newspapers.

At the same time there was another kind of formation: a popular market, served mainly by older popular forms: 'prognosticating almanacs', chapbooks, ballads and broadsheets. These had sold, since the seventeenth century, at a level well above that for books, and by the 1820s, as in the house of Catnach, really large sales began to be attained: the 'Last Dying Speech and Confession' of the murderer of Maria Marten sold more than 1,100,000 copies.

The true sociology of these different reading publics is very difficult to determine, except in the most general terms. There are obvious class differentials, but there is almost certainly also a crucial differential between urban and rural people, and – within the urban – between

London and other cities. Distribution methods, which would flatten these differentials, were not radically changed until the mid-century establishment of the railway network.

One changing cultural institution, the theatre, throws some comparative light on these questions. To assess it we need first to look back at earlier centuries. The medieval drama had moved from the church to the streets, becoming a genuinely popular but also strictly occasional drama. With the growth of London in the late sixteenth century, regular theatres were established for the first time, and between about 1580 and 1620 these served a predominantly popular, mixed audience.

From the 1620s there was an evident narrowing of the audience, related to the new indoor theatres, and there was then a sharp if not total break in the closures during the Civil War and Commonwealth. Under the Restoration there was a conscious narrowing. In 1600 there had been six successful theatres in London; from the 1660s, and, legally, until 1843, only two London theatres were licensed for the performance of drama. In fact, from about 1700, other theatres developed, in London and in provincial towns, serving an expanding middle and lower-middle class.[4]

Times of performances reflect the changing class of audience, moving from the early afternoon of the Restoration court and its circle towards the evening, when people could attend after business and work. By the early nineteenth century performances began at six and often went on for four or five hours. The old fashionable audience of the Restoration period moved, in the course of the eighteenth century, from the pit to boxes, and then often out altogether. Attempts to raise prices to keep 'the mob' out of the theatre led to actual riots, as at Covent Garden in 1809. In London, at least, even the patent theatres, and the minor theatres which, legally forbidden to perform drama, used many devices to come near to it, again had socially mixed audiences.

But meanwhile, in the early nineteenth century, there was a further significant development, within the rapid growth of London. New large theatres were built south of the river (the 'transpontines'), and in the East End; these undoubtedly served large popular audiences. It was in the minor theatres and in the transpontines that melodrama became a dominant popular form. In part this relates to the patent theatres' monopoly of 'legitimate' drama; the play with singing and spectacle was often devised to evade this restriction, with a consequent confusion of classifications. By 1832 the House of Commons had voted to end the patent theatres' monopoly, but were blocked by the House of Lords.

The repeal came finally in 1843.

Melodrama's reputation as sensational is well deserved, but as a form it shows interesting contradictory characteristics, of a kind directly relevant to the character of the popular Sunday newspapers.[5] Crime, adventure and spectacle were staples of the form. At the same time certain classic figures – the ruthless landlord, the rich seducer, the poor and innocent victim – are central. It is not that the melodrama was politically radical; Jerrold's *The Factory Girl* (1832) was pehraps the first piece of English imaginative writing to deal with the new industrial exploitation, but it was shouted from the stage. What is really there is a more generalised social radicalism, of a kind corresponding to the alliance between middle-class and working-class political forces before 1832, in which the rich and idle could be isolated as villains, but with innocence and magic (respectability and Providence) as the only effective alternative forces. It is significant that the Bastille plays, widely imported from France, were emptied of their political content and became simple dramas of imprisonment and escape.

One effect of the long-imposed separation between legitimate drama and other kinds of performance was the development of other popular forms: variety, pantomime, and circus. It was the variety element – singing, monologues, sketches – which eventually found a new home outside the theatres, developing from performances in pubs to the drinking music halls which began in the late 1840s and were to remain important into the twentieth century.[6]

Theatre and music hall remind us of a fact which can easily be overlooked in an analysis of the new urban popular culture from its surviving records. The print-culture – in books, pamphlets, magazines and newspapers – was, as we have seen, developing quite rapidly in the new urban conditions. But it was still at almost all levels a minority culture, and at certain levels it was significantly interactive with a predominantly oral culture, which in the development of the cities was itself assuming new forms.

By 1881 a majority of the British people were living in towns of 20,000 or more inhabitants. London had passed the million mark early in the nineteenth century; by mid-century its population was over $2\frac{1}{2}$ million and by 1900 over six million. The new industrial cities were developing at often even more explosive rates. Within these unprecedented conditions, old oral forms, such as the sermon, were extended and developed; and relatively new oral forms – the outdoor and indoor political meeting, now often of vast size, and the popular lecture series – became central elements of urban culture.

To the expanded political meetings we must add the newly significant demonstrations, from Peterloo to the Chartists to the Hyde Park 'riots' of 1867. These produced their own contributions to popular culture, in the remarkable development of banners: a trend also to be underlined in the growing trade union movement, whose elaborate banners are a significant form of popular art. Again, in the new urban conditions, the folk-song, in its old rural sense, was developing into the urban popular song, which, until very recently, has been significantly neglected or undervalued by song historians.

In the complex changes of the century, several if not all of these elements were incorporated into a new popular *commercial* culture, as is indeed most evident in the history of the press. Radical protest meetings were to develop, in part, into campaign meetings within the new electoral system. New forms of visual display were to be extensively incorporated into commercial advertising, from mid-century invading the city streets at an alarming rate, though still rigorously excluded, in its display forms, from the press. Local centres of song-writing and production were joined and often overridden by commercial song-writing and publishing of a more modern kind, significantly often in connection with the music halls and variety theatres. Again, from mid-century, organised sport, especially football and horse-racing, developed within the new urban culture.

The lecture is worth a special note, because it is so often overlooked or treated as an extreme minority form. It is significant how much of the important social thought of the century was in lecture form: from Coleridge through Carlyle and Ruskin to Morris. We know far too little about the audiences at these lectures, but in cases where research has been done – as on Ruskin's lectures at Bradford[7] – it is clear that quite large and general lecture audiences were a significant feature of nineteenth-century urban culture. It is also well known that in the Mechanics' Institutes the lecture was a centrally significant form. Some of these lectures have survived in printed books, others in verbatim reports in newspapers. They are a reminder not only of the relatively obvious fact that in the new urban culture there was significant expansion at every level of interest and quality. They also serve to remind us that within what can be distinguished as the new urban popular culture – that of the new urban working class and poor – the expansion also took place at every level of interest and quality, and thus in increasingly complex relations with the institutions and forms of a more traditionally organised culture.

Lord Ellenborough, explaining the Newspaper Stamp Duties Act of 1819, said that 'it was not against the respectable Press that this Bill was directed, but against the pauper press'. This frank distinction is crucial to an understanding of the history of the press in the first half of the nineteenth century: a history which has too often been written in a unilinear way.

The 'respectable Press' was not, as it happens, particularly respectable; there had been heavy direct bribery of journalists by Ministers, and official advertising was steered to papers favourable to Government opinion. Political independence, within the terms of established opinion, still lay some way ahead, as a general fact.

The 'pauper press' is quite another matter. After 1815, radical journalists – notably Cobbett and Wooler – reached a large, new audience, against every kind of attempt to repress them. Cobbett evaded the Stamp Duty – which in those years was primarily a political tax – by excluding news and publishing only opinion. His *Political Register* sold up to 44,000 at twopence weekly, and Wooler's *Black Dwarf* up to 12,000 in the years around 1820 when the circulation of *The Times* was rising to 7,000 and beyond. What is evident is the emergence of a new social basis – essentially a new social class basis – for a new kind of campaigning political journalism.

But, in the complex political history of the years between 1815 and 1848, the independence of this campaigning radical press was only sustained with great difficulty, being subject throughout the 1820s and early 1830s to every kind of intimidation and prosecution. A generation earlier, the effective ruling class had opposed, or sought through bribery and subsidy to control, a middle-class press. In the intricate shifting of political alliances through the 1820s and before the Reform Bill of 1832, an independent 'respectable' press began to emerge, led by *The Times*, as part of the same complex process within which the radical popular press was being harassed and confined. During the Chartist years, a radical popular press was again active; but several pressures were now combining to determine its development and eventual isolation.

It is this isolation of a radical political press and the steady incorporation and institution of a new commercial popular press which we must emphasise as the decisive developments within literate popular culture as a whole.[8]

One crucial factor was economic. When Cobbett and Wooler were competing directly with the respectable press in the years after 1815, the technology of the newspaper was still relatively undeveloped, and costs – at these levels of circulation – were in a reasonably competitive relationship for both kinds of press. The real social expansion of newspaper readership, which began in this period and which at first followed relatively clear class lines, was to be profoundly complicated, and eventually determined, by the costs and capitalisation involved in the precise technical developments on which any major expansion depended. Steam printing of *The Times* began in 1814 and speed of production was steadily raised by mechanical improvements. The eventual combination of rapid steam production with the new, fast distribution system made available by the developing railway network, produced the conditions for major expansion; but at a level of capitalisation which – indeed by definition – the 'pauper press' could not match.

Leadership in the press – hitherto, in spite of political repression, largely determined by simple competition for readership – was from this period until our own day inherently associated with access to ever-rising amounts of capital.

The technical developments – which were eventually to make possible the fully distributed popular press – occurred within precise social and economic relationships, which made the true competition for readership between a radical and a respectable press more and more unequal, and indeed – at some levels – pre-determined. In the course of the nineteenth century, the development of the newspaper from a small-scale capitalist enterprise to the capitalist combines of the 1880s and onwards was at every point crucial to the development of different elements of a popular culture.

Yet it was not an economic process alone. Market factors took their place within a complex social and cultural development. This can best be seen in the development of the Sunday papers, which provide an interesting comparison both with the 'respectable' daily papers and the true radical press. From the beginning of the century, in spite of many attempts to have them declared illegal, Sunday papers had circulations well ahead of the daily papers – a constant factor of press expansion down to our own day. Their readership was also wider, in social terms, than that of the daily press. They were bought in, not only by clubs and coffee-houses, but by such places as barbers' shops, where the working man's Sunday visit might often be his only opportunity to read a paper or listen to it being read.

Politically, most of the Sunday papers were for Reform, and this continued to be true well past mid-century. At the same time, as a cultural phenomenon, the *Dispatch* or *Bell's* is crucially different from the *Political Register* or the *Black Dwarf*. The Sunday paper, in fact, was from the beginning a commercial enterprise within the new urban (in fact predominantly metropolitan) popular culture. It included political and general reporting and foreign news but it had also a very specific content of reports of crime and scandal. Much of the popular content of ballads and broadsheets and last dying speeches – always ahead in sales of all reading material – found its way into this essential redefinition of the 'newspaper'.

The new Sunday papers of the 1840s – the *News of the World* and *Lloyd's* – show this development much more strongly; and there was some further effect on their content by the problem of Stamp Duty, which could be avoided if fiction, or sometimes back-stories, replaced actual news. The subtitle of the new *Bell's* was *Sporting and Police Gazette, and Newspaper of Romance*. It had at once a cultural and a technical continuity with the ballad and the chapbook. A front page of 27 February 1842 has the headline 'Daring Conspiracy and Attempted Violation' and a large woodcut above the detailed report – a layout typical of the earlier non-newspaper format.

With a combined circulation of about 275,000 (to be compared with a combined daily circulation of some 60,000), and with the great majority of its readership concentrated in London, this was a popular press of a new kind. It is strictly comparable, in social terms, with the contemporary London theatre, itself now largely popular in audience, and with melodrama as a leading form. Radical elements of a kind persisted – directed more against an old ruling class than against the now dominant industrial capitalist system – and were a crucial factor in the new popular cultural formation. The complexity of this formation can be studied in the work of G. W. M. Reynolds (whose *Reynolds's News* came down to the twentieth century as an organ of the radical Co-operative movement), who was a leading Chartist speaker, and who for a number of years outsold even Dickens with his serialised sensational fiction, centred on aristocratic scandals. The limits and pressures of the whole social development are well summed up in this contradictory but powerful figure and form.

'Popular', then, had three senses, which in practice steadily diverged. There was the old radical sense, of being 'for the people': the political press of Cobbett, Wooler, Hetherington, Carlyle, of the Chartists, of Blatchford in the 1890s, of the Labour Movement press of the twentieth century. Contained economically, by their inherent disadvantage in capitalisation, these elements came also to be contained culturally, to an important extent. In the very difficulty and priority of keeping independent political opinion extant, they often had no choice but to exclude other elements of the popular culture – in which millions of their potential readers were interested – including those which were the new positive enjoyments of urban culture as well as those which were seen as its exploitation.

There was, then, an intermediate sense of 'popular' – a skilful and vigorous combination of generalised political attitudes with the established popular reading material of crime, scandal, romance and sport.

Finally, with increasing pressure in the second half of the nineteenth century, and becoming predominant in the twentieth, there was the sense of 'popular' in purely market terms. This emanated from a steady movement away from independent political radicalism, itself deeply affected by the extension of the suffrage and the formation of new-style electoral parties; from a more and more open reliance on habitual tastes and markets, the alternative social and political visions of the genuine radicals pushed away to the margins and beyond them; and was now, decisively, realised by the new centralised production and distribution system, based on altered social relations between journalists and their readers, and between both and proprietors. The result was the popular newspaper as a highly capitalised market product for a separated 'mass' readership.

Within the general lines of development of a capitalist economy, the 'inevitabilities' of this process have a double edge. The trends towards high capitalisation, combine-ownership and the dependence on display-advertising revenue (effectively instituted by Northcliffe in the 1890s; the nineteenth-century newspaper before that decade, while relying on classified advertising, had vigorously resisted display) followed, very closely, much more general tendencies in the economy as a whole.

At the same time the repression, the isolation, the containment and eventually the incorporation of an autonomous popular press had nothing inevitable about them: they began as conscious political acts and continued as an effective deployment of financial resources to keep poor men's reading matter in rich men's hands. In the second half of the nineteenth century, the Sunday papers moved towards circulations around a million. And behind them came the 'new journalism' of the *Telegraph* from 1855 ('they naturally', Labouchere observed of its owners, 'sacrifice all decorum to the desire to make the journal a remunerative speculation'). Then, from the late 1860s to the 1880s, came the new cheap evening papers, which, incorporating the increasingly important sports news, are the real forerunners of the twentieth-century popular paper; and the new cheap daily papers, from the *Mail* in 1896.

WHAT I CAME TO SAY

At every stage of the development of newspapers, corresponding types of magazine and periodical evolved: from 1820, the 'scandalous' *John Bull*, but also the extraordinarily successful education penny-magazines (*Chambers', Penny* and *Saturday*) from the 1830s; the family magazines of the 1840s to the 1870s; the new *Answers* and *Tit-Bits* of the 1880s. The economic effects of new technical developments, which would eventually narrow the sense of 'popular' in magazines as it had from much earlier in newspapers, were not to come through fully until the mid-twentieth century.

The three senses of 'popular' are still crucial, and need always to be distinguished in the still-expanding culture of the 1970s. The complex historical development of different kinds of 'popular press' provides crucial evidence for the interpretation of our whole modern cultural development.

1978

Notes

1. See Joseph Kay (brother of Sir James P. Kay-Shuttleworth), *Social Condition and Education of the People in England and Europe*, 2 vols (London: Longman, 1850). See also Sir James P. Kay-Shuttleworth, *Four Periods of Public Education, as Reviewed in 1832, 1839, and 1862* (London: Longman, 1862); and C. Birchenough, *History of Elementary Education in England and Wales from 1800* (London: University Tutorial Press, rev. edn, 1938).
2. Raymond Williams, *The Long Revolution* (London: Chatto & Windus, 1961), pp. 184–99.
3. See A.S. Collins, *The Profession of Letters, 1780–1832* (London: G. Routledge & Sons, 1928); and Amy Cruse, *The Englishman and his Books in the Early Nineteenth Century* (London: Harrap, 1930) and *The Victorians and their Books* (London: G. Allen and Unwin, 1935).
4. See G. Rowell, *The Victorian Theatre* (London: Oxford University Press, 1956); and Raymond Williams, *op. cit.* (1961), pp. 253–66, and 'Social Environment and Theatrical Environment', in M. Axton and R. Williams (eds), *English Drama: Forms and Development* (Cambridge University Press, 1977).
5. See M. Willson Disher, *Melodrama* (London: Rockless, 1954).
6. See M. Willson Disher, *Winkles and Champagne: Comedies and Tragedies of the Music Hall* (Bath: C. Chives, New Portway reprint, 1974).
7. See M. Hardman; 'An Investigation into the Prose and Ideas of John Ruskin, With Special Attention to the Central Years 1857–66 . . .' (unpublished Ph.D. thesis, Cambridge, 1975).
8. See A. Aspinall, *Politics and the Press, 1780–1850* (London: Home & Van Thal, 1949); C.D. Collet, *History of the Taxes on Knowledge*, 2 vols (London: T. Fisher Unwin, 1899); S. Morison, *The English Newspaper 1622–1932* (Cambridge University Press, 1932); W.H. Wickwar, *The Struggle for the Freedom of the Press, 1819–1832* (London: Allen & Unwin, 1928); *The History of The Times*, i: '*The Thunderer' in the*

Making, 1785–1841 (London: The Times Publishing Co., 1935) and *The History of The Times*, ii: *The Tradition Established, 1841–1884* (London: The Times Publishing Co., 1939); and R. Williams, 'Radical and/or Respectable', R. Boston (ed.), *The Press we Deserve* (London: Routledge and Kegan Paul, 1970).

Film History

What is the history of film? In considering this question, we are likely to pass lightly over 'history' and put a defining emphasis on 'film'. 'Film' is the noun that brings us to our subject. Its history, or any other intellectual process relevant to it, seems to follow naturally from its already defined properties.

This has certainly been the procedure in most histories of film, or cinema. The properties of the subject are taken as known, and their components are then traced as precedents of these properties. In the simplest versions, film and cinema are treated as unitary subjects, which are then made to disclose their historical stages of development: an early technology and its institutions; the silent film; the sound film; films for television. In what appear more complex versions, tendencies or schools or (very commonly) national 'traditions' are identified within the more general phases: a form of history which can then be developed into a form of criticism – the identification of key directors, actors, techniques, described and then evaluated as leading factors in the general historical development. Collected writing on these bearings is now vast. Some, perhaps much, of it is obviously useful.

Yet there are hard questions underlying the assumptions within which such writing is undertaken. The hardest question is in the biggest assumption, if we stop and really consider it. This is the assumption that there is a significant unitary subject, film, with reasonably evident common properties. In fact the only unifying element, of a definite kind, is a particular material process or repertory of processes. Yet this, evidently, is not all that is indicated by a proposed history of film. There is a useful current distinction between 'film' and 'cinema', in which 'cinema' is used to describe the institutions of the production, distribution and reception of films, while 'film' is used to describe the material processes and the uses made of them by those who compose or watch them. This is a valuable kind of distinction, in its necessary discrimination within the loose unitary subject. But what can then happen is that 'cinema' and 'film' become, in their turn, unitary subjects, with known properties to be traced in the elements from which they are eventually assembled. There is 'social and historical' narrative and analysis, and there is also, but elsewhere, 'critical' narrative and analysis or, at more basic levels, 'formal' analysis. Some, perhaps much, of these different kinds of writing is again obviously useful.

History, however, is something else, both in practice and in any adequate writing. Particular areas of attention and emphasis have of course to be distinguished, not only in historical accounts but also in practical living. Yet in any full assessment of history it is necessary to be aware that these temporary and provisional indications of attention and emphasis – of 'subjects' – can never be mistaken for independent and isolated processes and products. For they are at best provisional intellectual identifications of significant areas of a common life. At worst, and frequently, they draw hard lines around certain areas, cutting off the practical relations with other 'areas' (which are indeed then seen only as 'areas' – 'the economy', 'the family', 'literature') which are in fact necessary if we are to understand not only the 'outward' relations – how 'the economy' affected 'the cinema' – but also the 'internal' relations and compositions, the supposed fixed properties of 'cinema' or 'film', which can often only be clarified if the specific processes are seen in the context of much more general processes. Lines have indeed to be drawn, to make any account possible, but it is always necessary to see ourselves as drawing them, and willing to redraw them, rather than to suppose that the marks on this one of many maps are hard features, of similar content and isolation, on the ground.

There are many ways in which this general proposition can be illustrated. I was myself very struck, reading histories of cinema, to see how indifferent most of them were to the preceding history of theatre. Indeed this was more than a hard line around the separated subject of film. It was often a defiant rejection of the idea that 'theatre', or 'literature', or any other of those marked areas, could have anything significant to do with the practice of film. Or should we then say Film, for what often followed was an account of how 'theatre' or 'literature' had diluted or destroyed the pure essence of 'Film', which was then not a name for a body of actual practice and works but an idealised projection of supposedly pure and inherent properties?

This is in fact the false form of what could, on different bearings, be an important argument: that certain cultural (or other) influences limited or misdirected actual practice and development in this specific material process or group of processes. But to write a critical history of 'film' which is actually going to exclude, on such grounds, those films which were 'really only theatrical or literary bastards' is a procedure so astonishing that it could only ever be undertaken in the same spirit of misplaced confidence that is shown in similar histories of Literature (excluding not only all 'non-imaginative' writing, but also most actual novels and poems which fall below the proper standard of 'literature') or of Theatre (restricting drama to one of its places of performance – the theatre – and to work of certain types, while excluding other places of performance and rejecting all other types as 'popular entertainment'). What we really find, in each case, is a categorical argument, based on what, if it were not categorical, could be openly offered as a justified opinion, which manages to reduce the actual diversity of its real subject and to offer its highly selective version as the whole real history of its now necessarily hard-line area. We can argue against such reductive procedures, but the best cure, usually, is to look up from these categorical histories and see the astonishing actual diversity within the practice itself. It is true that this can lead the historian to adopt the mode of an indiscriminate miscellany, in which the endless is finitely preferred. But in all real history, while the necessary starting-point and control lie in the recognition of diversity, the essential next steps are provisional analyses and groupings which are intended to clarify, rather than merely register, the diversity itself.

It is a disadvantage of the most common historical mode that the usual forms of such analyses and groupings are chronological periods, or types assigned to such periods. This method produces a kind of prehistory, devoted to early technological developments and uses of films, followed in order by the silent film, the early sound film, the modern film and so on. A linear view is set out in a linear way. But it is my own understanding of the history of film/cinema that while there are very significant periods of development, in which certain emphases and uses are possible or dominant, there are also, from the beginning (a notion that in itself must be examined), diverse actual elements and possibilities which often, and perhaps always, run through such fixed periods. If I then separate these out, to try to clarify them, it will be difficult not to suggest, or to be understood as suggesting, that these are steps in some development of fixed properties or known categories. What I shall in fact be suggesting is that the history looks very different according to the bearings that are chosen to run it on. It may then be through putting the bearings side by side that we can begin to distinguish an actual, rather than an ideal or categorical history.

The four bearings I shall use are: (a) the actual technology and its uses; (b) film and popular culture; (c) film and established culture; (d) film and modernist culture. These do not form a linear progression but a set of lateral and eventually interactive relations. What I shall write under each heading will, equally, not be a summary, nor an attempt at a definitive account, but an exploratory one. I shall finally try to indicate some of the diverse practical ways in which the bearings come together, in an actual and active rather than a narrated history.

It can reasonably be argued that the only true common property of film is its technology. But what we usually separate out as 'film' is a variable and, in fact, changing selection from a wider body of systems.

It may nevertheless still be possible to talk of a technology of film. This has to depend on a firm distinction between 'technical invention' and 'technology', which are usually employed interchangeably. A technical invention is a specific device, developed from practical experience or scientific knowledge and their interaction. Such devices have been carefully recorded in what is seen as the prehistory of film. Yet we have only to stop and look at these, as the narrative rolls them before us, to realise that the selection refers to what are at least two, and perhaps more, technologies. Thus there are a number of inventions and devices which belong primarily to the development of still *photography*; the daguerreotype; the sodium thiosulphate negative (for which the term 'photography' was invented); wet collodion; the gelatin dry plate; the nitro-cellulose roll (by which time the term 'film' was established for straightforward descriptive purposes); reflex and roll-film cameras. All these and further developments were eventually brought together, by exclusion, selection and improvement, into a systematic technology of general photography, embodied in major industrial and commercial enterprises. Equally, however, there are a number of inventions and devices which belong primarily to the development of the display of *moving images*: the technique of the *camera obscura* refined and extended to the magic lantern; the phantasmagoria, the thaumatrope, the praxinoscope, the zoetrope; the developments from still photography in sequences of cameras and revolving plates; the kinetograph and kinetoscope, using new celluloid strip film; the *cinematographe* and the vitascope. It can be said that these were selected, improved and developed into a systematic technology of 'film' or 'cinema', embodied in what soon became, in this field, major industrial and commercial enterprises likewise.

Yet the point is not just the obvious one that there were two major lines of development: towards the recorded and reproducible image and towards the moving image. It is that there is a problem of what we then say when we find the two lines of scattered technical development combined in the 1890s in the invention of 'cinema'. It is ironic that the often preferred term, 'film', comes from the group of photographic developments, with which it still shares certain physical properties. And it is interesting that the popular term, 'movie', comes essentially from the properties of the other group, the work on moving images. But can we then not say that the film camera and the associated projection systems mark a qualitative new stage, in which moving images can be recorded and reproduced?

We have of course to say something like that. For this is the point at which the diverse technical inventions were assembled and developed into a systematic technology which eventually attracted enough further investment to become an independent industry. Yet in the rush to that conclusion we can easily fall into a simple technological determinism. The inventions come along and 'make' a new industry and a new art. Simple historical retrospect shows everything leading to what we now have. But this is where the difficulties, and many of the interesting problems, start. For in fact we do not have, in that simple unitary way, a 'new art', or even, in any unitary way, a 'new industry'. Diverse and in some cases alternative possibilities, in both art and industry, are there in the material history from the beginning, and even after the qualitatively new phase of the 1890s. To put it at its simplest, a fundamental argument about the nature of film and its uses, which is still at the centre of many of our most serious discussions, is already inscribed in the diverse technical and technological history. Some say that film is a major medium because it can record and reproduce life and its movements, in a physical world, so clearly and permanently. Others say that film is a major art because, with it, an artist can compose with moving images. At their extremes these positions are often argued in typically absolutist ways: 'true film' or 'authentic cinema' is one or other of these seemingly opposed things.

Thus no account of the technical inventions, or even of the systematic technologies, can function as a prehistory to some unitary version of the history of cinema, whether presented either from any of these, or from any similar, positions. Already in the earliest years the basic elements of the technology were being used for the radically different purposes which were inherent in what was never a series but always a scatter of inventions. Lumière recorded events on film and projected them; Méliès used a different property of film to project tricks and illusion. Edison, meanwhile, wanted moving pictures to accompany his phonograph – the ironic opposite of the eventual development of silent into synchronised sound film. Nor are these simply early uncertainties. The whole subsequent practice of film shows both the intense development of the alternative emphases of record and illusion, in these simple senses, and the diverse development of many forms, taking these emphases into more complex uses or attempting simple and complex syntheses beyond them. Very little of this history is explicable or predictable from the technical history or the systematic technologies. Rather, these provided certain new possibilities, at times themselves entailing further technical developments, within the general pressures and limits of a wider social and cultural history.

Film – the 'motion picture' – has been used, throughout its period of availability, for strict record of a scientific or historical kind, and this remains a major use. But the early and most of the subsequent development of cinema has been firmly within the area usually defined as 'popular culture'. Most of the early shows were held in tents and booths, or in music-halls – while films made for purposes of factual record were screened in scientific institutions. Already by 1914 cinema had become the most widely distributed cultural form that there had ever been, and the scale of this distribution had been vastly increased by 1945.

Yet there was no simple transition from the technical prehistory to the new universal art form. Film took its place, and then made its own new place, in an already dense, complex and changing popular culture. In Britain this has been especially clear.

The 'popular culture' of a predominantly urban and industrial society comprises a radically different set of phenomena from preindustrial popular, or 'folk', culture. The latter is relatively traditional in form and content, and its contrast is with 'court' or 'aristocratic' – or 'polite' ('liberal', 'learned') – culture. Modern popular culture however is not only a response to predominantly urban and industrial living. It is also in its central processes, (1) largely urban-based, (2) an application of new industrial processes to a broad range of old and new cultural processes and forms, and thus (3) predominantly mobile and innovative, but with very complex relations to older and still persistent conditions and forms. Film arrived at the end of a century of such developments.

Two related areas can be briefly characterised. By the time of the first film-shows the newspaper press had been transformed, with popular Sunday, and then new daily papers, building up circulations of more than a million copies each. At the same time there had been an intense and novel development of both popular and 'society' drama.

The popular newspaper should not be primarily related to the need for information in a new kind of society, though it marginally served this purpose at different times in history. We misunderstand the press if we attempt to trace a simple line from the early newsletters to modern 'quality' newspapers. The most widely distributed newspapers, from the early nineteenth century onwards, were firstly those of a radical character, opposing the political establishment, and secondly, when these had been largely defeated by repressive legislation and by the rising costs of capitalisation in new methods of production and distribution, newspapers of commercial 'entertainment' (their main topics being crime, scandal, sport, pastimes and spectacle). The minor element of pure 'news' continued in the cinema through the equally minor medium of the newsreel, following much the same principles of selection and presentation but of course with major visual advantages.

The other elements of the popular press were congruent with much of the popular drama, and the development of cinema, in one of its main tendencies, has to be seen in relation to both press and drama. Yet we can usefully emphasise the congruence and even the continuity of certain theatrical forms which permit more direct comparisons.

These forms are often crudely summarised as 'melodrama', but the real history is more varied. Melodrama began in the established, 'legitimate' theatre, in about 1800. It was a form of play with music and with a large element of mime. If we try to generalise 'mime', or silent 'gestural' acting, from the conditions and achievements of the silent film, we overlook this whole previous history. In many early melodramas certain characters were represented as, for some reason, dumb, so that mime could be employed by the actors who took these roles. A whole rich tradition of predominantly visual acting, stemming from travelling popular entertainers with a very long history behind them, was thus taken into theatre and was again to be heavily drawn on and developed in silent film. As melodrama became popular, from the 1820s, its plots increasingly resembled events reported in the popular press: sensational crimes and seductions – though in melodrama these were eventually concluded by providential rescues and escapes – at times presented in a radical perspective. From the 1860s there existed in effect two broad kinds of melodrama: this well-remembered type, but also the earlier and always numerically more common 'costume epic', peopled by pirates, bandits, soldiers, sailors and 'historical' figures of all kinds. Each type was to contribute massively to cinema: at first by direct adaptation

(*Pearl White, Jane Shore, Ben Hur*); later by the cinematic adaptation of similar plots, themes and shows, and (as in Britain before 1914) by the addition of such new but congruent techniques as the close-up and the chase.

But there was more than melodrama in each of these kinds. In the established theatre, by the time of the first film shows, there was a century's tradition of extraordinary spectacle: the vast development of elaborate costuming, by period or for display; the great elaboration of 'sets' – the new (nineteenth-century) theatrical device of fully furnished places of action and rooms; the highly ingenious staging of mechanical and lighting effects, from fires and volcanic eruptions to shipwrecks, railway crashes and even naval battles. Film was to develop many even more ingenious technical resources, but mainly it was to show much the same things with even more 'spectacular realism' and conscious display. It is very difficult, when considering this line of development – as when considering the derivation of film from the two kinds of melodrama – to see any real qualitative change, though there were obviously more resources and possibilities once film had been mastered, and there were the usual changes of style over the passage of time, so that a contemporary film 'melodrama', essentially similar in form and plot to its nineteenth-century predecessors, may not seek to be 'melodramatic' in that older style. To these continuities, with their local variations, we have to add those elements which lay outside the 'legitimate' theatre: the acrobats, conjurors, tumblers and dancers, who carried on both old and new tricks in film; the performers of farces and sketches in the music-halls; the skilled horse-riders, prominent in the circus from the eighteenth century onwards and now finding new openings – in one special case, the 'Western', in a major way – in film.

Thus majority cinema, in both the silent and the sound periods, can be reasonably seen as the flowering of a whole body of drama, theatre and entertainment, which in its essential interests and methods preceded film but was then at once enhanced and made much more widely available by it. Indeed, the qualitative change can be seen less in what was done – there are really very few films, by proportion, for which there is not a nineteenth-century precedent in drama or entertainment – than in what then happened, in the genuinely new factors of multiple and recurrent reproducibility and distribution.

Film was to become the central art form of the twentieth century, but it took a long time – longer in some nations and in some classes than in others – for this centrality to be recognised in relation to already established culture. From its marginal beginnings, within both the content and the institutions of popular culture, it made its way to a qualitatively different position: not only or even primarily because of its individual qualities as art, but mainly because of the radical change in the means of artistic production employed.

In the early decades most cinema industries tried to move towards respectability within the terms of the established culture. The earliest settled sites of distribution were modelled on theatres, and often went on being called theatres. The process of the luxurious refurbishing of theatre interiors, which had been such a feature of theatre building and adaptation from the 1860s, was extensively continued in the period of the 'picture palaces', with a further continuity of characteristically aristocratic or exotic names. Most of the films shown in them were derived from various forms of the popular culture, especially the commercial popular culture. But there were also many attempts to draw on the more prestigious theatre (both in the enlistment of stage actors and in the adaptation of plays), on musical comedy and light opera, on novels in the established literary tradition and on other literary forms such as biography. As late as 1940 the quality of film was often evidenced from these borrowings and adaptations – a thin blue line above the assumed typical 'vulgarity' of the cinematic popular culture. Yet what went into film from these sources formed, of course, a real contribution to the medium. Dismissal of such work as merely 'theatrical' or 'literary' can only emanate from an arbitrary idealisation of film. In one cultural area after another, film, as it became (before television) the dominant form, was in effect a common carrier of many different kinds of art, and cinemas were the central institutions of this wide range of drama and entertainment.

Yet alongside these adaptive and incorporating processes something more fundamental was happening – something consequent on the nature of the new means of distribution. The prestige of the established cultures was very closely linked with the predominance of the old metropolitan centres. London and Paris, Berlin and New York were the places where high art, especially in drama, music and painting, was produced or exhibited. This situation corresponded with a phase of political and cultural centralisation and with the general dominance of orthodox metropolitan criteria. What happened beyond the metropolis – in what, during this whole phase, from the eighteenth century onwards, could be defined as 'the provinces' – submitted itself, for the most part, to these allegedly superior and fashionable centres. In fact however in some of the relevant arts, and especially in drama, this became an inherently false situation, particularly in Britain. During the period from 1870, when European drama was moving into a new great period, it was not from the fashionable metropolitan centres and the dominant national cultures that creativity was flowing. It was from what were regarded in most countries of Western Europe as marginal or distant cultures: Scandinavia, Russia, Ireland. In Britain the established theatre was locked into social fashion rather than into anything which could be even momentarily mistaken for high art. Indeed, the persistence of this enclosed and self-reflecting 'West End' is at least a contributory reason for some of the failures of British cinema, if only because its exceptionally class-marked enclosure raised, in its shadow, what was often a reductive and self-impoverishing 'provincial' and popular culture.

One major factor shifted the old kind of metropolitan dominance, and eventually, and ironically, produced a quite new form of dominance. The central material characteristic of film was that its productions and performances could be fixed, and could then be distributed in standard multiple forms. Thus, quite apart from its new technical capacity to enhance and extend older forms, there could be a simultaneous high investment of both talent and resources in any single production, and, when such a production was achieved, very widespread and indefinite reproduction. Obviously this matching of potentialities made sense in financial terms also. Thus the dominant centres of production became, first, less dependent on the established metropolitan centres, and, in all later phases, in effect dominant of them. In the theatre the old kinds of prestige persisted, in remarkably reproductive ways, but whereas they had previously dominated all relevant activity elsewhere, they were now in a less important position, with major new institutions and forms surpassing them – nationally, and, even more crucially, internationally – in the eyes of newly enlarged, regular audiences.

The results have been complex. In relation to the established culture – a very different matter from traditional culture – film and cinema have been in general quite remarkably liberating. Yet, quite apart from the effects of new kinds of centralised dominance, which must be separately examined, there has remained a certain parasitism on established forms and styles, often most noticeable when the 'industry' has taken itself most seriously and produced 'serious' films. It is clear that in much mainstream cinema there have been nothing like the cultural breaks that might have been predicted from the new possibiltiies of the technology and from its new and potentially new social relations. There has been some evidence, from time to time, that this situation may be changing, but the continued prestige of 'theatre', as opposed to 'film', is remarkable after a half-century in which it is quite clear that film has produced much more important new work. Moreover, deference towards the forms and styles of the established culture seems continually to re-establish itself within cinema, for predominantly social rather than artistic reasons.

Yet the history of film looks different again when we relate it to modernist culture, itself the conscious antagonist of established culture in every field. Such a relation however is necessarily complex.

It has always seemed to me significant, since I first noticed the dates, that the years in which the motion-picture camera and projector were being effectively developed – the 1880s and 1890s – were also the years in which there was a decisive break, within avant-garde drama, towards new kinds of mobile and dynamic composition. To read Strindberg's *Lady Julie* (1888), but even more his *The Road to Damascus* (1898) and the later *Dream Play* and *Ghost Sonata*, is to find a stage dramatist writing what are in effect screenplays, embodying shifts of location, sequences of images, fragmentations, transformations and dissolves which were only just technically possible (if that) in the most experimental kinds of stage production, but which would eventually become even commonplace in film. There is hardly any evidence of direct influence either way. The experiments were going on in widely separated and non-communicating sectors. The correspondence, or even congruence, is at a different level, where not only experiences of mobility, dislocation and alienation, but also an intense curiosity about movement and about newly possible dynamic forms, were parts of a deeper and more general cultural movement. The same underlying movement can be seen, for example, in the paintings of Munch; it went on into expressionism and in fact quite directly into early German cinema. The profound perceptual shifts embodied in a whole succession of movements in the visual arts, from impressionism to cubism, belong to the same general cultural transformation.

The hostility of this kind of modernist culture to the characteristically fixed and enclosed forms of the established culture was intense. What are much harder to analyse are its then very complicated relations to the forms of popular culture, and beyond these to the altering social relations within which both tendencies – at first sight so far apart – were trying to develop.

There is a quite clear line of development from the subjective expressionism of Strindberg and Munch, with its uses of dynamic distortions and dream imagery, to a whole body of expressionist and surrealist film. But there is also a very different yet related line, also within general modernism, in two tendencies which came to define the most influential modernist film-making: on the one hand, shifts of location, point of view and perspective in narrative, including non-linear time sequences (all of which had been developing in modernist fiction, and continued to develop interactively in both fiction and film); on the other hand, the more specifically filmic use of composed and associated (linked or contrasted) images, whether in the original theory of montage $(A + B = C)$ or more generally. In the kinds of film developing (with other differences) through Griffith and Eisenstein, these new processes of dispersed narrative and edited imagery led not only to a modernist cinema but also to a repertory of film techniques which were eventually incorporated into mainline cinema in its still basic adaptations to the established non-modernist culture. They were then commonly perceived as the specific properties of 'film'.

Yet there was also a more diverse progeny in the general anti-bourgeois character of modernism. In the formal senses already referred to, modernism broke up the fixed frames and images of established bourgeois art. But its commitment to the dynamic was never solely, and not always even primarily, formal. Its rejection of the forms of bourgeois theatre and representational painting was often combined, in ways that break up the conventional formal categories, with an interest in popular forms, in two senses: (1) popular movements in history, whether explicit revolution (as in early Soviet cinema) or a more general extension of the actions of history to the characteristic and technically possible 'crowds' of the 'epic' film; (2) the non-representational and non-realistic elements of popular culture, which had by now become available in silent film comedy and melodrama. The outcome of this complex of conflicting influences has been, as might be expected, very complicated indeed. The 'art film' of one kind of modernism (composed images, or dispersed narrative with composed images) has to be set beside forms which appear, at first sight, to be wholly in contrast with it: the revolutionary epic, which used the mobility and scale of developed cinema and also composed non-representational images within these; but also what came to be called the 'documentary', in which the specifically 'theatrical', the 'staged' event, was so thoroughly rejected that a new, apparently unmediated, relation between 'the camera' and 'reality' was proposed and created. The old dual potentiality of film – (1) that the camera could create illusions and that the film itself could be worked on to create new visual effects; (2) that the motion-picture camera made possible the most accurate and thorough representation and record of real life – has thus been recognised and used, selected from, combined and recombined, in extraordinary and unprecedented ways which ought not to be reduced to apparently separate and distinct 'periods' and 'genres'. What is necessary, by contrast, is to distinguish those genuinely modernist elements (over the range from expressionism and surrealism through dispersed and extended narrative and symbolic montage to the documentary and *cinéma-vérité*), which have been used for conscious social and artistic purposes in a diverse and continuing series of films, from the more common 'technical' or 'professional' adaptations of this or that method or device which were uncritically incorporated into an apparently neutral technology of 'film'.

It is clear that when we look at the history of film on these different bearings – the material processes; the relations with popular culture; the relations with established culture; the relations with modernism – we find something very much more complex, but also more interesting, than the ordinary categories of film history or film criticism can contain. Moreover there is every reason to resist the temptation of arriving at some synthesis of which these elements are components. All are real in the sense that they describe actual work in actual places at actual times. But no present place or time can be permitted to absorb or order them, because what they are, in practice, has been and remains contradictory in the full sense: diversely alternative and often irreconcilable practices, within the diversity and opposition of actual and foreseen social and cultural relations.

This sense of diversity and contradiction must be firmly sustained against the forms of any unitary 'aesthetics of film' or unitary developmental history – and, as urgently, against the industrial and commercial structures which, with their command of means and resources of production, impose more practical forms of (marginally varied) unification.

What needs emphasis in this context, where the question of the industrial and commercial structures is concerned, is the effect of the decisive material factor in film – its indefinite and multiple reproducibility. Within capitalist and state-capitalist economies, it came to seem natural that this led, by a familiar financial logic, to an extreme concentration and relative monopoly of production: massive production costs made affordable by a controlled system of mass distribution. Yet the material factor itself could, within different general relations, lead as easily to more diverse centres of production, beyond the old metropolitan fixed points, and to a radically extended and more diverse distribution of this wider range. Thus there is no technological determinism running from 'film' to 'Hollywood', or to anywhere else. And whatever may be said about the past, there are now new opportunities for diversity in the increasing distribution of films through television, though they can only be exploited if the television institutions are themselves consciously reformed to make independent production and extended diversity more possible. This remains a more hopeful line of development than what has hitherto been settled for: the fusion of commercial popular culture and established culture in a massively organised capitalist cinema, which in turn adapts to control television and video-cassettes and discs. The alternative, at the fringe, is of a festival and art-house cinema, as a conscious minority culture.

It is how this fusion relates to the bearings already examined that needs emphasis. Popular culture should not be romanticised, either that which existed before the coming of film, or after. Neither 'melodrama' nor 'mime', music-hall song nor icon, is a simple fixed element. Most of the ways in which these forms were put together were absorbed, without effort, into what became an established popular culture of commercial consumption. That they did not have to go this way, and that the 'popular audience' is not predisposed to what is eventually made of it, is better evidenced from film than from any other area of the culture. At the same time the radical elements in modernism, widely apparent in many areas of minority culture, have been expressed more generally – and with less specific ties to social minorities – in film than in any other medium. Yet the tendencies to monopoly, to incorporation and to agency or outpost production in terms of the dominant centre have been so strong that only relatively brief periods of fully independent production, and then more often than not in 'national' terms, have escaped them. At the same time, as in the related case of twentieth-century theatre, it has been almost wholly in these comparatively independent centres that work of real value has been done. What has been lost, in the whole process, is not so much the consciously modernist work, which can find a not uncongenial place at the margins, but the fully autonomous development of native popular cultures, which keep showing their strength whenever there is even a half-chance, but which have been denied any mature expression and growth by the pressures and prestige of a skilfully homogenised and falsely universal cinema: popular *cinema* rather than popular films.

Yet it is important to realise that the old economy of the cinema is beginning to break up – under the pressure not only of general economic, but also of mainly new technical, developments – and that some new kinds of opening are becoming apparent, in which the history, already in any full sense of the term so diverse, can be reinterpreted by being changed.

1983

The Future of 'English Literature'

Still, often, I find myself surprised that English studies are so controversial. I mean that the interests which bring people to the subject are so unusually strong and substantial, involving poems, novels and plays, enjoying discussing them, thinking about them and even making them; and in a way an English course seems, as the continual strength of applications demonstrates, so ideal a continuation of those interests that begin for many of us so early and seem quite central to our understanding of life. At first sight, what is waiting in a university course, after certain of the constrictions of the school syllabus, seems an endless prospect of doing more of that same kind of thing and having a chance of discussing these strong interests with people who've spent their life doing it, of having access to a library in which one can be sure that the supply of that kind of stimulus will never dry up. And how can it *be* that a subject like that should have been, almost throughout, a source of chronic irritation and indeed a series of acrid public disputes and *causes célèbres* – some of which I've analysed, one or two of which I've taken part in? And yet occasionally even then it's as if a gear slips and I find this surprising – why *should* it be so?

I sometimes try to explain it to myself by analogy with another experience which I remember very well when a friend visited us in California at the time when a number of men were forming groups for personal discussion in reaction to the widespread formation of women's groups, of 'women only' groups. So men were meeting and discussing, and this friend went to one such meeting and was told at the beginning, 'There's only one rule about these encounter meetings: that we can say anything we like, there are no boundaries, no limits. We talk about our experiences.' And indeed they did. They talked fluently and candidly about their relationships, their physical experiences, their anxieties and so on. And fairly late in the session he said, 'Well, what I feel actually is that we're all victims of a kind of petty-bourgeois guilt and anxiety within the social crisis of late capitalism' (he was my friend, after all). The moderator jumped up and said, 'You can't say that!' And he said, 'But you said at the beginning you could say anything you like.' 'Yes, anything you like, but not *that*!' He came in a state of great worry and sense of transgression back to tell us this story, and until my wife burst into laughter at that whole situation, it had a hold on him, he really felt he'd transgressed.

Now this isn't too unreal an analogy with what is, after all, within the British university system, a quite strong sense of liberal openness. You come here to discuss, we expect you to read so that you know what to discuss. There *is* openness, and yet the source of most of the really serious disputes has been that somebody who's done the work, who's read, who's thought, and then has a point of view to put forward (it may be as bizarre as my friend's perhaps correct, perhaps incorrect analysis of the Californian trauma), *puts* that forward, and there is the sudden introduction of a limit that had never previously been noticed. The familiar case in English after all being, 'That is not a literary point. That is not a point about literature.' In other words, a definition of what *is* a literary point has been built in, although the whole ideology was one of openness, that we simply respond as we feel, as we think, as we relate to whatever experiences or ideas we find. That you could demonstrate something to be entirely irrelevant, that this or this – anything but *that* – may be said is a sense which I think a number of people have been coming to. It is because of this that it's so difficult to push into an area where these people – not merely academics who have invested their life's work in a certain kind of study, simply want to reproduce it, and are then very suspicious of others who are going, as they think, to remove or diminish it – but even people with more real tolerance of mind are anxious. This is why I took that analogy. It is clear that in that otherwise harmless discussion one way of understanding the issues being debated touched raw nerves. Nothing else in my opinion can explain the ferocity of responses to certain mild critical interventions – especially when you compare them internationally. You find that what has been proposed in one place is already common practice somewhere else. It *must* be touching some raw nerve.

Now the nerve it tends to touch would in my opinion need a lot of tracing; it's connected to a whole cultural and social situation. It's not surprising that the notion of something called 'Englishness', even 'essential Englishness', is continually hovering around the discussion of a course in English Language and Literature. Given that there are real problems about understanding and valuing or, for that matter, accepting Englishness or essential Englishness, in the rapid pressures and tensions of our recent social history, it's not surprising that some of these connections are really at some distance from the ostensible subject matter. Many people who are resisting syllabus reform often feel that they are defending some last identity, some last bastion of civilisation and social achievement against what they claim and easily see and sometimes describe as barbarians, as crude irruptions from other kinds of interests. But whether that is so or not, and it varies – in some cases it is almost pathological, in others it's merely a confusion – it is at some distance from concerns which are more properly professional. And it is these professional issues that I'd like now to address, because I've heard the argument about them so often.

The fact is that what is waiting at the end of the road I was describing earlier – where having read books of all kinds, you see a path ahead in which there will be more of that kind of activity, more people and more experienced people to discuss it with in a continual expansion and interchange, in all the many stimuli and pleasures of different kinds of writing – what is waiting is of course the *syllabus*, and this requires rather precise definition. I don't think you could simply say, we've all developed these strong kinds of personal interest in reading and can come to a university where there's a library and we can all pursue our individual courses. I mean you *could* argue that position, but it's difficult really to make the case for a university if that's what you do mean. Sometimes when you hear some of the more ideological defences of Practical Criticism, you really do feel that there is no need for an institution. If the encounter of naked reader with naked text is a sufficient basis for the understanding of many kinds of writing, then the reader can be provided with the text and intermediate institutions are really hardly necessary. But people say there are other things to learn, and this is how a syllabus gets shaped. And in the sense that there ought to be some common activity, that there is very much positively to be gained by it being a common activity, by being an institution – however blocking any institution may at times feel – that *is* an advance, though there were times in the arguments of the 1960s when people were essentially advocating the dissolution of the course into – what would it be? – at Cambridge 750 different courses which are, precisely, *not* courses but individual readings and encounters. It evades the real problems to say that there shouldn't be a syllabus, a constructed course. And yet immediately you look at a syllabus you see that the limits that my friend encountered at the men's group are in fact inscribed in it, and this is the most difficult professional point. For a syllabus is always offered as if it were a fairly common-sense, self-evident description of what is agreed common ground in the study of the subject – English Literature. It is not offered as a matter for argument but rather as the way the subject as it were constructs itself.

Now of course nothing constructs itself in that way. The map of English Literature which people carry around in their heads, which in a sense underlies the orthodox syllabus, its division into periods, its tag-names of certain kinds of writing in certain periods – that map is a construction. Moreover, it is a construction which has been laid down by discoverable generations of scholars and critics, often not so much reconstructed in each generation as layered – new layers being put onto the older types of construction. It is what I often call, in practice, a 'selective tradition' in which there is selecting and reselecting going on all the time. And nobody, whatever course they offer you, nobody in any Faculty on earth, speaking of the need for coverage, has read enough English writing to say that this is unproblematically what is there. Nobody could do that. A lifetime's reading of the most devoted kind would not give you enough to be able to say, the map *is* the substance. Nobody knows – you may only say that the map represents a consensus of opinion. When you look at how much of it was essentially laid down in the late nineteenth and early twentieth century in those disciplines of English Literature which then began to come through, and see that that map is still there essentially unrevised, you realise that you simply cannot for *professional* reasons – nothing to do with the irritation about compulsion – accept that what has been offered is simply a self-evident, common-sense description of the subject.

Let me just develop that point. I think that it is extremely difficult to talk about English Literature before about 1500 as in any significant sense a constituted subject to which certain definite boundaries can be fairly confidently assigned – though people do. And it is for quite different reasons difficult to talk about it after about 1880. Before 1500 and for 500 years before it, the literature of these islands was being carried on in at least four or even five languages. To understand the work of that extraordinary period, when there is something you could call a centralised State, as being *English* literature is a very narrow, shallow response indeed. This is to say nothing of the literature of these islands *before* that centralising English State, the way in which the older literatures of the islands – their *oldest* literatures, the Welsh, the Irish – fed into that extraordinary contemporaneous writing in four or five languages which went on from the Norman period through to, say, the mid-sixteenth century. Now at that time the English thread is an important one to trace, nobody doubts that. But then the English thread is often woven from these other materials, including Latin and the translation often through Norman French from Welsh and Irish. The English of that period is part of a multi-culture, so that to call it in this flat way 'English' Literature, in the sense that from 1550 you can reasonably begin to do, is mistaken. It's a problem; it's what people interested in it ought precisely to address, without it being self-evident.

If one misses those other elements, intent on following through the thread of Englishness, then one is really quite unprepared for the other and very ragged end of this relatively straightforward central literature. From 1550 on there had of course been continuous Welsh, Irish, Scots, whatever, contributions to what was still on the whole an inter-changeable tradition, without very consciously separated areas from it. But from about – there's no great merit in any of these dates, but as a sighting-shot – 1880, not only is there very clearly in Ireland and a bit later in Wales and Scotland the constant recreation of literatures that they now begin to think of as national – Irish literature, Scottish literature, *in* the English language but not *of* it, and in the Welsh language, Welsh literature. But at the same time the crucial North American contribution, which up till somewhere there – perhaps it ended rather earlier – had been aligning itself with the English literary tradition, broke away, as of course it was bound to do on the way to its subsequent great strength; it was now the *American* literature. Almost only the English – left you might say in possession of the field, though there was now no such field to possess – still thought they inherited, and still in a sense commanded, that common body which all these different streams had been contributing to – and which were now, in these changing circumstances, separating. The process continues in the twentieth century, with writing in the English language on the Indian subcontinent, in Africa, in Australia, New Zealand. It is now perfectly clear that, however you may want to define it, to go on talking of English Literature as unproblematical all the way through from the earliest work you find in a language still traceable as English right to the latest thing is not self-evident.

If you decide to organise a syllabus in that way, as a simple continuity which we're dividing up conveniently by date, you are evading precisely the questions which the offer of coverage can validly pose. Those questions, say, which make one wonder why it is after 1880 that the revised official account of the progress of English Literature, Leavis's Great Tradition, veers very sharply off from English writers. It veers into expatriate Americans, expatriate Poles, there's the odd surviving

Englishman like Lawrence, but suddenly modern English literature is no longer the creation of some relatively centralised culture. But in terms of the syllabus, academics sit down and say, educationally it is not sensible that people should be able to take an Honours Degree in English Literature without knowing the really major works in their literary tradition and some general sense of its historical moves and shifts. Yet if it is set down in this simplified way, of picking out English from the multi-lingual, multi-cultural medieval work, then of not noticing what has happened to English in all those overlapping meanings of 'English' since about 1880, then one is precisely not doing what one is claiming to do, is not in fact offering 'coverage' at all.

In his introduction the Chairman raised the issue of compulsory Anglo-Saxon, compulsory Old English. Now there's no question that if one is to understand, in however provisional a way, the various streams which fed that complex and rich tradition of writing, one needs the Anglo-Saxon. But one needs also, as a matter of fact, the Old Welsh and the Old Irish, and one needs the transition of them through Norman French and Church Latin. Just imagine, for example, that you were trying to trace the extraordinary resonance of the Arthurian theme through English writing. You cannot do that unless you understand the complex transition from the status of that material in Welsh, through Norman French, precisely as a counterweight to Old English. Because of course the whole claim for Arthur, the Norman claim for Arthur by those Norman writers writing in Latin, was that at least he was a British king and therefore not a Saxon, and therefore this gave a kind of Norman legitimacy to the suppression of the Saxon element in the culture; it was consciously used in that way. Now if you're busily and professionally tracing your single thread from Old English through, picking up Chaucer on the way and coming to Malory or whatever, and not knowing what else has happened, then precisely the charge that is raised over and over against syllabus reformers – that you are selling out knowledge – is the charge one has to return with interest. Because it is precisely a construction of 'English', ultimately of an ideological kind, that has excluded that other work. You may then go on to say that now I'm making the thing impossibly large, that one would need to look at early Welsh and Irish, British Latin, to know early modern French and very specifically Italian in the crucial Renaissance intervention, that one would need to know all these things to do the work adequately and that it's impossible. Certainly, I think, as a requirement at the level of a specialist, it must be impossible for any undergraduate course. But access *to* these areas, and this kind of access on the basis of options which allow people who want to go that way to specialise, to acquire the spread of mastery that a few want to do and can do, this is the way a university course should go, rather than the notion of picking out *one* of these necessary elements and then insisting that by a process of drill people become proficient in that one single thread.

It is in all these ways, then, that you realise that we have inherited a constructed syllabus from just the period when the simpler received shape of English Literature was itself rapidly changing. If you read those late nineteenth century literary histories, you are looking in effect at the residual modern syllabus, in which indeed what was then called Anglo-Saxon nationalism was often a strong element. For the study of the language was then heavily influenced by German scholars who were far ahead in studying English and who thus gave a persistent Germanic bias to the understanding of both the speech and the writing of these islands. It's then that you see that on the basis of what seems the unproblematical offer – here is a neutral description of what is there, let us see how much of it we can reasonably study in a fixed period of time – you are actually studying the constructions of . . . what would it be? I can't work out the generations – your great-great-grandfather's? It goes that far back. That's why these new young men and women who are pushing in a restless intemperate way are pushing at something which should have been evident for 80 to 100 years. Indeed, something that *was* evident at just the time that, in this residual academic way, a whole situation about to change was being set in what some people would defend as a kind of eternal statute.

And when you've got the shape, all these contested shapes – I'm not going to ask anybody to accept the literary-historical pattern, pre-1550 and post-1880, that I've just outlined as some ultimate last word – what kinds of consideration then arise? Well, first there's the problem which I once described as the fact that there have been 600 years of English literature and only 100 years of English literacy – where evidently I'm talking about English in slightly different ways, I'm using different adjectives. I'm not saying that English hasn't been written for 600 years, it's been written for longer. But I *am* saying that there's a real problem about that 600 years of English literature when it is regarded as the creation and expression of the whole people. After all, that is what the claim to Englishness, essential Englishness, is: that in learning this you learnt the real fibre of your people, they almost said 'race'. And yet, we must then insist, not until the last 100 years or so could the great majority of the people of these islands have been in any significant sense contributors to that literature, or readers of it, responding in the way in which readers do, helping both to constitute it and in some sense to shape it, giving certain shapes, affecting certain tones which involve the historical transaction of writers and readers.

One doesn't raise the *only* as a 'political' issue, as people say, fighting an old cause, fighting the cause of a people consciously kept illiterate – though of course that's what it was. The struggle for literacy was as real a social struggle as any struggle for subsistence or food or shelter. It was at several points viciously beaten back, and then in a sense only admitted on terms which are again becoming highly fashionable and contemporary: because people would need to read instructions and even to write down certain things in the way of record to be able to work. One might save the committee now being set up to study the teaching of English in schools a lot of trouble by simply photocopying from the debates about 1810 and submitting it as evidence. Literacy was crucial because, apart from these 100 years, only a few people were fighting through with great difficulty into that period of written literature, only a few people somehow got to read, and there are some remarkably heroic individual examples of this. But in general that was *not* happening, and to what extent – it's a question I consistently ask – does that affect the way *we* read works produced within that curiously asymmetrical situation? When we hear certain tones, certain rhythms – those rhythms which if you have a strong literary sense are supposed to be internalised and reproduced – from earlier writing in that asymmetrical position, what does that do now to our ways of speaking and writing in this society and therefore our ways of relating to others? Are not these questions about those works as *real* questions as the things one is invited to discuss about plot and character and imagery? Is not that deep substratum of the language-situation, not in a technical sense of language but in a social sense, a major issue in itself?

Now it's in all these ways that the existing orthodox syllabus reveals itself as a stabilisation before the very forces that are now visibly disturbing it, disturbing the situation, in some ways ending the situation. Don't those forces, especially as they come through in new media, in the return of a predominance of the oral, in new kinds of imaginative creation, force the rethinking of what is there to be covered? Just consider the point that during that dominance from 1550 to 1880, which was among other things the dominance of writing or print, and of reading print, you got the invention of a notion as uncomprehending as 'oral literature' for all that extraordinary work that preceded it – much of which was oral – and indeed for all the work during the main printed period in drama, in a whole body of sermons and lectures which constitutes a surprising amount of the activity, in many of the verse forms which have singing or speaking very near to their necessary forms. Just consider what the definitions of the print period did to the possibility of people's understanding the complexity of the oral – which is not naive in comparison with writing but is more complex, involving many different relations. Or to the understanding of something as central and at the core of any syllabus as Shakespeare; the habits of a study of the written text have simply effaced many things which are quite obvious if one doesn't bring that prejudice to it, and which are necessary parts of the work's real formation.

I think it could be argued on these professional and intellectual grounds that in a number of different ways we need a course in which certainly we are gaining knowledge over this important, indispensable central culture, but also recognising that in its very constitution, in the constitution of the very categories which are used to describe it, there are crucial issues of a serious, in some senses more intellectual kind. And much of the construction of a syllabus should be aimed at not only making access to the text, provable knowledge of the text, a joint and commonly accepted end, but should provide just those examples which from a number of different points of view are the cruces of these arguments about what it is we have as 'English', as English writing; it should be constantly asking these questions. About what it is we have in the present situation where there is more writing for other media than print than at any time for five centuries, I suppose, when the writing many people will proceed to if they go on after their course to write is at least as likely to be in various other media as in the one that for a long time has solely constituted the context of their study of imaginative writing. We must argue for the injection of these cases, the test cases, which can be suggested from very diverse intellectual points of view, as those which could be analysed and argued about, as illuminating and for some of us deciding these issues.

If that is the case for syllabus reform, it is in the end inevitable. If it is made simply in the form that these are undesirable restrictions of my total individual freedom of choice, then it will not get through because it concedes too much. It concedes the notion that we have some common responsibility to knowledge and its maintenance; it concedes the sense of a certain necessary organisation as a basis for much more individual choice and options which lead out from that. The case is stronger when it doesn't concede these points, which are almost the only serious points left to the defenders of the status quo; and they defend it the more easily if the challenge is not primarily an intellectual one, with the examples that make sense from our own reading, problems and discussions. So that when one *does* speak – whether or not you choose to say it's petty bourgeois anxiety and guilt – and the moderator gets up and announces, 'you can say anything but that', then you say, as I'm afraid I've often had to, 'after all, that is what I *came* here to say'.

1987

A talk given to Oxford English Limited, 1987

Adult Education and
Social Change

There are two ways, perhaps, in which we can interpret the matter of the relation between Adult Education and social change. One, the evident and obvious one, is that Adult Education was instituted, developed and altered by social change in the sense of movements of the larger society. The other, less obvious but I think quite inner to its history, is that Adult Education offered to be, and at times was, part of the process of social change itself. It is much easier to talk about the history in terms of the first, in which Adult Education is the bottle with the message in it, bobbing on the tides and waves of history. It has its good phases and its bad phases and so on. But I think that kind of history and that kind of interpretation of its relation to social change, although inevitable and full of evidence, diminishes it. For, though in very different ways and leading into controversies which are not yet over, the central ambition of this process which was eventually called Adult Education was to be part of the process of social change itself. At many times, and especially by those who had become eminent in one of its previous phases, this ambition was denied or played down. Nevertheless I think the true dignity of its history is not to be found in what it was influenced by, although of course being so often marginal, precarious and under-funded, it was continually influenced in this or that direction – momentarily encouraged, often thwarted. Its dignity is in the more general sense that it kept this ambition to be something other than the consequence of change and to become part of its process.

I remember a key meeting of the Oxford Delegacy at which G.D.H. Cole, very much a surviving voice of an older tradition, said, 'I don't give a damn about Adult Education, I am only interested in Workers' Education.' That was one of the interpretations of Adult Education as being part of the process of change which was at just that time colliding with the need which Cole, to be fair, did not see, for a kind of Adult Education which was wider than that of Workers' Education in the strict sense. But it was colliding also with a newly anxious respectability in which it was Adult Education that was expected to assimilate to the changed manners of the University rather than in any sense the other way round. What was at stake was the whole history of the educational challenges that Adult Education had made to those institutions which, in a way, because they do their own jobs so well, are always in danger of acquiring a very restricted and privileged and stagnant view of the world. The tension had to be worked through, the challenge had to be made, between equals. Whereas always in practice there were those unnoticed superiorities which do not belong to matters of the mind but to control of resources and committees and so on. The superiority always seemed to be coming from this other end and one of its results was that the very notion that an Adult Educator was contributing to the process of social change became suspect. This was so especially in that period of the 'forties and 'fifties when almost everybody put their intellectual resources well under cover. For it was a politically dangerous time.

Every such notion was controversial, and besides it was not made any easier to resolve by the fact that there were some crude versions of that active role around. There were indeed crude versions which would have converted this educational practice into ideological training and propaganda. But we can never be satisfied with that kind of argument between two false positions. The true position was, always essentially was, that the impulse to Adult Education was not only a matter of remedying deficit, making up for inadequate educational resources in the wider society, nor only a case of meeting new needs of the society, though those things contributed. The deepest impulse was the desire to make learning part of the process of social change itself. That was what was important about it. How to do it was always in question and always being changed, but if one forgets that underlying intention then it becomes just one of many other institutions with an essentially different kind of history.

It is true that the conscious organisation of a more literate and scientific culture in the nineteenth century was bound to throw up new kinds of institutions and eventually something that could be consciously called Adult Education. But I often recall a remark of Cobbett, at a very early stage, when people were collecting money for one of the early Mechanics' Institutes and he sent along £5, which is quite a substantial subscription if you translate the currency from the early nineteenth century. However he added, 'I gave my £5 as a mark of my regard for and my attachment to the *working classes of the community* and also as a mark of my approbation of anything which seemed to assert that these classes were equal, in point of intellect, to those who had the insolence to call them the "*Lower Orders*". But, I was not without my fears that this institution may be turned to purposes, *extremely injurious to the mechanics themselves.* I cannot but know what sort of people are likely to get amongst them ... Mechanics, I most heartily wish you well but I also most heartily wish you not to be *humbugged*, which you most certainly will be if you suffer anybody but REAL MECHANICS to have anything to do in managing the concern. You will *mean well*; but, many a cunning scoundrel will get *place* or *pension* as the *price* of you.'

Now Cobbett on Education is no kind of automatic authority. He was a great adult educator in his own practice, a remarkably self-educated man continually engaged in the real business of adult education before it was officially named. But at the same time he was deeply suspicious of the process in ways that anticipate many of the later arguments, because he was never prepared to say that education was an unambiguous good. He didn't have that kind of intellectual swoon before the very notion of a leavening of cultivation. Always it was the true content of education and the relations which as a process it was itself instituting which seemed to him to draw the line between whether it enabled people to understand and have better control over their lives or whether it was part of what he called more generally and abusively and often loosely 'the comforting system'. This was to be echoed in that slogan of the Plebs' League, a hundred years after Cobbett: 'Do you suffer from too much class consciousness? Come to Oxford and be cured'.

I often think of Cobbett's phrase 'I cannot but know what sort of people are likely to get amongst them.' It is part of the real history of adult education that some very remarkable people have got amongst the mechanics and their successors and have contributed enormously to a better understanding of the world and an ability to act in it. It is also true that some of the people Cobbett foresaw got there too, and got there because they could see the sort of process it was going to be. The necessary entry of a new kind of organised learning for adults in an increasingly literate and scientific culture didn't stay at the early institutional phase. What interests me most is the very mixed case – I have thought about it a good deal in trying to understand my own practice and that of others – in the next phase, which really inaugurates the history of what we now directly call Adult Education, particularly as it began to relate to the Universities. It was obvious that there had to be some relation to the Universities. In that second phase, particularly in the hey-day of the Extension Movement in the last third of the nineteenth century, there was a very curious thing which I think helps one to understand that crucial difference in British culture between two ideas which sound so like each other that we often confuse them: on the one hand *social conscience*, and on the other *social consciousness*.

There is no doubt that a very large part of the Extension Movement was the product of a certain kind of social conscience, and this is in a limited way to be respected. People saw not only hard-working men living in poor and deprived material conditions but hard-working men of considerable intelligence and interest in learning deprived of the least opportunity in any sustained way to fulfil that kind of resource. If what followed from that included a missionary sense, the sense of going out to remedy a deficit, it has still to be respected but certainly not submitted to. For it sent out many good people who tried to humanise their own learning and to bring it into real relations with this hard-pressed environment. But also necessarily, and it is true of the majority in that phase (I would not like to estimate how long that kind of confidence persisted), they believed that they were taking *understanding* to people. Not taking the tools of understanding; not taking the results of certain organised learning; not putting these into a process which would then be an interaction with what was often very solid experience in areas in which the learned were in fact ignorant; but rather a taking of learning itself, humanity itself. It is surprising how often in the writings of that period people whose individual lives we can respect, talk about 'humanising' or 'refining' people, of course mostly poor people. But the fact is that the real situation was never of that kind.

Everyone notices, in an unequal education system, the facts of deficit; notices the people who could do with more or better, more sustained education and who are in that sense deprived. But what few notice, because to have the opportunity to observe both sides of this divide is not common, is that in a society in which learning is unequal certain distinctive kinds of ignorance accumulate in the very heartland of learning. This heartland defines itself; it defines what learning is; it deems what is a subject and what is not. It knows what is evidence and what is not. We find Cobbett, if I may quote him again, thinking just about this in relation to history. The Histories of England, he says, 'are very little better than romances. Their contents are generally confined to narrations relating to battles, negotiations, intrigues, contests between rival sovereignties, rival nobles and to the character of kings, queens, mistresses, bishops, ministers and the like.' He was talking, he tells us, to a very clever young man who had read the history of England by many different authors and 'I gave the conversation a turn that drew from him, unperceived by himself, that he did not know how tithes, parishes, poor rates, church rates and the abolition of trial by jury in hundreds of cases came to be in England'. 'It is not stuff like this', Cobbett argued, 'but we want to know what was the state of the people, what were a labourer's wages; what were the prices of the food, and how the labourers were dressed?'

Now, again I don't quote Cobbett as an authority but the point he made was made again and was instanced without being made in hundreds of subsequent cases. For although the manifest relationship was that taking learning to a class seen as in deficit, or to certain stranded exceptional individuals as it was often interpreted, it was rarely noticed that the real deficit was on both sides of the account. For there was a positive deficiency in the centres of learning themselves. There were areas of the life of their own people about which they were profoundly ignorant. When adult education was seen only as the process of humanising and refining, when people who went out in that missionary spirit hit (as they sometimes did, although they often got a lot of submissive respect, but as they sometimes did) the hard talk of men who did ask (and it wasn't a utilitarian question although it often tended to be reduced to it) 'Where does this learning tie in with my life?', then the notion of refining and humanising could become anti-educational.

There was the anti-educational notion that you should soften the terms of the discussion; the anti-educational notion that you should exclude controversial current material. There was also the support of certain subjects, in that period and since, precisely because they moved people away from those areas which would put the status and nature of official learning in question.

Yet if you look at the next period from the turn of the century, there is not only that bust-up between the Plebs' League and the WEA, in which the Plebs' League saw the WEA as at one time they called them 'Lackeys standing in front of the university trying to divert the workers into this kind of university consciousness'. There is also what the WEA did, through its best tutors, to meet that centrality of response without, at least without intending, the responses of refinement or of humanising a rather raw population. For that is not where real social change lies. As it came through with harder, better organised people, it has been true of the best Adult Education in this century that the idea of learning itself has been changed, and this has been one of the processes by which learning has contributed to social change rather than simply reflecting it.

The case of Tawney is now classical because Tawney had the intellectual honesty to admit that as already a major professional historian there were areas of the history of his own people about which he knew little. It happened later, I believe, in economics. It certainly happened after the war when – if I may tell you this as a story – when I moved into internal University Teaching, when at about the same time Richard Hoggart did the same, we started teaching in ways that had been absolutely familiar in Extra-Mural and WEA classes, relating history to art and literature, including contemporary culture, and suddenly so strange was this to the Universities that they said 'My God, here is a new subject called Cultural Studies'. But we are beginning, I am afraid, to see encyclopaedia articles dating the birth of Cultural Studies from this or that book in the late 'fifties. Don't believe a word of it. That shift of perspective about the teaching of arts and literature and their relation to history and to contemporary society began in Adult Education, it didn't happen anywhere else. It was when it was taken across by people with that experience to the Universities that it was suddenly recognised as a subject. It is in these and other similar ways that the contribution of the process itself to social change itself, and specifically to learning, has happened.

Now it is very important to say this when we come to the post-war period in which the notion of deficit was dropped. It was said that since there was now universal education, since there was now every opportunity of access for what was still in that twinkling way called 'a bright child' to go wherever he wished, then there was a diminishing or vanishing deficit. The cannibals thus appeared to be dying out and there was therefore less demand for missionaries. The rough, naturally intelligent but unlettered were becoming a very small number, and the ones who were still like that didn't want to know anyway. Therefore – as indeed if that had been its only premise – adult education had reached its natural limit. It was the kind of thing that could be safely dropped and mythologised. Mythologised it was but also there were really very serious attempts to drop it, and still are.

This brings us to a real complexity, the relation between willingness and ability to learn and the forms of learning that are at any time presented. What is usually offered, in the crude state of official educational thinking, is the proposition that there is something called academic education and there is even something called the academic mind and, God help us, the academic child. Thus academic institutions exist for those potential academic persons and academic children, and those who are not academic persons or academic children will be very much happier not to be bothered. Under this wonderful alibi word 'academic' the problems about education which Adult Education and others raised can be simply evaded. For life is not like that, of course. It is not some simple process of offering and reception. There are always some blocks on learning. One of them is the relevance of the learning that happens to be available to what *you* want to learn. These complications eat so deeply into all educational systems that only somebody up to no good ever draws the stupid conclusion that you have reached the limit of the educable.

Actually the last time we had any records on this was in that otherwise unregretted period of National Service, when they gave recruits intelligence tests; not that we should put any great faith in them but they indicate something. It is very interesting that then, in the late 'fifties, in National Service recruits' intelligence tests, half of those who were put by the tests in the highest intelligence categories had had no more than a minimum education. Yet this was in a period when if the institutional alternatives which were talked about as having ended this deficit had really done so, at least a good number of them would have been picked up. This is one kind of objective support for my own very strong belief that it is not just a matter of available intelligence and available learning interest, but that there is still an extraordinary lottery in the interlock between those and the kind of learning that is at any time available and the time of life at which it comes up. This is a point that adult educationalists have of course often made. It defeats the crude, ideological attempt to write the last chapter of adult education because all the bright boys and girls have gone through the system and up the ladder. Or rather it should defeat it, but in practice the crude ideology can be one of those self-fulfilling prophecies, as you put less resources into education, or as people subtly change their own attitudes to it and then you get less significant response and that seems to confirm the initial assumption.

Such changes are very different from the movements of large, objective forces such as the nature of work and the rise of modern communications systems and all those other things which have quite evidently changed the nature of education in any case. All of us must adjust to those, but this is very different from adjusting to the anti-educational ideologies. Indeed I sometimes feel when I look at the actual cannibals who are now powerful in the world of ideas and educational provision, that we could do with a few missionaries again, simply carrying social conscience towards deficit. But then if we accept their kind of analysis of the history, we shall be quite unprepared to analyse the very critical and complex situation that anything now offering to call itself Adult Education finds itself in.

It is very interesting in spite of the persistent echoes of that symbolic dispute between the Plebs' League and the WEA, and later the WEA and the Labour Colleges, about the feel, the tone, the content of education, and about who should control it, that although the WEA was the better founded organisation and had the key assistance of the universities and of official recognition, nevertheless people entered it, especially in the 1930s with a strong sense of Adult Education as contributing to social change. These were people, and in my experience they were almost all good people, who went into Adult Education because they wanted to change the society in some specific ways. They were driven not by social conscience, in the old sense. It wasn't the missionary position of feeling sorry for the unfortunate. Instead they were interested in the process of building a social consciousness of an adequate kind, as they saw it, to meet new crises, the crises that were then defined as war and unemployment and Fascism but that in any case were seen as the crises of modern capitalist society. It was almost invariably seen like that, but they went into Adult Education, not to propagandise – they could have done that more easily in other institutions – but with that necessary consciousness as a kind of priority. The resulting complications – the emotional, intellectual and social complications of that generation, which entered with that kind of intention – have still, I think to be fully analysed. Because quite apart from the simplest things one can say about it – that it didn't turn out like that, that it became politically very difficult, and so on – the whole problem was that people arriving with a message, their kind of message in the bottle, had to learn, if they were to enter in any sustained way the experience of Adult Education, that even people who agreed that the point of Adult Education was the building of an adequate social consciousness didn't, in that sense, want messages. I mean they didn't want the conclusions of arguments: they wanted to reach their own conclusions.

But also in a rather later period the whole problem was not whether the message would be accepted or rejected or modified but – and I don't mean this satirically – what the message should be. I mean that the very broadening of the material and of the subjects of Adult Education which occurred in that generation, was, we can say in retrospect, a kind of thinking arising from the complications of practice. It was a question not what the message should be so much as what would be the kind of evidence, what sources would you look for?

I would instance, for example, the shift that has happened in thinking about symbolic values, as in thinking about Art and Literature. Something of this kind had always been done in this work but usually as reflecting what happened elsewhere in the society. The new thinking was about just these practices, in any period, as part of the way in which a general social consciousness is formed, the way in which it actually gets embodied, not from other sources but from some general source in social life and yet they are still unmistakable as themselves and can only be addressed as themselves. The shift to that is part of the complication. There was a time as an adult tutor when you felt a second class citizen if you were not teaching Economics or Politics, because that had been the first interpretation of what the business of creating social consciousness was. I know in my own case the first four Tutorial Classes I had were all in International Relations and in some curious way in the next year they had all become classes in Literature. The process by which this happened has never been satisfactorily explained. Yet I didn't get what might be called approval about this. And after all you can still see the case. Suppose you say now, 'What do we most need to be conscious about, since we are starting a class this winter?' You might easily ask if there is anything worth discussing this winter but the problems of nuclear disarmament and the problems of the British and world economy – I am not running any of those issues down – I am just saying the old assumption was that there and there only, and in those ways, was consciousness formed. And this was the curious change that happened in this post-war period, of which some of the political results are now taking some of the people who never noticed this shift by surprise. If I can again give one example, when I was teaching classes and writing about newspapers and advertising in the 'fifties one of my political friends said, 'Well, I suppose it's amusing enough but what does it have to do with politics?' But if you look back from the 'eighties, having seen what newspapers have to do with politics, you can recall the really virgin innocence of people who thought themselves hard, mature, political analysts.

For the process of real social consciousness is always complex, and learning and getting through to the centres of consciousness of one's own time is always a matter of *contemporary* analysis. This will certainly renew many received things but it will also draw on kinds of evidence, kinds of influence, kinds of change which had previously been excluded. Yet the other pressure on us was to feel that this was the nice, good stuff, as against the chaotic and dismal muddle of Politics and Economics; that this was the beautiful material, these were the real achievements of humanity. But to be able to see in the shift of a style of painting or in the shift of a method in architecture or in a shift in a major literary form, that social relationships and people themselves are changing, and that people's symbolic values have a crucial effect on the ways in which they interpret all their other values and their other relationships and therefore contribute necessary evidence to it, this was the kind of change that eventually occurred. The simple version, that you went into Adult Education to build social consciousness, changed, not in its ideals but in its methods. Of course there were then also all the other changes: the supposed ending of the deficit; the development of an educational bureaucracy; the pressure, backed by funding, to train people for roles and jobs as preferable to the general education of human beings and citizens. Through all this there was also the pressure to make adult education respectable, in such limited terms. The old humanists were pushed away; the industrial trainers arrived; but still, under difficult conditions, the new humanists – the true public educators – survived.

The building of social consciousness is of real consciousness, of real understanding of the world. And it extends beyond the simpler areas that were externally defined as Political and Economic. It is in work like that that real Adult Education justifies itself. It is reduced if it is seen as merely the second-order consequence and reflection of social change. At its best it has truly contributed to change itself, and continues to contribute in a social order which has more need of it, being less conscious of its real situation than I think has ever been the case. For this is a social order which really does not know in what crucial respects it is ignorant, in what crucial respects it is incompletely conscious and therefore in what crucial respects this collaborative process of Adult Education is still central.

1983

The Tony McLean Memorial Lecture, September 1983

The Red and the Green

Some very important changes in socialist ideas are now beginning to come through in Europe. Yet at the surface of politics they are invisible in Britain, even though there are those here who have contributed to them. Where they have become visible at the surface, as most notably in the rise of the Green Party in the German Federal Republic, they are still commonly interpreted as a local 'ecological' variation, without long-term effect on the main body of socialist institutions and ideas. Similarly, the difficult argument about relations between the Left and the popular campaigns for nuclear disarmament – description of these as the Peace Movement raises the precise point – is often displaced to the idea of a 'single issue', which leaves the main body of politics intact.

It is impossible to predict what will happen to these ideas and to the movements within which they are active. But it will clear the air if we can begin to recognise that they are an attempted redefinition of the whole socialist project, on the basis of a new kind of analysis of the systems which are being opposed. From this point of view, it is arguments about the relations between the Labour Party and the Militant Tendency, or between the parliamentary versions of socialism and social democracy, which are local and residual. Similarly the long argument about Soviet Communism and its consequences, though it has many vested interests on both sides, is no longer central: its lessons, rather than its enclosed antagonisms, have been placed in a new perspective. The most difficult term in the redefinition is 'ecology'. As this has come through, in its most obvious forms, it is indeed a set of special issues: campaigns against industrial pollution, environmental damage, dangerous technologies such as nuclear power, and the exploitation and waste of scarce resources. All these command growing support but are widely seen as either non-political or at the fringes of real politics. Even when they are brought together as the crisis of industrial society, there is still no obvious engagement with our orthodox political forms, within which a commitment to this form of society is taken for granted. What is then new in the new socialism is that it takes the ecological arguments through to the point where they engage with the arguments of economics, and so to new positions about industrial capitalism and world production and trade.

It is at first, for many, a strange intellectual experience. The familiar starting-points, in the Labour movement or in the radical tradition, become stages in an argument which has set out from a much wider base. The interlock with established politics is obviously difficult, and is still unresolved. But it ought at least to be an intellectual responsibility to look at what this movement is really saying.

Rudolf Bahro, who wrote *The Alternative* and was imprisoned and then released in East Germany, is one of its most articulate spokesmen. He is a Marxist who has taken a position in classical terms but with far from classical results. What he is saying, in these terms, is that in the old industrial societies 'external contradictions' have become more important than the 'internal contradictions' on which the traditional labour movements were founded. This probably needs to be translated, since many people have got into the habit of switching off when Marxism or a term like 'contradiction' is mentioned. Specifically, then, the argument is that all human societies are now dominated by three active conflicts of interest: between 'East' and 'West', in the special form of the arms race; between 'North' and 'South', in the special form of the world economic and monetary crisis; between 'humanity' and 'nature', in the special forms of the exploitation of scarce resources and of widespread environmental damage. The effect of these definitions on socialist ideas and movements is that these conflicts must take priority over the internal conflict, to do with wages and the distribution of national production. Indeed Bahro returns the charge often made against ecological or disarmament or feminist campaigns by saying that 'if there is anything today that really does deserve the label of a single-issue movement, it is the institutionalised wage struggle.'

It can be objected that these definitions of the three major conflicts merely restate well-known problems, without contributing to a solution. In evocative campaigning this is indeed often so. It is occasionally a weakness even in Bahro that the moral challenge represented by naming these conflicts, supported by the deep emotions now provoked by the evils of war and poverty and disease which they cause, is seen as leading to what is in effect a movement of conversion. An analogy with the situation of the first Christians is often directly made. Styles of campaigning, in the peace movement and also in ecological and 'Third

World' demonstrations, are often visibly of this kind. What is offered is witness, in a call to turn away from unarguable evil.

Yet it is a fact that, working mainly at this level, the movements have already made a difference to orthodox politics. The disarmament campaigns, especially, are now being taken very seriously by the most orthodox parties. The instant diagnosis, however, is that they are all primarily 'emotional' campaigns: understandable, but at best raw material, at worst hysterical distraction, in terms of 'real politics'. Some elements of this diagnosis are themselves evasive, but at a certain level the challenge is real. It is not by evoking these conflicts and dramatising their dangers that their central political processes can be altered. What is necessary is a unified theory, and then a unified movement, within which the three major external conflicts, and then necessarily the continuing internal conflict, can be seen as interconnected. Such a theory may now be in sight. Its basis is the progressive unification of economics and ecology. It is not industrial production as such which has led to these major contradictions. That is the weakest side of the ecology movement, which has correctly identified current symptoms but supposes that these can be removed by some option for a pre-industrial or post-industrial order. The root cause is not in the isolated forces of production, but in the mode of production as a whole. Its most evident damage has been in the relentless drive for profit and the accumulation of capital, but underlying even this has been a basic orientation to the world – at once its resources and its peoples – which defines it as raw material. The idea of 'resources' may itself often include this orientation. What is seen is not life-forms and land-forms, in an intricate interdependence, but a range of opportunities for their profitable exploitation, which at certain definite technical stages becomes, on a rising scale, a form, not only of production, but of destruction and self-destruction.

It is true that the major phase of this long history has been the specific combination of capitalist drives for profit and ever more powerful technologies of transformation. But this cannot reduce the argument to one against the property forms of capitalism. If that were true, we would have no way of explaining the continuing appropriation and exploitation of the world as raw material – again including people as well as other life-forms and land-forms – in the 'Communist' economies: what Bahro calls the societies of 'actually existing socialism'. It is crucial to the whole argument that what the orientation involves is not only or even mainly the exploitation of the resources of the earth, but, as the critical factor which makes it practically and powerfully destructive, the use of actual majorities of other people as the raw material without which the material processes could not be carried through. Thus the subordination of such majorities, by military, political or cultural means, is a central element of the whole orientation, which cannot be reduced to its 'material' or 'industrial' results.

It is ironic that what is now seen as the central problem of the old industrial societies, in rising unemployment, is actually a phase in this general development, in which an increasing number of the people previously seen as raw material are being classified, through various technical changes, as 'surplus to requirement' and therefore, in that most significant term, 'redundant'. Bahro continues to argue, against other Marxists, that the concept of the revolutionary proletariat has failed, and that other agencies of change or challenge must be found. In some obvious ways he is right, but it is still much too early to know what will happen in the working class of the old industrial countries, seen by Bahro as tamed and incorporated by the wage-bargaining of a relatively successful capitalism, when more and more workers are forced beyond these forms, by being turned out of their jobs and the styles of life which these supported. In his anxiety to get beyond an old ideology, he may be failing to notice a now rapidly changing situation.

Yet it remains true that the existing institutions of nationally based labour movements, whether in trade unions or in political parties, are peculiarly unadapted to the scale of the current crisis in the world economy. All that they can generate is a set of defensive campaigns, aimed at restoring previous stabilities and resuming what they see as only temporarily abandoned policies. Yet whether the general crisis is seen in economic or in ecological terms, and all the more when these terms are combined, it is probable that those stabilities are permanently lost, and with them the relevance of the traditional policies. This is only one of several instances of the otherwise surprising political fact that the hard Right and the hard Left are now addressing the same levels of problem – in each case with a conviction of radical discontinuity and the consequent need for radical change.

It is primarily in seeing the crisis as that of a world economy that this divergence from more familiar political forms arises. Yet as between hard Right and hard Left there is then an even more important divergence than the obviously different directions of interest and policy. For the Right talks the same apparent language as the Centre, when it bases its policies on economic growth. Its difference from the Centre is that it sees this as possible only by harsh reductions in all other areas of social policy, and by the development both of more aggressive marketing and more intransigent competition with all other economic forces, in the 'Communist bloc' and among 'Third World' suppliers of commodities. The international Left, by contrast, is increasingly resisting growth of that unequal kind. When the ecological argument is added, there is some significant divergence. One of its forms is suspected of being, and often is, a further discrimination against the poor countries, in its campaigns against development and in its concentration on population growth as a primary cause of poverty. Bahro's position is quite different. The industrial drives which are already causing environmental damage, and which are threatening to cause ecological disaster or even collapse, are firmly located in the old but still dominant industrial economies: the same source from which the dangers of nuclear weapons and of indiscriminate arms export also proceed. Thus it is in these powerful societies – Western capitalist but also Eastern 'Communist' – that these drives must be halted and turned back. A new broad social movement, as distinct from the received socialist or social-democratic forms, has then to be built in these countries, around the central issues of ecology and peace. This is the new radical form of the red and the green.

Such movements are now growing, in many countries, and are beginning to co-operate with each other. Yet there are still problems of interlock with the existing and dominant political processes. Moreover, the problems vary in different societies. The Greens in the Federal Republic have the advantage, which might also in some circumstances be the disadvantage, of proportional representation and thus entry into the parliamentary system. It is what they do when they get there, in the complications and pressures of coalition politics, that has still be be judged. It seems safe to say that there would be a Green Party in Britain within a year of any introduction of proportional representation, but then with the same problems ahead of it. Meanwhile its potential members, against the odds but with many formal successes in the adoption of policies, are looking primarily to convert the Labour Party. It is again too early to say, but this may prove at least as difficult as Bahro's policy of a more general public conversion.

1982

Review of *Socialism and Survival* by Rudolf Bahro (1982), *Capitalist Democracy in Britain* by Ralph Miliband (1982) and *Socialist Register 1982* edited by Martin Eve and David Musson (1982)

Communications, Technologies
and Social Institutions

When we think of modern communications we think at once of certain technologies. A whole series of effective inventions seem to have changed, permanently, the ways in which we must think of communication. Yet, at the same time, communication is always a form of social relationship, and communications systems have always to be seen as social institutions. It is then necessary to think, very generally but also very precisely, about the real relations between communications technologies and social institutions.

Consider first one common and influential way of thinking, or appearing to think, about these relations. People say 'television has altered our world', or 'radio altered the world', or, reaching further back, 'printing altered the world'. And we usually, at first, know what these statements mean. Evident and widespread social effects have undoubtedly followed the uses of all these inventions. But then, in expanding the statements in this way, we have already – and sometimes without noticing it – introduced a further category: that of 'uses'. The argument can then go in several directions. It can be said that what has altered our world is not television or radio or printing as such, but the uses made of them, in particular societies. Against this, or partly against it, it is then often said that once the invention has been made it will be used, and that the general effects of its use are at least as important, and may indeed be much more fundamental, than more local and more particular applications.

There are no simple ways out of the argument at this point. One main reason is that the terms in which such initial propositions are made are inadequate. A very complex set of relations and interactions is being reduced to interpretation in two simple terms: 'technical invention' and 'society' ('the world'). Using these simple terms, we can make such opposing statements as that 'technical inventions change society' or that 'society determines the uses of technical inventions'. But then the

172

argument often gets stuck at this stage of apparently opposing assertions, or at the further stage when selections of the historical and empirical evidence are assembled in support of either. For what the terms and their assumptions often prevent us from seeing is that technical inventions are always made *within* societies and that societies are always more than the sum of relations and institutions from which, by a falsely specialising definition, technical inventions have been excluded.

These fairly obvious facts are further obscured by the common tendency to use the terms 'technical invention' and 'technology' as if they were equivalent. This is particularly so in the adjective, when people describe some element of the development of a device – in engineering, for example – as a technological problem or a technological breakthrough. But the distinction between techniques and technologies is crucial, especially in the context of this general inquiry. A technique is a particular skill or application of a skill. A technical invention is then a development of such a skill or the development or invention of one of its devices. A technology by contrast is, first, the body of knowledge appropriate to the development of such skills and applications and, second, a body of knowledge and conditions for the practical use and application of a range of devices.

These two definitions of technology can be theoretically distinguished, but they are in fact substantially connected. They relate to overlapping stages: the body of knowledge, both theoretical and practical, from which the skills and devices (technical inventions) come, and the body of knowledge and conditions from which they are developed, combined, and prepared for use. What matters, in each stage, is that a technology is always, in a full sense, social. It is necessarily in complex and variable connection with other social relations and institutions, although a particular and isolated technical invention can be seen, and temporarily interpreted, as if it were autonomous. As we move into any general social inquiry, we then find that we have always to relate technical inventions to their technologies, in the full sense, and, further, that we are starting from one kind of social state or institution – a *technology* – and relating it to other kinds of social state and institution rather than to a generalised 'society' so pre-defined as to separate or exclude it.

Two Kinds of Resource in Communication

The general technology of communications is full of fascinating examples of these real relations. Yet, before we can properly understand them, we have to take account of one fundamental distinction in human communications in general. The earliest forms of human communication, like the forms of almost all animal communication, made predominant if never perhaps exclusive use of inherent, evolved and constituted physical resources. The human body, in its full sense, is the set of resources from which this major kind of communication was developed. This is true of both verbal (oral) and non-verbal (physical expression and gesture) forms. It would be confusing to speak of the systems that were developed from these inherent physical resources as 'technologies', yet we can never afford to overlook the important systems of knowledge, skill and training applied in the development of these inherent resources – the great systems of rhetoric and of training in acting are the most visible because most specialised forms – alongside the other systems that we can designate as imitation, custom or habit.

This point becomes very important when we come to emphasise the fundamental qualitative change in communications systems which occurred when men began using and adapting – and in the end quite extraordinarily extending – objects and forces outside their own bodies as major means of communication. For, even as we insist on this qualitative change – the beginning of the true *technology* of communications – we have of course to recognise that those earliest forms, dependent primarily on immediate and inherent physical resources, are still today, in many kinds of social relationship – the family, the immediate community, everyday business and travel – either predominant or central. Even in other kinds of social relationship – larger societies and larger economies – they are combined with specific technologies which reinforce them. Meanwhile, of course, other systems, quite differently based, have acquired an increasing importance. But the distinction between systems based on inherent physical resources and systems based on the development and application of objects and forces outside the human body is fundamental to understanding the complex history, including the social history, of communications technologies.

We can now make some preliminary distinctions of the most general types of communications systems, by function. Thus some systems are of an *amplifying* kind – megaphoning or telephoning or broadcasting the still autonomous human voice; transmitting voices, expressions, gestures and actions, as in television. Other systems are of a *storing* kind – recording in more or less permanent form actual human voices, as in sound recording, or expressions, perceptions, gestures and actions, as in much painting and sculpture, or both aural and visual elements in videotape and film. Still other systems are *instrumentally* alternative to the use or representation of inherent physical resources, even when they offer to be equivalent to them, such as the record and transmission of information and ideas in locally autonomous material systems, as in writing, printing and teletext.

These are not simple distinctions between 'ancient' and 'modern' communications. Some uses, however simple, of each of these types occurred very early indeed in human cultural evolution. There were and still are skills of pitching the voice to carry long distances, and methods of choosing prominent places to amplify voices and gestures. There was 'lasting' representation, 'storing' at least in effect, of such human actions as hunting, as in the cave paintings. There were also very early instrumental communications, as in the setting up of stone markers or the making of marks on trees, and again in the adaptation or invention of physical objects to transmit sound, as in shells, drums and horns. All these very early skills and devices presuppose social relations, but it was in the storing and especially the instrumental types that they moved most evidently towards systems. For obvious reasons, it is in the storing and some of the instrumental modes that there has been most survival into later periods, yet it is notorious that many of the surviving marks and representations are very difficult to interpret, largely because their elements of inherent system have been lost. The possibility of interpretation is, indeed, quite precisely related to the extent to which such elements became fully systematic, rather than conventional processes still directly attached to lived and living social relations.

But we can see very early, in some cases, some direct relations between systems and institutions, as distinct from more general relations between skills or devices and the fact of social relationships. Thus we find the mnemonic, indicative or initiation devices of early calendars and genealogies, topographical plans, and above all cult modes and objects. There can be no doubt that these are discretely systematic, in direct relation to social organisation. But there is then an intensification of system, and a move towards its generalisation, in the development of writing systems in the temple cities and then in the extending trading areas. It is significant that these major advances in what was already becoming a communications technology are predominantly of an instrumental kind, and there are direct relations (as already in tribal societies, in the case of the cults) between the increased complexity and efficiency of the system and its social specialisation: 'it was the complexity of the writing that confined its systematic use to a well-trained set of "scribes",' whose position also rested upon the fact that they were largely trained by priests. At the same time the primary uses of the system were directly related to the same form of social organisation: 'the records mainly refer to the property and accounts of temples'. The further development of writing systems was directly related to the development of specific kinds of urban economy: 'nor was it simply a consequence but also a condition of that development'. But with the expansion of trading areas, new writing systems, and above all the alphabetic, took the possibilities of instrumental communication beyond local institutional systems, extending at once its range and its content, and indeed making possible the general social dimension rather than the specialised craft of literacy.

Techniques and their Realisation

Yet there is then an evident asymmetry between the social possibilities of the new instrumental system and the actual institutions which could alone provide access to it. For many centuries, though writing had spread beyond the specialised scribes to a more general educated class, it still spread only to minorities of the actual populations in which, in matters of law, property, history and ideas, it was now a major organising force. Thus, not for the first or the last time, a communications system and its technology stood in contradictory relations to the institutions which employed and controlled it. In the earliest human communications, use of and access to the various systems, whether amplifying, storing or instrumental, had been relatively generalised, since the relations between the systems and quite general immediate social skills and resources were necessarily close. The increasing complexity of the systems, indeed the movement from techniques to what can properly be called early technologies, made the new relations at best problematic. It was not now by being a person in a place that relative access to the central communications systems of the group was assured. Increasingly, in certain important areas of life, there was a network of institutional arrangements, most evidently in selective educational institutions, which determined the possibility of full communicative resources and access, and this organisation of differential access to the most developed communications systems both corresponded to and was itself an integral part of general social organisation.

The increased range and the greatly expanded content of written communications only deepened this stratification. For a very long time after writing systems developed, large areas of cultural life were still primarily oral: but, alongside these, are power and continuity of written bodies of law, history, social and religious thought and literature were steadily increasing. By the time of the invention of printing, and its first applications, the asymmetry between the abstract possibilities of the new technologies and their actual, institutionally controlled uses was remarkable. The alphabetic script, the pre-print technologies of reproduction and distribution of writing, and then the printed book itself all contained abstract possibilities (all eventually to be realised in certain societies). At each stage of the development of the actual techniques and technologies these possibilities were not only not fully used but were in many cases deliberately arrested. A simple history of the developing technologies, considered in isolation, might indicate a steady generalisation and strengthening of human communication. But technologies, as we saw earlier, can never be considered in isolation. The technique of writing is one thing, but the *technology* of writing involved not only the development of writing instruments and materials, but also the development of a wider body of knowledge, and specifically of the skills of reading, which was in practice inextricable from the most general forms of social organisation. Thus it should come as no surprise to us that 'access to books has contributed to the structuring of a hierarchical social order'. Effective use of the new technology, at the level of reading, required a 'long apprenticeship' which presupposed, for several centuries, a relatively privileged social position: an initial privilege which, 'yielded returns which could be reinvested to further advantage'. Thus the relations between a technology and its most general institutions became the ground, first, of specific social differentiations and later, inevitably, of social conflict.

Between the invention of printing, in the 15th century, and our own day, there has been a long and complex series of institutional changes and conflicts in the uses of this powerful and often decisive technology. Frequently these changes and conflicts have represented major issues in the whole development of societies. Thus the long and seemingly endless battle for the freedom to write, print and distribute our own thoughts has been, in one society after another, a key issue in the development both of free intellectual inquiry and of political democracy. Every kind of measure has been adopted against it, from systems of state licensing and the ecclesiastical controls of the *imprimatur* through to general legal provisions in such areas as security, libel and obscenity and organised political censorship. Important gains have been made in some constitutional provisions for the freedom of the press, but in world terms the freedom to print is still extremely uneven and in many societies still does not exist. The tangled and bitter history of the struggle for freedom to print is of course inseparable from the related struggle for the freedom and capacity to read. Yet these relations are not always direct. Some of the most bitter struggles against state licensing and ecclesiastical controls occurred when the majority of people were still unable and unlikely to read. On the other hand, in certain societies, the balance eventually struck between freedom of the press and a minority reading public was deeply disturbed when social and technical changes were beginning to expand the reading public. A good example is the political crisis of English newspapers in the early 19th century. After repeated struggles, most importantly over the right to report the proceedings of Parliament, the relative freedom of some minority newspapers had been established. But in the political crisis from the 1790s a whole new press, written for and often by the new urban working class, grew up alongside newspapers of the older type, and new and severe legislation was enacted against them. This was still at a time when less than half the population could read. Comparable situations and struggles can be found in, for example, the Germany of Bismarck and early 19th-century Spain.

But of course the distribution of print was not limited by ability to read. In the early 19th century, at once because of reading difficulties and because of the expense of buying books and newspapers, formal and informal group reading – reading aloud – was very common. The interaction between written and oral forms was indeed very complex. The church sermon, often later printed, retained a central importance. Its secular successor, the public lecture, was just entering its major social development. In these varying ways, the real public for what was in effect the combined operation of oral and printed communication was becoming very large. It was a quite different social situation from that of the relative predominance of print in the period 1890–1940.

By the later period, in the most advanced societies, systems of near-universal education in literacy had been established. This relative specialisation of education to literacy of course had its own effects. Since the Renaissance, though then for more limited numbers, the defining quality of education had been this mastery of reading print, by comparison for example with the substantial elements of oral training, as in the great systems of rhetoric, in the medieval curriculum. The problem of the relations between this newly central skill and the other relevant skills of adult life became acute as education was extended to whole populations. Some of the consequences of these particular relations are still being critically experienced in the late 20th century. There was of course much resistance to the institution of popular education, on anti-democratic political grounds. But, sometimes confused with this, there were both generous and ungenerous questions about the relations between this central skill of reading and most types of adult work. What eventually carried the day for reading was a combination of three rather different considerations: first, and perhaps especially in the Protestant countries, the desire for moral instruction and moral improvement by the capacity to read the Bible; second, the increasing need, in the new industrial economy, to read printed information and instructions; and, third, the political need for access to facts and arguments in a developing political democracy (a case made from both sides: by the popular forces, that the press was the engine of liberty; by the anti-popular forces, at this late stage, that the new voters must be properly instructed). There were many social complications. Some of those arguing that the poor must be able to read the Bible, as a means to their moral improvement, overlooked the fact that there is no way of teaching a man to read the Bible which does not also enable him to read the radical press. The consequent disillusion was considerable. Again others argued that the poor should be taught to read, in the interests of moral improvement and working efficiency, but that there was no need at all to teach them to write, beyond the capacity to append a signature, since it was evident that they would have nothing to communicate on their own account. Out of these mixed motives and considerations a system of general literacy eventually emerged. Elementary literacy in England, for example, rose from some 50 per cent in the 1820s to some 90 per cent in the 1890s, and this trend is broadly characteristic of other West European societies in the same period.

Types of Popular Culture
But there were now quite new problems in the relations between the technology and the institutions. Over a long period, elements of an earlier oral culture – 'ballads and "street literature"' – had been incorporated into print, and new popular print forms, such as almanacs, had been developed. This long period marks the phase of an established popular culture being translated and developed into printed forms. Early popular newspapers bear many of the marks of this inheritance. But the eventual establishment of a widely distributed

commercial popular press inaugurated a new phase in the relations between oral and printed cultures. This phase is of course inseparable from general social changes, and in particular the rapid development of predominantly urban and industrial economies. Organised sport (mainly football and horse-racing) and organised commercial entertainment (popular theatres and eventually cinema and television) were not only newly important institutions in urban industrial societies; they became major items of news of all kinds in the new popular press. Their combination with earlier kinds of item – reports of notorious crimes and of scandals – produced a distinctive modern cultural form which still, very obviously, makes some definitions of 'newspaper' ambiguous. The claim of the press to be a 'fourth estate' in political life was sustained by one kind of newspaper, which took its central material from political and economic affairs. By contrast, much of the new 'popular press', though including some of this material, became a specific form which offered to represent, at its chosen level, the general cultural interests of the whole society. These alternative forms of development, important everywhere, are especially evident in the history of the press in the United States, which produced the most influential examples of the latter form. The transition from a 'folk culture', or indeed from a 'popular culture' in the older sense, to a modern type of 'popular culture', now basically derivative from organised central institutions, is a remarkable example of the interaction between a major technology and major social institutions: a history in print which has since been widely repeated in later media.

It is in this perspective that we have to look again at the complex relations between communications technologies and social institutions. For of course this new popular press was made possible only by significant technical developments: steam printing, cheaper production of paper, the telegraph for news-gathering, the railways for rapid distribution. The first two of these were specific to the development of the press, and were, as inventions, specifically sought; in neither area was there mere random technical discovery, which then changed a wider world. On the other hand, their development was closely bound up with the more general changes which were producing the conditions in which the new social and cultural form was necessary: changes which were by no means fully foreseen. Steam printing was an evident application of the more general development of steam engineering for pumping, textile manufacture and loco-motion. Improved paper production was a development within the general advance of the chemical industry. Improvements in type-setting and graphic reproduction, on the other hand, were more specific. Improvements in signalling systems had originally been sought mainly for military purposes, but the coincidence of the electric telegraph with the new situation of the newspaper was decisive. The railways, of course, were primarily developed for moving people and goods, but, once built, transformed the social relations of newspaper distribution. The whole interaction is exceptionally complex, with no simple cases of cause and effect, either way.

Yet the general consequences of these interrelated technical and social changes included, in largely unforeseen ways, important changes in the character of the cultural institutions. The amounts of capital required to take full advantage of the new technical and social opportunities led to profound changes in the social character of the press. The English example is extreme but not unrepresentative. In the second half of the 19th century the ownership and control of newspapers moved, in the majority of cases, from small and often local family businesses to a more concentrated corporate stage, in which whole strings of newspapers and magazines were owned and controlled by a few powerful individuals or groups. This contradiction between the democratic potentials of the technology and the specific social and economic conditions which determined its full application and development has been very important indeed, throughout the 20th century.

Communications in the New Market

Moreover, within this type of development of the press, there was to be a further development of a major and novel communications system. In many early newspapers, the taking of small commercial notices – what we now call 'classified' advertising – had been a significant factor in revenue and an important element of the newspaper's services. Such advertising was characteristically related to small businesses and to certain novel imported products. The great changes in manufacturing which occurred in the 19th century were very late in being reflected in newspapers. Indeed the new larger-scale advertising looked for every other way to reach its new urban public, from processions and hoardings to fly-bills, since the newspapers, with their quite rigid column layouts, were unwilling to include the 'display' advertising which the new larger manufacturers wanted and which they were already exhibiting elsewhere. But in the last years of the century, with great consequent change in both the layout and the economics of newspapers, display advertising at last penetrated the press. Page layout, type sizes and graphics were all affected, and there was a complex interrelated development of new advertising and journalistic styles (the headline and the slogan; the designed page rather than the assembly of columns; altered relations and proportions between images and print). Increasingly, in the 20th century, income from advertising became a major rather than, as earlier, a minor factor in newspaper economics. Circulation studies and media market research developed in attendant institutions. Advertising agencies changed from booking offices to skilled originators of material and whole campaigns. By the mid-20th century the suitability of a newspaper for effective advertising was to become a major, and in some cases a dominant, criterion for its survival in its original function. Criteria for economically viable circulation changed remarkably. To sell a million copies of a popular newspaper was, by the 1950s in England (where the concentration of 'national' papers was extreme, by international standards), not nearly enough, though to sell less to a public whose buying habits were of more interest to advertisers, as in local newspapers or papers read mainly by higher-income groups, was still quite effective. Thus the specific interrelations of a technology and its social and economic conditions produced results which were in no sense determined by the nature of the technology as such, and which might even, as in this case, in some respects contradict it. The technology which had promised both extension and diversity had, in these circumstances, produced a remarkable and specific kind of extension (what came to be called the 'mass' public) and, by comparison with its own earlier stages, an actually reduced diversity.

Yet while this was the major and indeed dominant line of development, it was always possible to maintain a certain level of oppositional and alternative production. The battle for the big publics had been won by the most advanced print technologies in a context determined by centralised capital, combine ownership and distribution, and a planned interlock with corporate advertising. Yet in the 19th century, as in the 17th century, the culture of the pamphlet and the oppositional newspaper was still intensely active. Indeed at the level of production its technical means were continually improved and made more accessible; it was mainly at the level of distribution that it had been outclassed and in effect marginalised. This situation persisted in the 20th century, but from the 1960s there were important changes. Because of competition from other media, the high point of development of the 'mass newspaper' had been passed, though, within an overall decline of circulation, more intense competition and still further simplification, towards the standard 'tabloid', were evident. In the most centralized print cultures, and especially in Britain, the 'mass' newspaper market began to shrink and there was a flow of new vitality at two different levels: the commercial local press, and new kinds of community and alternative publications. While the centralised press went through fierce and sometimes disabling internal conflicts, significantly centred on the problems of adopting the new, faster, capital- rather than labour-intensive electronic print technology, these other sectors were able to make relatively rapid (in the case of alternative publications, extremely rapid) use of new printing and reproductive techniques.

These are still only marginal changes in the inherited general situation, but they probably indicate the lines of a more general change. They are a useful reminder of the fact that while there can be historical plateaus in which there are settled and apparently permanent relations between a developed technology and certain social conditions and relations of production, there can also be sudden scarps in which a whole set of institutional arrangements, exploiting a technology in determined and established ways, can be seen to be in crisis: a crisis which may at first be seen in isolation, as problems *within* such institutions, but which shows itself eventually as a very complex interaction of innovating technologies and quite general social and economic factors. In the case of print, such a plateau occurred not only in the history of the newspaper but in the history of the book. From the late 18th century to the mid-20th century, improvements in printing and paper and binding technology made possible a remarkable expansion and also a remarkable cultural diversity in publication and readership. But from the mid-20th century onwards, certain crucial cost factors in the traditional technology began moving the other way, and there were more or less rapid institutional and cultural changes. On the one hand there was a sharp and persistent move towards combine publishing, as distinct from the earlier range of small to medium independent publishers: a move which repeated, structurally, what had happened to newspapers in the second half of the 19th century. At the same time there was the decisive innovation of the paperback book, at first as cheap reprints; later, though still insufficiently, as original titles. At the level of technology alone, the paperback represents a decisive lowering of costs, but of course the technology never does stand alone. The determining factor of distribution, at the level of a new equation between production cost and selling price, led in combine conditions to quite new definitions of the effective size and speed of sale of editions. These definitions, rationalised as the technology but in fact a combination of the technology with determinate economic institutions, brought market considerations to a much earlier stage in the planning and writing of books. At the same time, while institutions of increasing size and cultural predictability came to dominate the general market, there were new opportunities, in the many left-over areas, for new kinds of small publishers using new electronic and reproductive technologies. This complex development, in book publishing, is still at this stage occurring within a general expansion, by contrast with the beginnings of a general recession in newspapers.

The Interaction of Technologies

It is convenient to follow the relations between technologies and institutions in a single medium, as here with print, but of course the real situation has for nearly a century been much more complex and interactive. The crucial modern developments of the technologies of extended sound and extended image have had very deep but also diverse institutional effects. Thus it is interesting that by contrast with the centralising and standardising institutional effects of the 'popular' press and later broadcasting, the telephone was a technology which not only permitted but encouraged direct person-to-person communications. Much the same can be said of the private photograph, within extended and now often separated families. These are especially interesting in cases, in that we can see the problems of cause and effect in an unusually long sequence. Thus both the telephone and the photograph were consciously sought, as inventions, though as usual in such cases the precise forms were not always exactly foreseen. The social and economic conditions which made both technologies desirable were thus already present, as a shaping general context.

In the case of the telephone, the proximate causes are more evident: the general increase of trade, and social specialisation into desirable and undesirable residential districts, within the turbulently expanding industrial cities. These were already the effects of other productive technologies and their specific social relations. But then the telephone, designed for this business use, contributed directly to an acceleration of the newly emerging patterns of settlement – of the business quarter, the skyscraper and (here quite subsidiary to transport technologies) the commuter suburb. Moved beyond its business use, it was then an available technology for personal contact within the new conditions of dispersal of friends and families.

The proximate causes of photography are more predominantly scientific and technical, though the intense interest in reproducible images – and especially in images of persons – is almost certainly itself a response to quite new problems of perception and identification within a society characterised by wholly unprecedented mobility and change. To these basic factors were then added the effects of the vast dispersal of families in the generations of emigration, colonisation and urbanisation. Within this dispersal, the cheaply reproducible personal image took on a quite new cultural importance, at the same time that more internal cultural effects, in the new social psychology of the image, were also strengthening.

But then the use of the private telephone and the private photograph, within this socially and economically determined area, were the means to new kinds of contact and response, of an assuring and confirming kind. We have only to imagine a modern large-scale metropolitan society without the technologies of the personal telephone and the personal photograph (and the associated personal letter of modern postal systems) to realise that these technologies, produced and developed within a vastly dispersed and (in received terms) dehumanising social tendency, were seized on as at least to some degree mitigating such conditions; and, more, were the means to wider and more varied personal and social contacts than had been possible within older and more settled communities.

But then, at a quite different level, the predominant general (as distinct from individual) technologies of extended sounds and extended images passed at the same time, though in quite different ways, into new kinds of social and cultural institution. The case of the cinema is especially interesting. For here already, within the new urban and metropolitan conditions, there had been a remarkable expansion, quite pre-dating cinematic technology, of new institutions of everyday entertainment. It was in the 16th century that drama changed, as a social process, from an occasional to a regular provision. The performance of plays at set times of the year, usually as part of a religious festival, came to be replaced by a repertory of productions in new kinds of theatre. In England, for example, the first commercial theatres were built in the last quarter of the 16th century, significantly at the approaches to the City of London, to catch a passing as well as a resident trade. Their physical structure followed precedents in performances in the courtyards of inns. Thus the transition from the occasional drama to regular drama was directly associated with a more mobile, trading society. In different social conditions, in 16th-century Spain, municipal professional theatres were rapidly extended beyond the capital city. The subsequent development of theatres of this modern type was closely associated with the development of modern cities, first metropolitan, then provincial. The major period of general expansion was in the urbanising and industrialising societies of the 19th century.

The arrival of the motion picture was within this structured phase. At first it occupied the fringes of the show-business world, as had the music-halls and 'out-of-town' theatres of earlier decades. But the power of the motion picture, and especially its capacity to realise effects which had been repeatedly attempted, but with more limited success, in the advanced technology of the stage theatres, soon brought a decisive central establishment: the 'motion-picture theatre' – 'movie house' or 'cinema'. A crucial technical advantage – rapid multiple distribution of a filmed production – then put it almost at once ahead of the stage theatres. The same technical factor made possible, and in important ways led to, a novel centralisation of production and, in relation to the capital costs of these reproducible productions, conditions of relative monopoly: not only within societies but, because of the factor of rapid reproductive distribution, paranationally, as in the relative monopoly of American production.

Thus the institutions of everyday entertainment, long associated with the city and with the form of the stage theatre, were at once extended, with a certain continuity – the distribution of films, until a much later stage, with the predominance of television, was through *theatres* – and, in the process, from the factor of centralised production of indefinitely reproducible performances, transformed. Cultural tendencies towards monopoly from a fashionable centre, clearly visible in European and American stage theatres throughout the 18th and 19th centuries, were heavily reinforced by the new centralising technology and then by the specific paracultural qualities of the North American cultural process: the simultaneous integration of newly urbanising and newly immigrant people. The conjunction of these conditions pushed the institutions of cinema in a certain direction (that of relative monopoly) and selected, for dominance, certain modes of artistic use of the technology. At the same time, in relatively subordinated or protected or privileged areas, other artistic uses of the technology became evident, though the problem of the relations of such 'minority' films to the predominant institutions was persistent and often insoluble.

In the same period, though always at a relatively later phase, the technology of sound broadcasting entered its own problematic institutional development. The development of the actual technology was related to pre-existent official and business uses. And in this case there was no prepared alternative, as in the music-halls and theatres, to take in and adapt to the new technology. Instead, a new set of social conditions both made possible, and in a sense required, new kinds of communicative relations. Theatres and cinemas (like sports stadiums and commercial and cultural exhibitions) had belonged to the phase of urban and metropolitan accumulation. They depended on bringing together, by prior assembly or by new regular transport systems, significant numbers of people in designated public places. Yet there were now two further factors. Within the cities there were very many people, at many times of the day and night, who were unable, for various reasons – hours of work, family responsibilities in homes, shortage of money – to go, at all regularly, to the places of regular public entertainment. Moreover, outside the cities, and outside the suburbs, there were large numbers of people for whom opportunities of this kind were still, in effect, occasional at best, non-existent at worst, yet who, because of the decisive general development of predominantly urban and industrial cultures, were already or were becoming socially, culturally and politically attuned to the dominant centres. The technology of radio broadcasting, initially developed for quite different purposes, was adapted to these conditions by investment-directed development of the domestic receiver. Soon the whole range of pre-existent communicative relationships – the long-standing and now fully-developed institutions of public assembly, from theatres and concert halls to public meetings and lectures, but also the second-phase institutions of centralised production and rapid physical distribution or reproduction, such as the press and the cinema – was challenged by this new set of relationships: the domestic receiver in direct relation to a centre or centres of regular broadcasting; the inclusion of several hitherto separated functions – news, opinion, music and drama – within a single technology, first in radio and then, even more powerfully and generally, in television.

Types of Large-scale Communication

It is crucial to distinguish between these two phases of modern communications institutions, which are usually blurred by the overriding and vague concept of 'mass communications'. There are decisive social differences between three types of communicative institution: (i) public assembly; (ii) variable distribution of reproduced central products; (iii) direct distribution of a centralised range of products. It is open to argument whether the metaphor of 'mass' is best applied to one or other of these phases. Its first application was to (i), public assembly, with the 'mass meeting' taking on new social tones in an epoch of democratic mobilisation. Its second application was in a context of reproductive centralised ('mass') production – specifically, the automobile assembly line – corresponding to (ii). But this shaded, within particular marketing conditions, into considerations of the size and generality of the public reached, with effects from the centrally-determined character of the product and from the integration of hitherto separated cultural functions – as in (iii). The reduction of all these variable factors, relations and historical phases to the single concept of 'mass communications' obscures these crucial and effective distinctions. It also encourages simple, all-purpose responses to a very complicated set of phenomena. It tries to assimilate a set of very different technologies, with inherently variable functions and potentials, to a generalised 'mass communications technology' which then appears to have determinate rather than, as in fact, specifically determined and both variable and alterable social and institutional effects.

The need to retain the real distinctions, and to resist the reductive generalizing concept is, as it happens, especially evident in the case of broadcasting. It is well known that even in societies which chose the eventually predominant form of the domestic receiver – as distinct from societies like Nazi Germany which made major use of radio as a form of street address – the nature of broadcasting institutions varied considerably. Variable answers were given to the questions raised by the social character of the new technology: its relations to official communications channels; its problems of funding. The latter question was acute. Earlier types of institution, whether those of public assembly or of the distribution of reproduced products, could operate direct charges for each use. This was impracticable, at that stage, in broadcasting (though it has since become technically practicable in television systems). The solutions adopted did not follow, except at this most general level, from the character of the technology, but from the predominant political and economic institutions of different societies. Thus there could be direct State funding, with corresponding State control of output, as in communist and some other systems; indirect State licensing, controlling both transmission and reception but, within the degree of indirectness, permitting relatively independent but still largely centralised production; or, as in the United States, funding by a complex interaction of the manufacturers of domestic receivers and general advertising interests. Each funding solution had inevitable effects on productive content, which, as the cultural history of radio shows very clearly, was in only very general ways determined by the technology alone.

What is particularly striking about the history of broadcasting is that, unlike all earlier communications technologies, it was available as a major distributive system before there was any important definition of what was to be distributed. It took many years to move broadcasting from its two earliest practices – *amplifying* sound events which were already occurring, in other institutions and forms; or simply *filling-in*, with improvised material, to maintain the service or retain the audience – into what was eventually specific autonomous production. In news, opinion and drama, especially, radio and television eventually produced work of very high quality – as well as much else, of course. In music, interacting with the new technology of sound recording by discs and eventually cassettes, it radically changed both the distributive relations and eventually some important elements in the production of music. But, by this time, the generality of its systems was such that the technology was, at least potentially, a common carrier.

To understand the opportunities and the problems of this stage we have to look again at some fundamental distinctions between communications systems. From the beginning of writing through to the 19th century there were certain inevitable relations between uses of the technologies and the acquisition (itself socially determined or controlled) of the relevant specific skills. Even with the eventual coming of general literacy, there was a continuing direct relation between a specific training and the uses of print. What then happened, or can appear to have happened, was a radical shift of the relations between systems of social training and access to the products of the new technologies. The most basic social skills, of a kind acquired in quite primary development and relationship, gave access to the motion picture, the radio broadcast, the television programme, at the level of reception, while very easily learned skills gave more general access, including some production, to the photograph and the telephone.

Thus the new technologies were inherently more general, and less apparently subject to systems of training. Much of their popularity undoubtedly derived from these facts. The para-national character of much of the cinema, the developed para-national character of some radio, took people across some cultural frontiers and barriers, but of course still largely in determined conditions. It was not only that the institutions of the new technologies, in the very course of their development, and especially of autonomous production, became, in themselves, training systems. In immediate ways, types of speech, points of view, catchphrases, jingles, rhythms were in effect taught. Less immediately, some conventions of relationship, of behaviour, of personal and social perspectives, were disseminated by reiterated practice. What had been true of all communications systems was now more generalised by the very fact that the new systems meshed so readily with unspecialised receptive skills. And then the further area of determination, at this stage, was the unprecedented relative monopoly, for audiences of this size, both within and across national societies. Major uses of the new technologies came to depend on unprecedented concentrations of communications capital, and there were then very complex and at times contradictory relations between these new systems and the more normal (State, church, school, family) networks of social and cultural training.

No simple balance can then be struck. In some ways, themselves highly variable according to the character of local institutions, new cultural choices, and effective if still limited processes of cultural mobility, were undoubtedly achieved. The relatively late case of the portable transistor radio, taking the machine out of the family home again, is striking. In other ways, at the stage of relative monopoly – local, national or international – some, perhaps many, of the new choices and mobilities were much more deeply determined than those who first experienced them realised. Some at least of the new horizons were put there to be found: programmed and indeed marketed.

One crucial response to this complex situation was the development of new or adapted institutions – from censorship, through codes, through advisory committees, to media research and education – which sought to control, monitor, or even, occasionally, understand what was happening. Typically much of their attention went to children, who were only the most evident case of those many who now had alternatives, or apparent alternatives, to the normal systems of social and cultural training. For many of the urgent issues being discovered in media practice were at least forms of deeper issues of social and cultural change in a much wider dimension. To the extent that this is realised, the usefulness of monitoring and critical responses can be at once affirmed and defined. For they are necessary responses to communications as centralised propaganda or centralised marketing systems, yet until they have engaged with the real processes and the really new technologies of social change and mobility they cannot be much more than marginal.

From the 1960s, and now at what is technically a rapidly increasing pace, certain factors of the technologies have begun to change. The high capital costs of the productive and reproductive technologies, following in part from the centralising directions in which they had been steered by investment, but following also in some respects from the actual technical stages, are beginning to be succeeded by a period in which (in part from the development of the next stage of the high-capital productive market) *means of production* (as in video) *are themselves being distributed*, or are becoming accessible to more diverse, more autonomous, more voluntary and self-organising institutions. The problems of this phase are still complex and still emerging. Some of the new 'means of production' are, like most photographic cameras, effectively a stimulus to the use of relatively centralised and profitable processing facilities. Others are a kind of unloading of new domestic machines as marginal consumer products. Neither development, of this kind, implies any significant institutional change.

Yet there could, with enough thought and effort, be quite radical institutional innovations. The epochal change, if it could indeed be achieved, would be a moment beyond the two previous major stages of communications technologies and institutions. The stage of minority instrumental systems (writing and printing) has already been joined and in some sectors succeeded by majority systems (print in generally literate societies, cinema, radio, television) in which the typical relation is one of a few producers to many consumers: a repetition, in new technical forms, of a major division of labour: the reproduction, in communications, of profound social divisions, and of effective (if relative and changing) social domination and subordination. In this second stage, the limited distribution of specialised products has been overtaken by the wide distribution of generalised products. What may now be possible is a qualitative change to the wide distribution of *processes*: the provision of equitable access to the means and resources of directly determined communication, serving immediate personal and social needs. The limited mobility of choice between specialised and generalised products could be steadily and in some cases dramatically extended to the full mobility of a range of communications processes which in all their aspects – amplifying and connecting, storing and reminding, alternative and extending – would be the means and resources of a qualitatively different social life.

It will not happen without precise thought and effort, nor without very widespread discussion and quite public decision-making: the inescapable means to its specific end. The institutions of direct democracy and of personal liberty – and of their complex interrelations in self-managing communities and societies – are in communications, as more generally, still largely to be explored. But we are now at one of those historical moments when the relations between communications technologies and social institutions are a matter not only for study and analysis, but for a wide set of practical choices. It is not only (though it will often be presented as) a matter of instituting new technologies. The directions in which investment in research and development should go are now, in this field, fundamental social decisions. The effort to understand and take part in them is more likely to be made, as against the bewildered reception of new products and processes which 'just happen', if enough of us realise the scale of the communicative and thus social transformation which is now becoming, though still in ways to be decided, technically and institutionally possible.

1981

III

Marx on Culture

There is an initial paradox. Few would now remember Karl Marx for any direct contributions he made to cultural theory. Yet it is clear that the contribution of Marxism to modern cultural thought is widespread and influential.

This problem can be interpreted in very different ways. Thus it is often said that the influence of Marxist cultural thought is a by-product of the success of Marxism as a critique of the capitalist social order and as the decisive philosophy of revolutionary socialism. This can then be either a recognition or a dismissal: an acknowledgment of the major effects which this body of thought and this transforming movement have had on an area of human practice to which they have always, in fact, given considerable attention; or, conversely, a rejection of the distortions which this primarily political, economic and sociological theory and practice have imposed on works and interests which they can only misunderstand and damage.

Or again it is said that while the practical success of Marxism has for obvious and integral reasons been primarily in the political and economic spheres, its central contribution has always been much wider and indeed that the distinctive effects of its political and economic influence can only be understood when it is seen that these are the expression of a much more general interpretation of all human activity and of ways of understanding and changing it. From this emphasis it follows that Marxist cultural theory is not a by-product of a political and economic movement but one of the main areas of the theory and practice as a whole. It can then of course still be rejected as wrong, and even among those who are broadly in sympathy with it there can be divergent attitudes. There have been many, including too many in power, who, while repeating the most general claims, have in practice reduced cultural theory to a relatively dogmatic application of political and economic positions. There have been others who have seen the preoccupation with cultural theory, which has been a feature of Western Marxism since the 1920s, as an indication of the (temporary) failure, in such societies, of the central revolutionary political and economic movement. On the other hand, an increasing number of Marxists now believe that cultural theory has become even more important, in modern social and cultural conditions, than it was in Marx's own day.

Finally it is said that the evident influence of Marxism in modern cultural thought is indeed a *contribution*, whether welcome or unwelcome: that it has, in combination with some other intellectual and social traditions, established certain distinctive positions and interests but has in practice combined these with other forms of thought which have no particular basis in Marx but which can still be swept up in the general Marxist classification. This would be one kind of explanation of the fact that there are now not only divergent but contending and incompatible schools of Marxist cultural thought. On the other hand, from either of the earlier positions outlined, what is emphasised is not the combination with other forms of thought but this or that *interpretation* of what Marx really said or meant, and the consequent argument against other interpretations. This happens even in areas in which Marx wrote extensively and systematically, so it is not surprising that it also happens in relation to the more scattered and less systematic indications of a cultural theory.

It is not likely that any of these problems can be authoritatively resolved in a relatively brief essay. Yet perhaps something can be done, if its purposes are declared and its limits acknowledged. My main interest will be in what Marx himself wrote in this general area. Yet this is not an interest determined by some wish to provide legitimacy for any subsequent position. Necessarily, as a way of understanding what Marx wrote, I shall refer to what others have understood him to have written, but I am not attempting, here, a history of the Marxist tradition of cultural thought, which is not only a vast subject in itself but in which there are writers who, on these matters, are at least as important as Marx himself. If all were in one way or another inspired by Marx, still the most important of them looked to his work not for legitimation of their own, or for some title of authority, but as to a great colleague, in a social and intellectual enterprise much wider than any individual contribution. That enterprise is now part of a continuing and necessarily conflicting world history. We look at Marx in that context but still primarily, for present purposes, at Marx himself.

We can define three aspects of Marx's contribution to cultural thought.

First, there are his own incidental but very extensive comments on a wide range of writers and artists. Second, there is the effect of his general position on human development, which can be taken as at least the outline of a general cultural theory. Third, there are the unfinished problems, the questions raised and set aside or only partly answered, some of which are still important in their own right.

The first aspect needs emphasis, against many hostile or merely ignorant accounts. It is not only that he was an intense and lifelong reader of so many of the great works of world literature. Professor Prawer's *Karl Marx and World Literature*[1] gives extraordinary evidence of this, of a kind to impress even those who knew the general fact. It is also that much of his early writing was directly concerned with literary and aesthetic subjects, and that as late as 1857, with other major work in progress, he planned and read for an essay on aesthetics, though he did not write it.

What has then to be asked is how these facts bear on his more general work. It is a difficult question to answer. The student poems, the fragment of a novel, the sketch of a Platonic dialogue, the projected but unrealised journal of dramatic criticism, are too slight and local to sustain any positive indications. They testify to his intense interest in writing and can be said to show two characteristics – a Promethean daring and an irrepressible critical irony – which are central in the mature writer. On the other hand it is too easy to read back such characteristics, from the later achievement. There must have been thousands of student writers who did as much but did not go on to the very different work of the mature Marx.

Can we say the same of the lively early journalism, and in particular the *Rheinische Zeitung* articles on censorship and freedom of the press? Not really. The attack on the Prussian censorship is rather more than conventional liberal protest:

> The law permits me to write; it asks only that I write in a style other than my own! I am allowed to show the face of my mind, but, first, I must give it a *prescribed expression!*[2]

This becomes a shrewd analysis of the familiar pressure or demand for 'moderation' of tone:

> Freely shall you write, but let every word be a genuflection toward the liberal censor who approves your modest, serious good judgment.[3]

Or again, in a far-reaching comment:

> The moderation of genius does not consist of the use of a cultivated

language without accent or dialect; it lies rather in speaking the accent of the matter and the dialect of its essence. It lies in forgetting about moderation and immoderation and getting to the core of things.[4]

Similarly, in his observations on the freedom of the press, an important but relatively familiar position –

> In no sense does the writer regard his works as a *means*. They are *ends in themselves*; so little are they means for him and others that, when necessary, he sacrifices *his* existence to *theirs*[5]

– is set in the context of a more original and still relevant argument:

> It is startling to find *freedom of the press* subsumed under *freedom of doing business... The first freedom of the press consists in its not being a business.*[6]

There is shrewd insight, also, in the essay on Sue's *Les Mystères de Paris* which Marx contributed to *The Holy Family*. The essay works, with some inconsistency, at several levels of analysis, but is especially interesting in the use of analysis of vocabulary to clarify what would later be called the ideology of the tale, and in analysis of its internal contradictions.

These are the more isolable pieces of Marx's early literary and cultural writing. They are still, at their best, important now only because of the later work of their author. The same is true, really, of the evidence of Marx's wide knowledge of world literature, not only from documentary records but in the long use of allusions, quotations and references, and in the use of certain writing techniques in his major philosophical and historical works. That Marx was such a man, learned and cultivated, deeply devoted to literature, is a fact against certain ignorant travesties. But the centre of the argument about Marx and culture cannot be displaced to such a dimension. Marx himself would have been among the first to say that it doesn't primarily matter how well-read a man is, a fact that is often only the indication of his social and cultural position and mode of life. What matters much more is what is done with that reading and knowledge, at levels more decisive than learned and apt allusion and habits of style. If Marx was, indeed, an exceptionally cultivated *bourgeois*, he gave most of his energy to becoming or making possible something different: never in a renunciation of reading and learning, but always in the transition from a possession of knowledge to its transforming use.

One further observation on this aspect of Marx is necessary. It has been so widely alleged against Marxism, both as theory and as some twentieth-century practice, that it is an enemy of culture, especially in respect of the freedoms of its creation, that it has been tempting for some Marxists to produce the old man himself, reading and re-reading Aeschylus and Ovid and Dante and Shakespeare and Cervantes and Goethe and so on, as if that were sufficient answer. But it would be a guilty admission of the faults of Marxist cultural theory and practice if the central argument were shifted to the private or semi-public cultivation of their founder. On the other hand it is true that it should be necessary for some of those who claim the authority of Marx, either for their own bureaucratic illiberalism or for that reduced version of Marxism which treats culture as *a priori* marginal or dependent, to come into contact with his mind in this vigorous, uncompromising and persistent part of its range. Except, of course, that the early work especially can be conveniently diagnosed, by friends and enemies, as pre-Marxist, with special bearing on the fierce (and in fact lifelong) assertions of the liberty and autonomy of cultural work. There is a serious question waiting there, as the mature theory is seen to develop, but it cannot in any case be solved, from any position, by the assembly of facts about his reading or by the tactical use of this or that quotation. It will be solved, if at all, by direct inquiry into the long, massive, unfinished, often contradictory work which we now call Marx.

There is a preliminary problem, of wider import than either Marx or Marxism. I have been using the term *culture*, in this essay, in one of its predominant twentieth-century senses, as a general term for artistic, literary and intellectual work. There is no comparably adequate general term, so the use can be readily justified. But it is well known that *culture* is also used, in anthropology and sociology but also more generally, to describe a distinctive way of life, then including arts and learning but also much more general practice and behaviour. The complexities of the word are in fact even wider than this, and have been explored elsewhere.[7]

Now from certain positions it can be objected that any particular use of *culture* is misleading: too broad, too narrow, or simply too confusing. Yet the difficult history of the word is in fact an indication of a very general and complex intellectual movement, which happens to be especially though by no means exclusively relevant to Marx and Marxism. The variations and conflicts around the meaning of *culture* are central elements of a long, specifically modern inquiry. It is precisely the relations between, on the one hand, the arts and learning, and on the other hand a more general way of life, that are argued through, beyond and behind this term, in what in any local instance can seem intolerably confusing ways. Moreover the relations between *culture*, either as the arts and learning, or as a more general way of life, and that state or process widely defined as *civilisation*, have also been intensively explored and argued, again through, beyond and behind the vital words. There has been the use of *culture* as inner spiritual development, best externally exemplified in the arts and religion and responses to them, in contrast with the external and material achievements of *civilisation*. On the other hand the distinctiveness of particular ways of life, in their more general aspects but including their arts and ideas, has been emphasised as the diversity of *cultures* by contrast with the often unilinear and uniform version of *civilisation* (or as some would now say, *development*). Again, however, and in fact in the work of a German contemporary of Marx, G.F. Klemm in his *Allegemeine Kulturgeschichte der Menschheit* (1843–52), the general progress of mankind was traced through phases of *cultural* history, in which basic forms of social life were seen as rooted in historically changing and developing conditions. Such phases were also traced through the key word *society*, as in the American Lewis Morgan's *Ancient Society* (1877), which so impressed and directly influenced both Marx and Engels.

This actual history quickly shows us that it is not possible, in any simple way, to answer or even ask the question: what does Marx say about culture? Yet at the same time it shows us that the questions he actually asked, in this initially indeterminate area, belong to a very widespread and active area of philosophical, aesthetic and historical inquiry, which undoubtedly preceded him and which has certainly continued after him, not only 'inside' and 'outside' the Marxist traditions but of course primarily as a central issue in itself, where the effects of any particular intellectual tendency are for obvious reasons difficult to disentangle.

What this means in practice, for the study of Marx himself, is that the real history is not one of isolated innovative work: that it finds, in Marx, certain strikingly original questions and answers, but finds also his answers to the questions of others, questions persistent from work with which he otherwise disagrees, to say nothing of borrowings, provisional syntheses, notes and sketches. This in no way diminishes him, but it restores, as against the isolated authoritative master, that which he was himself always concerned to show: a concrete, shifting, at times contradictory historical process, temporarily and provisionally high-lighted in this great and singular figure.

'There is no history ... of art.' Or, to give the sentence in full, 'There is no history of politics, of law, of science etc., of art, of religion.'[8] This is a manuscript note, rather than a considered statement, but it at once introduces a major emphasis in Marx's thought and raises a central problem in interpretation. The intended emphasis becomes clear in its full context. It had been and is still commonplace to generalise certain human activities as if they were distinct and autonomous, and from this to assert that they can be regarded as having their own independent history. And this had been especially the case in cultural activities, which had been regarded not only as the originating, directive impulses of all human development but also, in certain powerful intellectual traditions, as themselves originated, by revelation or by inspiration, by forces beyond human beings. The whole thrust of Marx's reading of history was then, first, to insist that all cultural processes were initiated by humans themselves, and, second, to argue that none of them could be fully understood unless they were seen in the context of human activities as a whole. That is the initial and least controversial sense of the argument that 'there is no history... of art': that the real history is always of human beings making art, from their own human resources, as distinct either from the history of a 'reified' Art – the sum of certain human activities seen as if it were a self-evolving product or an internally developing abstraction or a result of extra-human direction – or, where these more extreme projections were not in question, from that kind of specialising history which deliberately ignored the general conditions within which the specialised activity was practised. It is an important part of the legacy of Marx, but then also of a wider movement of modern thought, that these initial emphases are now very widely accepted.

But there are then further and more controversial senses of Marx's argument. These can be seen from the way in which the argument was put by Marx and Engels in *The German Ideology* (1845–6):

> Morality, religion, metaphysics, and other ideologies, and their corresponding forms of consciousness, no longer retain therefore their appearance of autonomous existence. They have no history, no development; it is men who, in developing their material production and their material intercourse, change, along with this their real existence, their thinking and the products of their thinking.[9]

It is here that the central problem is joined. But we should first be clear about a problem of formulation, which is potentially very misleading. It is easy to read such sentences as 'they have no history, no development' or 'there is no history... or art' in the irrelevant and obviously untrue sense that these activities do not change and develop and thus have no history. This would be directly contrary to what Marx meant, but the rhetorical form of the statements, made as they were within explicit polemic against those who taught that the history of these 'spiritual' activities was the essential history of all human development, can in some respects mislead. What is at least initially being argued is that these activities are not separate and autonomous, and that they have all been carried out by actual human beings, in the whole real conditions of their existence.

Yet this readily acceptable sense of the argument is also, evidently, not Marx's whole sense. This can be seen in the sentences which immediately precede those quoted:

> We begin with real, active men, and from their real life-process show the development of the ideological reflexes and echoes of this life-process. The phantoms of the human brain also are necessary sublimates of men's material life-process, which can be empirically established and which is bound to material preconditions.[10]

Sympathetically read, this can be taken as little more than a strong form of the argument that all human activities, including the 'cultural' and the 'spiritual', have their origins in the whole real conditions of human existence. This general argument would be widely accepted. Yet is is obvious that other distinctions are being made: notably between 'real' on the one hand, and 'reflexes', 'echoes', 'phantoms' and 'sublimates' on the other.

There are again strong and weak senses of this argument. The weak sense offers little more than the argument that the most refined forms of human thought necessarily occur within more general human activities in definite material preconditions: that human beings have to gain the resources for physical existence as a condition of doing anything else. In this weak sense there is no room for serious doubt. Yet the language of at least this early formulation indicates a stronger and more controversial sense. The language of 'reflexes', 'echoes', 'phantoms' and 'sublimates' carries the inescapable implication of a secondary activity, and then, it would seem, of 'consciousness' as a secondary activity. We have again to remember that this was part of a polemic against the assumption that the whole of human history was determined by ideas, whether human or extra-human in origin: an assumption which complacently and cruelly ignored the long history and present facts of human labour, through which the necessary physical existence and survival of human beings were gained and assured. The counter-emphasis, that human labour is central, necessary and thus genuinely originating, remains as Marx's major contribution to modern thought. But what can then be seen as happening is a way of formulating this emphasis which, ironically, is in danger of converting human labour – its 'material preconditions', 'material production' and 'material intercourse' – to, in its turn, a specialised and even reified element of human totality.

This comes out clearly in the next preceding sentences in *The German Ideology* (the argument is being deliberately read backwards, as a way of progressively analysing its assumptions):

> In total contrast to German philosophy, which descends from heaven to earth, we here ascend from earth to heaven. That is to say, we do not set out from what men say, imagine, or conceive, nor from what has been said, thought, imagined or conceived of men, in order to arrive at men in the flesh. [We begin with real, active men ... etc.][11]

As a statement of philosophical presupposition this is clear and admirable. It is wholly consistent, in its general emphasis, with the argument that we must begin any inquiry into human development and human activities from actual human beings in their actual conditions. But then rather more than this is actually said. The rhetorical reversal of metaphysical thought, in the proposal to 'ascend from earth to heaven', has the extraordinary literal effect, if we are reading it closely, of shifting 'what men say, imagine or conceive' and 'what has been said, thought, imagined or conceived of men' from earth to ... heaven! Of course Marx did not literally believe this. It is a by-product of that particular polemical rhetoric. Yet a more serious question underlies the idiosyncrasy of the particular formulation.

In this way of seeing the problem, and in fact against other emphases by Marx elsewhere, there is a real danger of separating human thought, imagination and concepts from 'men's material life-process', and indeed of separating human consciousness from 'real, active men'. Taken crudely and literally, as indeed it has sometimes been taken, this is, ironically, a familiar position of bourgeois philistinism, of the kind satirised by Brecht as 'eats first, morals after', or more seriously of the kind now regularly propagated by apologists of capitalism, in the argument that we must first 'create wealth' and then, on the proceeds, 'improve the quality of life'.

Marx's central emphasis was so much on the necessary totality of human activity that any reduction of this kind has to be firmly rejected. In the matter of human labour in general it is indeed from him that we can most clearly learn a more adequate conception. Thus:

> We presuppose labour in a form that stamps it as exclusively human. A spider conducts operations that resemble those of a weaver, and a bee puts to shame many an architect in the construction of her cells. But

what distinguishes the worst architect from the best of bees is this, that the architect raises his structure in imagination before he erects it in reality. At the end of every labour-process, we get a result that already existed in the imagination of the labourer at its commencement. He not only effects a change of form in the material on which he works, but he also realises a purpose of his own that gives the law to his *modus operandi*, and to which he must subordinate his will.[12]

This convincing account of the specifically human character of work includes, as will be seen, not only the foreseeing concept of what is being made but ideally integrated concepts of how and why it is being made. This is intended to enforce Marx's conception of what is truly human in labour, and thus to provide a standard from which it is reasonable to describe certain forms of human work – those in which the worker has been deprived, by force or by the possession by others of his means and conditions of production, of the necessary human qualities of foresight, decision, consciousness and control – as degraded or sub-human, in no hyperbolic sense. Thus 'real, active men', in all their activities, are full of consciousness, foresight, concepts of how and why, or to the degree that they are not have been reduced from this fully human status by social and economic conditions which practically diminish their humanity, and which it is then a central human task to change. The revolution of labour, to achieve this fully human status, is of course Marx's central political perspective.

But then it remains very strange that in the early writings, in which he wrote most directly of what we now call 'cultural' activities, Marx worked with so reduced and so vulnerable a definition of consciousness. It can of course be argued that what he then had mainly in mind was not the integrated consciousness of necessary human labour and genuine production, but what he and others could see as the phantasmagoria of religious and metaphysical speculation or the self-justyifying systems of law, politics and economic theory which ratified oppression, privilege and exploitation. What he wanted to argue, we can agree, was that any and all of these impressive systems of ideas must be placed or replaced in their true social and material context, and that in that sense we should not first listen to what men 'say, imagine or conceive' – thus limiting ourselves to these selected and abstracted terms – but should rather look at the whole body of activities and conditions within which these ideas and systems were generated. When we put it like that, we are in fact describing Marx's central and most influential argument.

Yet, with many serious subsequent effects, this was not all that he actually said. His contempt for what some kinds of men 'say, imagine or conceive' – self-justifying, indifferent or fantasy-ridden accounts of a world that was after all open to fuller and more direcct examination, and especially that world of necessary labour which underpinned and made possible all such apologia and speculation – rushed him into weakening his own most essential case. This case was that

> the whole previous conception of history has either completely neglected this real basis of history (the real process of production, starting out from the simple material production of life) or else has considered it as a secondary matter without any connexion with the course of history. Consequently, history has always to be written in accordance with an external standard; the real production of life appears as ahistorical, while what is historical appears as separated from ordinary life.[13]

That received and fundamental error was massively corrected, but at the cost, in some formulations, of making intellectual and cultural production, of any kind, appear to be 'immaterial'.

For, of course, even for the historical record of the real processes of production, 'the simple material production of life', it is necessary to attend, critically, to what men have said, imagined and conceived. There is important non-verbal evidence of human material production, as, most notably, in the total absence of verbal evidence, in the essentially material inquiries of prehistoric archaeology. But we have only to move from those illuminating analyses of pots, tools, weapons, work in earth and stone, to analyses which are able to include verbal records of production, social relations and change, to realise that Marx's positive emphasis, on the inclusion of material production as historically central, is greatly enriched when we have evidence of what men of the time, in ways that of course need critical interpretation, quite materially 'said, imagined and conceived' – in practice necessarily in material ways, in writing and in work with stone, pigment and metal. The persuasive philosophical presupposition, that we must begin from active human beings, in all their evident social and cultural diversity, rather than from some abstractly imagined and conceived concept of Man, must not be weakened by what would in the end be the philistine dismissal or relegation of what actual people, in definite material conditions and by unarguably material processes – writing, printing, painting, sculpting, building – said, imagined and conceived.

Thus, at the root of the problem of Marx's contribution to a theory of culture, and with critical effect on the subsequent development of a Marxist tradition, we have to restore the practical activities which we now generalise as culture to the full social material process on which he insisted. Against the tone of some of his formulations, and against much influential subsequent interpretation of these activities as merely reflective of and secondary to the then abstracted and specialised 'material production', we have to emphasise cultural practice as from the begining social and material, in ways with which in fact he might have been among the first to agree.

It is possible to clarify these difficult problems and arguments by making a distinction which obviously comes to mind: between those intellectual and cultural processes which, as we have seen Marx arguing, are necessary elements of any form of truly human labour, and those other forms of intellectual and cultural production which are undertaken in their own terms, not as elements of another more general process but as what Marx had called in his *Rheinische Zeitung* articles 'ends in themselves'?

The distinction seems to give us some early advantages. We can all see the difference between the exercise of intelligence and foresight in ploughing a field or planting a crop or breeding a certain type of animal and, on the other hand, the processes involved in writing a poem or composing a symphony or making a piece of sculpture. It is true that there are some obviously intermediate cases, such as making and decorating a cooking pot, or building a house with attention not only to its function as shelter but also to its appearance and style, or making clothes which not only cover us but are intended to enhance our appearance or to signify some social position. Yet it might still be possible to distinguish between work which is intended to satisfy a manifest physical need and work which, whatever its other uses, is not directly related to manifest physical need in anything like the same way.

Yet the distinctions being made here have in the end to be submitted to Marx's conception of the totality of the social process, which makes any simple extraction of certain practices as 'ends in themselves' very doubtful. There is some genuine uncertainty here in what Marx meant. The central difficulty is a confusion or slide between a simple and overwhelming assertion of the fact that human beings must eat and ensure the material conditions for their physical survival and reproduction, and the only apparently similar argument that human labour is the production and reproduction of real life in this persuasively restricted sense. It is not only that in modern economies the greater part of human labour is applied for purposes which go far beyond the assurance of food and of the conditions for survival and reproduction. Marx in fact showed very clearly that the satisfaction of basic needs, through a definite mode of production leading to certain definite social relations, *produced* new needs and new definitions of need, which in their turn became, beyond the bare necessities, the forms and objects of further production.

But it is also and more fundamentally, from the historical, anthropological and archaeological records, that even at stages of minimal or subsistence production, though then in highly variable ways, human beings apply energy not only to the isolable physically necessary tasks but, in varying degrees of connection with these, to social and cultural purposes which are from the beginning part of their distinctively human organisation. We may now think we can separate their carved 'cult' or 'fertility' objects, their ceremonial practices in initiation and burial, their 'symbolic' presentation or representation of facts of kinship and identity, their dances and masks, their narratives or 'myths' of human and natural origins, as 'magical' activities or, in some of the surviving objects (the famous cave paintings are an obvious example) as 'art'. But it should be clear, if we have taken Marx's sense of the total social process, which is richly justified when any of these practices are seen in living and lived relationships with other practices, that the external categorical distinction between 'necessary material production' and other forms of activity and practice is radically misleading. On the contrary, just because the necessary material production is human and social, it is cast from the beginning in whole human and social forms: indeed precisely in those forms, which are at root forms of the practical organisation and distribution of interest and energy, which we now call 'cultures'.

In its central sense, Marx would not only accept but emphasise this position:

> The production of ideas, of conceptions, of consciousness, is at first directly interwoven with the material activity and the material intercourse of men, the language of real life. Conceiving, thinking, the mental intercourse of men, appear at this stage as the direct efflux of their material behaviour. The same applies to mental production as expressed in the language of politics, laws, morality, religion, metaphysics, etc., of a people. Men are the producers of their conceptions, ideas, etc., – real, active men, as they are conditioned by a definite development of their productive forces and of the intercourse corresponding to these, up to its furthest forms. Consciousness can never

be anything else than conscious existence, and the existence of men is their actual life-process.[14]

Yet there are in fact still several problems, if we are to get this full central sense, and its complex implications, clear.

First, in an area that has already been discussed (for this passage again directly precedes the 'earth to heaven' and 'reflexes and echoes' formulations previously examined), there is the description of conceiving and thinking as 'efflux', which, when read in association with the later formulations, is undoubtedly reductive, not only from the observable record but from the much more acceptable earlier formulation of 'directly interwoven'. It is in the movement from a sense of the simultaneous and fundamentally indissoluble human process of conception and labour, labour and conception, to the narrower polemical sense of what is in effect a two-stage process – associated human labour, but then as its 'efflux' or 'echo', or, worse, 'phantom', the consciousness which might be seen as the very process and condition of association but which can now be virtually a by-product – that all the difficulties of Marx's own and many Marxist conceptions of culture can be seen to begin.

Then, second, there is a very puzzling combination of historical and categorical argument. The historical element is initially very clear: 'at *first* directly interwoven'. This connects with one of Marx's most important cultural arguments, that the real relations betwen culture and society, or between art and labour, have always to be seen in terms of the particular mode of production and social order within which the relations practically occur. Thus the emphasis on 'at first directly interwoven' has to be understood in relation to his arguments about the effects of an historically subsequent *division* of labour, to the point where, very notably in modern class societies, 'mental labour' – intellectual and artistic work – can be both categorically and practically separated from 'manual labour'. This results not only in the degradation of what is marked off, in dominating and exploiting ways, as 'mere manual labour', deprived of its human conditions of conscious purpose and control, but in the false separation of 'mental labour', now held to be restricted to a certain class. The effect is not only the undervaluation of manual labour – in practice of the millions of manual labourers – on whom in fact the maintenance of human life still absolutely depends. The effect is also on the character of 'mental labour' itself. In its separation from the basic processes of assuring human existence it is inherently more likely to develop false conceptions of both general and specific human conditions, since it is not as a matter of necessary practice exposed to and tested by human activity in general. Even more, since the fact of the division of labour, in this basic class sense, is not just a matter of different kinds of work but of social relations which determine greater rewards and greater respect for 'mental labour', and of these relations as established in and protected by a specifically exploiting and unequal social order, the operations of 'mental labour' cannot be assumed in advance to be exclusively devoted to 'higher' or 'the highest' human concerns, but are in many or perhaps all cases likely to be bound up, in greater or lesser degree, with propagation, ratification, defence, apologia, naturalisation of that exploiting and unequal social order itself.

This is one of Marx's most powerful arguments, and we must return to it. But at this stage it is necessary to notice that what is already, at least in embryo, an historical formulation of the variable relations between necessary material production and 'what men say, imagine or conceive', becomes, too quickly, a categorical assertion of a merely 'reflexive' relation between what is primary and what is its 'efflux'. This loss of direction in the argument is, however, in practice less important than the apparent conceptual scheme which then distances the argument from real history, by the implicit postulation of two states: 'at first directly interwoven' and then 'in conditions of the division of labour'. The contrast is rhetorically striking, as in many Romantic and Utopian (and as it happens also Christian) conceptions of a primal integration and a later fragmentation or fall. But so broad a contrast cannot in fact be substituted for the more complex and differentiated history of different kinds of integration and different kinds and degrees of division of labour, which are not the categorical but the practical and historical forms of the 'activities of real men'.

Marx would not have disagreed with this. In his studies of economic history he continually sought and exemplified the processes of specific development, within his central emphasis.

> This method of approach is not without presuppositions, but it begins with the real presuppositions and does not abandon them for a moment. Its premises are men, not in some imaginary condition of fulfilment or stability, but in their actual, empirically observable process of development under determinate conditions. As soon as this active life-process is delineated, history ceases to be a collection of dead facts as it is with the empiricists (themselves still abstract) or an illusory activity of illusory subjects, as with the idealists. Where speculation ends – in real life – real, positive science, the representation of the practical activity and the practical process of development of men begins.[15]

Yet, because of the directions he gave to his major work, in an understandable choice of emphasis on the crisis of poverty and exploitation, the recommended kind of inquiry is not carried out in relation to art and is only partly carried out in relation to intellectual systems and ideas. It would be absurd to blame Marx for this, in view of the massive achievement of the work to which he gave his primary attention, but the result has been that his occasional relatively general pronouncements in these other areas have frequently been taken in a sense quite contrary to his own emphasis on method: have been taken, that is to say, as general and then abstract presuppositions about the relations between the material process and art and ideas. The worst consequence of this is in fact the neglect of the real social and material history of the *production* of art and ideas: a form of production which, like everything else, has to be studied as 'the practical activity and the practical process of development of men'. Yet, before we can do this, in anything like Marx's terms, we have to look again at his underlying position on the division of labour.

It is clear that, at different times, Marx meant rather different things by this crucial concept. His most influential use, in relation to culture, could hardly be more emphatically expressed:

> The division of labour only becomes a real division from the moment when the distinction between material and mental labour appears. From this moment, consciousness *can* really imagine that it is something other than consciousness of existing practice, that it is *really* conceiving something without conceiving something *real*; from now on consciousness is in a position to emancipate itself from the world and to proceed to the formation of 'pure' theory, theology, philosophy, ethics, etc.[16]

It is a powerful emphasis, with important possibilities for analysis, but it is clear that its formulation involves two intellectual operations which actually work against Marx's central emphasis. The first of these is the significant term 'moment': a received concept from schemes of universal history and in this kind of use essentially idealist. The effect of such a term is to flatten or altogether evade the highly variable relations between 'material' and 'mental' labour, in actual history, and to substitute an ideal and ahistorical contrast, of a simple kind. It is then not surprising that, within the language of the same mode of thought, the second operation follows, in which not actual people, in specific social relations, but 'consciousness' – that now ideal category – begins to 'imagine' and to 'conceive' and can even 'emancipate itself from the world'. Even when, as before, we have allowed for the polemical intention, in an argument against the proponents of 'pure' theory, the effect of this way of thinking, even when it has reversed the relative valuation of the categories, is to confirm their prepotence, and then in practice to hide the continuing determinate and thus variable social and material conditions of all 'mental labour', including that which is offered as the most 'pure'.

Indeed we do not have to go beyond Marx to make the point. In thinking about production in general, he was clear that historical evidence must prevail over categorical assumptions:

> The organization and division of labour varies according to the instruments of labour available. The hand mill implies a different division of labour from that of the steam mill. To begin with the division of labour in general, in order to arrive at a specific instrument of production – machinery – is therefore to fly in the face of history.[17]

But then this same point is highly relevant to the actual processes of 'mental labour'. Even if we retain, at this point, his categorical distinction between 'material' and 'mental' labour (overriding, as we shall see, the diverse social and historical conditions within which this distinction is variably practised and theorised), it soon becomes clear, from historical evidence, that the productive forces of 'mental labour' have, in themselves, an inescapable material and thus social history. Thus there are obvious differences between 'mental labour' which is still fundamentally oral in its production and distribution, and 'mental labour' which is produced and distributed through systems of writing and printing. The most obvious difference is that in predominantly oral conditions the actual process of 'mental labour' is at least in principle accessible to all normal members of a society. The faculty of speaking and of understanding speech has been a normal function of the most general socialisation The faculties of writing and reading, on the other hand, have to be specifically acquired, for the purposes of taking part, in whatever degree, in the social processes of 'mental labour'. It is then no surprise that one of the most common forms of the division between 'manual' and 'mental' labour is socially and materially specified in the capacity or incapacity to write and read. What in general argument may appear to be a categorical division has this precise social and material set of conditions. A history of writing and reading, not in the narrow technical sense but in its full social and material conditions, is then a necessary element of any 'real, positive science, the representation of the practical activity and the practical process of development of men'.

But then the division of labour, though fundamentally influenced by such developments in the forces of production, cannot be reduced to a history of technical means alone. It would, for example, be rash to claim that before the invention of writing there was no 'division between material and mental labour' in the important sense that Marx intends, which is at root a form of class division between those who have practically appropriated the general human faculties of consciousness, intention and control and those who have been made the objects of this appropriation, as the manual instruments – the 'hands' – of these other men's 'mental' decisions and intentions. The whole record of slavery in predominantly 'oral' conditions, to take no further case, argues against this. At the same time it is evident that the invention of a specific technical system, writing, provides obvious conditions in which an increasing part of the historical records, the laws and the ideas of a society, is embodied in a communicative system to which the majority of people have no or no independent access. That is a very practical form of a socially and materially inherent division of labour.

Yet again it would be rash to assert that the results of the long popular struggle for literacy – a struggle which still today is very far from complete – have abolished the underlying division between 'manual' and 'mental' labour. To be able to write and to read is a major advance in the possibility of sharing in the general culture of a literate society, but there are still typically determinate conditions in which the exercise of these faculties is differentially directed. Thus in late eighteenth-century England it was argued that the poor should be taught to read, but not to write. Reading would enable them to read the Bible, and to learn its morality, or later to read instructions and notices. Having anything to write on their own account was seen as a crazy or mischievous idea. Again, in our own time, there is an enforced division of labour, even among literate people, in the organisation of modern newspapers, in which there is one class of men – editors, journalists, correspondents – who *write* and another class of men whose proposed sole function is to *print*. Any attempt by the printers to have a say in what is written is denounced as interference with the 'freedom of the press', although it is then obvious that this freedom has been wholly formulated within the enforced division of labour. It is ironic that the possessors of capital, who can buy or hire whole newspapers – the material means of production and the services of journalists and printers alike – are able in practice to intervene and define the conditions of this supposed freedom, enforcing an even more fundamental form of the division of labour, between those who possess or can purchase these means of intellectual production and those who do or can not. It is not 'consciousness' which is in a position to emancipate itself, in the production of 'pure' news or a 'free' press; it is a precise class of men, within conditions which do not at all derive from the sphere of 'mental' labour alone but from the whole social and economic relations between capital and labour of any kind.

Further, that once critical form of an historically specific shift in the division of labour, in the long and varied change from oral or primarily oral to literate and authoritatively literate material and social conditions, is not categorically reversed when, as increasingly through the twentieth century, modern 'oral' forms, in radio and television, become as important as and in the end probably more important than print. One general condition is restored, at a higher level. The capacity to receive and to transmit, through speech, is again a function of normal general socialisation; it does not depend, as in the case of writing and reading, on particular forms of instruction which may be differentially distributed or altogether withheld from actual majorities. In this sense the cultural shift is radical. More people can and do express their ideas directly, and more people, with measurable social and political effects, find themselves listening to *other men and women* rather than reading, at first or second hand, written opinions described and prescribed as authoritative.

Yet a fundamental division of labour still exists, at two levels. First, because the ownership and control of these powerful systems of transmitted speech are subject to the general conditions of political and economic organisation, and are in practice normally directed by state or capitalist institutions. Second, because, as a form of this, there is an attempted and typically successful distinction between those who have 'something to say', in their own right – leaders, personalities, celebrities, presenters, official performers – and what is then called 'the public' – 'the listening or viewing public' – who if they speak at all speak in that assigned capacity.

Marx would have understood the spectacle of the degeneration of that phrase of the democratic ideal – *vox populi*, the voice of the people – into the resigned or cynical *vox pop* of professional broadcasters: the essentially random selection and collection of voices at a different level of substance and recognition from those who, within the division of labour, have 'something to say'. He would also have understood, very clearly, those negative versions of an undifferentiated public, a 'mass', which find their most memorable expression in the use of 'you' to describe everyone who is not a professional journalist or broadcaster, or the limited group they recognise as individuals. 'You Write', they write, above a selection of letters from some readers, whether 'you', reading it, have written or not. 'Your Reactions', they say, introducing similar selections, whether 'you', listening, have reacted or not. There was an old radical recognition of fundamental social divisions, based in the division of labour, as 'Them' and 'Us'. Within the altered conditions of modern communications systems, there is a profoundly unradical recognition of that division of labour which has persisted even after the generalisation of basic communicative skills and the development of new, relatively direct media: 'Us' (writing or speaking); 'You' (reading or listening). This is not a categorical 'moment'; it is a precise social and material form.

What then of the relation between the 'division of labour' and the attempted distinction between forms of mental labour which are aspects of more general productive processes and those other forms which were seen, at least by the young Marx, as 'ends in themselves'?

The examples taken thus far belong mainly to an area which is not easily distinguished by a simple contrast between 'general production' and what can be specialised, on the basis of 'ends in themselves', as 'high culture'. Most of them belong, in fact, to an area of quite material production which is yet distinguishable from certain obvious kinds of 'material production' in Marx's most limited sense. We have already looked at the problem this limited sense raises, in its too easily taken implication of 'material labour' as (only) the production of the absolute material necessities of life. In all his practical analyses, Marx was quite exceptionally aware of the profound, prolonged and intricate interaction between these basic productive processes and the social order to which, in his view, they gave rise. His famous or notorious metaphor of 'base' and 'superstructure', to express this fundamental relationship, has the effect, it is true, of underemphasising or even hiding the forms of interaction which he characteristically recognised. If we take the metaphor literally we find that what we have, ironically, is a classic and memorable assertion of a categorical, as distinct from an historical, division of labour. The material activities all occur in the 'base'; the mental activities all in the 'superstructure'. As a polemical point against the general assumption that all human history was directed by autonomous ideas the metaphor retains its relevance and force. But as a method, or as a set of tools for analysis, it leads us in wholly wrong directions.

What we have seen in the case of general communicative (cultural) institutions is a form of activity which is in its immediate processes indissolubly mental *and* material, and in its central functions directed not only to the production of ideas but to the manifestation or ratification of a social order within which, necessarily, all the most basic material production is in practice carried on. It is possible, as a hypothetical 'moment', to define an initial situation in which human beings can do no more than provide for their absolute physical needs, and then to see all history as dependent from that material necessity. But it was Marx more than anyone else who showed 'man making himself', affecting and eventually transforming both human and natural conditions, by the processes of associated labour. Then in the fact of that association there is the outline of this or that social order, and as one of its central elements – in story, dance, marks of community and identity – a set of cultural processes. If we can begin from this real situation, in all its actual historical variety, we can avoid the pointless play of categorical priorities and begin to examine what is really in question: the process of *determination* within different but always and necessarily connected activities.

This analysis of real determinations is inevitably complex. We should not assume in advance that the basic structural relations between different kinds of activity are themselves ahistorical, yielding regular uniformities and laws which can then be applied to any specific social and historical situation. Marx had already in effect recognised this when he described the 'moment' – which in his perspectives can only be a moment in human history – 'when the distinction between material and mental labour appears'. And it is again in practice unlikely that he would have held to the idea that this is a single moment, a categorical shift, rather than the diverse and complex historical process, illuminated but neither explained nor examined by the categorical distinction, in which the true social relations even between the extremes of 'manual without mental' and 'mental without manual' labour but more significantly between the very variable degrees of 'manual with mental' and 'mental with manual' can alone be discovered.

This argument bears heavily against the most widely known cultural proposition in Marx, in the formula of 'base and superstructure'. Yet of course it bears just as heavily against the dominant modern proposition that there are forms of 'mental labour' which can be assumed, categorically, to be 'ends in themselves': that proposition which, as we saw, Marx in his earliest writing picked up and repeated. It is then not a matter of trading adversary quotations within Marx's own work. The least useful form of the important argument which these alternative propositions introduce is also, unfortunately, the most common form, in which indiscriminate and absolute, non-historical positions are pitted each against the other. What Marx himself did, to make possible a more discriminating inquiry, was in this area relatively sketchy and unfinished. But we can look in more detail at what he actually did, first in relation to art and then in relation to ideas.

Two discussions of art stand out: that on Raphael and others in *The German Ideology*, and that on Greek art in the *General Introduction* (1857) to the *Critique of Political Economy*. First, on Raphael, where he is arguing against Stirner:

> [He] imagines that Raphael produced his pictures independently of the division of labour that existed in Rome at the time. If he were to compare Raphael with Leonardo da Vinci and Titian, he would know how greatly Raphael's works of art depended on the flourishing of Rome at that time, which occurred under Florentine influence, while the works of Leonardo depended on the state of things in Florence, and the works of Titian, at a later period, depended on the totally different development of Venice. Raphael as much as any other artist was determined by the technical advances in art made before him, by the organisation of society and the division of labour in all the countries with which his locality had intercourse. Whether an individual like Raphael succeeds in developing his talent depends wholly on demand, which in turn depends on the division of labour and the conditions of human culture resulting from it.[18]

This, as far as it goes, is an identifiable 'sociological' position, readily translated into a particular kind of 'art history'. It would be very difficult to deny its most general propositions, which are now in effect commonplace. It is useful that Marx includes 'technical advances in art' as well as more general social and historical conditions, but this is not much more than a passing reference, to what within Marx's general perspective should be seen as a central fact: the material history of painting itself, of which the painters themselves were very much aware in its immediately accessible form as techniques of work (labour). More emphasis is given to general factors of social environment and demand, which can certainly be confirmed from this and similar histories. But there is then an evident gap, between the briefly mentioned technical dimension (in fact the 'manual labour' of painting) and a general environment. And in fact it is in that gap, in that area of actual intersections between a material process, general social conditions, and the unmentioned assumptions about the purposes and content of art within those conditions, that the decisive questions about the art itself are to be found. By including the specific social and historical conditions Marx has usefully broadened the scope of the inquiry, but he has not then made it.

In fact, in his argument against Stirner, he passes at once to a different though related case:

> In proclaiming the uniqueness of work in science and art, Stirner adopts a position far inferior to that of the bourgeoisie. At the present time it has already been found necessary to organise this 'unique' activity... In Paris, the great demand for vaudevilles and novels brought about the organisation of work for their production, organisation which at any rate yields something better than its 'unique' competitors in Germany.[19]

This is a potentially important point, but it is hurriedly and even carelessly made. It is indeed a fact, against simple assertions of all works of art as 'ends in themselves', that a major part of modern cultural production is commercially organised, and that at least some work has from the beginning this commercial intention – the work of art as a saleable commodity – while much other work has a mixture of commercial and other intentions. Moreover this is an historically traceable development, from conditions of state and ecclesiastical patronage to the conditions of a developing capitalist market (I have described these historical conditions and phases in *Culture* [London: Fontana, 1981]).

But then, precisely because these conditions have a real history, with consequently variable relations between artists and their societies, the argument cannot be conducted, positively or negatively, around simple general propositions. Moreover, Marx's persuasive recognition of the extent to which modern cultural production has been 'organised by the market' remains relatively external. What does it mean to say 'the great demand for vaudevilles and novels'? Everything that Marx wrote elsewhere about 'demand', in the complexities of changing modes of production, must prevent us accepting any 'great demand' of this kind as some sort of primary cause. The conditions not only of demand but of production, and these within much more general social conditions, need to be specifically analysed before the argument can be rationally pursued, and the danger of course is that the merely polemical position can become, quite quickly, a reductive account of the making of art, against which, in its turn, a sublimated account, taking little or no notice of conditions which have unquestionably influenced and often determined actual production, is complacently reasserted. This is the more likely in the tone of Marx's remark about 'a position far inferior to that of the bourgeoisie', which gives bourgeois arrangements altogether too much credit and merely evades the persistent problem: that at least some art, made within determinate social conditions, is not reducible to their most general character but has qualities which attract such descriptions as 'uniqueness' or 'ends in themselves'.

217

In a later argument, Marx seems well aware of this:

> It is well known that certain periods of highest development of art stand in no direct connection with the general development of society, nor with the material basis and the skeleton structure of its organisation. Witness the example of the Greeks as compared with modern art or even Shakespeare. As concerns certain forms of art, e.g., the *epos*, it is even acknowledged that as soon as the production of art as such appears they can never be produced in their epoch-making, classical aspect; and accordingly, that in the domain of art certain of its important forms are possible only at an undeveloped stage of art development. If that is true of the mutual relations of different modes of art within the domain of art itself, it is far less surprising that the same is true of the relations of art as a whole to the general development of society. The difficulty lies only in general formulation of these contradictions. No sooner are they made specific than they are clarified.[20]

This is some of Marx's most developed thinking about art, yet it is obviously still uncertain and unfinished. It has the great merit of recommending specific analysis, and of recognising the problem which he had defined in an earlier note as 'the unequal relation between the development of material production and, e.g., artistic production'.[21] Yet it is limited by what are really preconceptions rather than ideas of 'progress' and 'development'.

Marx did not want to apply the idea of material progress to the history of art; his attachment to early Greek art was much too strong for that. All he can then fall back on, however, is the extraordinary proposition that 'in the domain of art certain of its important forms are possible only at an undeveloped stage of art development', which, insofar as it means anything, leads straight to an identification of art with naivety, and is then no more than a familiar kind of reactionary Romanticism. In fact he goes on to explain the continuing aesthetic appeal of Greek art in terms of the Greeks as 'normal children', its 'eternal charm' as inseparably connected with 'unripe social conditions'. He even generalises this as 'the historical childhood of humanity'.

It is difficult to believe that this is the Marx of the major work. His recognition of the problem is important. It belongs to the breadth of interest that we recognised at the beginning. But his offered solution is absurd. It is not only that Classical Athens was not, by any timescale, the 'historical childhood of humanity'; it is altogether too late for that. It is, more crucially, that the forms of Greek art and writing of which we have knowledge are unarguably mature, in their own terms. It is their long prehistory, only sketchily available, that might attract analysis of development, but even then it would be real development, in specific social and material processes, rather than the hazy idealism of an 'undeveloped stage of art development'.

There is indeed need to recognise what Marx called 'unequal relations' of development. But the underlying problem here is the two possible senses of 'unequalness' or, better, 'unevenness'. Thus it can be argued and indeed demonstrated that in particular social orders there is uneven development of various human faculties and practices. Such unevenness is wholly open to Marxist analysis, which can show how particular social orders and particular modes of production select certain faculties and practices for development within determinate general conditions, and by the same token neglect or even repress certain others. Moreover this can also be seen as more than conscious selection, or neglect and repression. In some important cases the character of the basic material production processes makes possible the development and extension of certain kinds of art (steam-machinery, the chemical industry, electronics are obvious examples), and there is almost always some significant relation between material production in general and the material processes in art. In either case, the uneven development of human faculties and practices has a discoverable social and material history.

On the other hand 'unevenness' can be construed, as in fact in Marx's argument about the Greeks, in terms of a generalised world history, where the problem is the evident lack of correlation between *increased* material production and *qualitatively better* art. But it must then be asked why this is seen as a problem at all. It is only from a very crude and undiscriminated idea of progress that it could ever be assumed that there is a regular relation between increased production and the quality of art. Marx was at once attracted to a notion of increased production as an index of general human progress (obviously in some senses a reasonable idea but at times involving ambiguities and even absurdities in the historical judgment of social orders which have increased production through increasing exploitation) and at the same time deeply committed to an idea of the general development of all human faculties and resources. When he took this uncertainty, between what are at times incompatible ideas, into the question of art, he could do little more than restate or evade it, though the necessary way through the problem, in terms of *contradiction*, was elsewhere one of his major methods of analysis.

For it is a fact of historical variation that art in general, and then arts of different kinds, are differentially valued in different social orders and in their own internal phases. It is this historical specificity, rather than a generalising progress, which is the ground for any history or historical analysis of the arts. There is still the problem of quality, but here Marx simply reverts to the received idealist notion of absolute, indeed 'classical', quality. It is not necessary to deny the effectively permanent value, within traceable historical and cultural continuities, of certain works of art from many historical periods, to be able to argue that *judgment* also, in its real terms of accessibility, recognition, understanding of theme and form, comparison, is itself an historical process. This need not mean that all judgments are relative, though that many of them are, including some of the most confident, is easily proved from the record. But it does mean, in ways which Marx elsewhere would quickly have recognised, and indeed in some other areas discovered and taught, that the processes of reception and judgment, quite as much as the processes of original production, occur within definite social relations.

Moreover, in the case of art, where simple physical consumption is not in question, no work is in any full practical sense produced until it is also received. The social and material conditions of the original production are indeed stable: the material object (painting, sculpture) or the material notations (music, writing) are there, if they survive, once for all. Yet until a further (and in practice variable) social and material process occurs, necessarily including its own conditions and expectations, the objects and the notations are not fully available for response. Often the varying conditions and expectations of response actually alter the object or the notation as it is *then* perceived and valued. Yet there are also some important continuities, which in Marxist terms do not relate to some unchanging pre-given human nature, nor to notions of the 'childhood' or 'maturity' of humanity, but to a range of human faculties, resources and potentials - some of the most important based in a relatively unchanged human biological constitution; others in persistent experiences of love and parentage and death, qualified but always present in all social conditions; others again in the facts of human presence in a physical world - with which certain works connect, in active and powerful ways, often apparently beyond the limited fixed ideas of any particular society and time.

Thus the question of value, in Marxist terms, while often a matter of direct and immediate social analysis - as in practice Marx exemplified - can be also, in more complex cases, a combination, in varying proportions, of such direct and immediate analysis and a more extensive, more open recognition and analysis of forms of material production - *works* of art - which embody and activate elements of that range of human faculties, resources and potentials which is factually wider than the determinations of any particular social order and which, both as historical evidence and as revolutionary aspiration, is the practical expression of actual and possible human development. This ultimate point of reference, not ideal but practical in those forms of material production which we distinguish as major art, is of course very relevant to Marx, who drew from it, sometimes with explicit reference to art as its evidence, his ideas of the overcoming of human alienation (from its own possibly fully human conditions and resources) and his most general ideas of the necessity and object of social revolution.

To move from Marx on art to Marx on ideas is to enter a very different and much more authoritative dimension. It is here that his major contribution to cultural theory was made.

> In order to study the connexion between intellectual and material production it is above all essential to conceive the latter in its determined historical form and not as a general category. For example, there corresponds to the capitalist mode of production a type of intellectual production quite different from that which corresponded to the medieval mode of production. Unless material production itself is understood in its specific historical form, it is impossible to grasp the characteristics of the intellectual production which corresponds to it or the reciprocal action between the two.[22]

We have already looked at some of the fundamental difficulties in the *categorical* distinction between, and then separation of, 'intellectual' and 'material' production. Yet, while retaining the necessary emphases that were then made, we can look at this part of Marx's work as a way of understanding his critical concept of *determination*.

It is already, as this passage shows, a matter of historically specific determinations, rather than some categorical law of regular determination, of the kind indicated by crude application of the 'base-superstructure' metaphor. But then this recognition is relevant to some of his other arguments on this matter. Thus:

> The ideas of the ruling class are, in every age, the ruling ideas: i.e., the class which is the dominant *material* force in society is at the same time its dominant *intellectual* force. The class which has the means of material production at its disposal has control at the same time over the means of mental production, so that in consequence the ideas of those who lack the means of mental production are, in general, subject to it.[23]

This early formulation can be read as a categorical proposition, but it can more usefully be taken as an *historical* proposition, which can then be tested by specific evidence. As such it is in practice of great value. Marx's welcome emphasis, here, on 'the means of mental production', as distinct from other abstract uses of 'mental production' as if it were an unlocated 'consciousness', shows us where to look for certain fundamental conditions of intellectual production and distribution. And then we do find, again and again, that such conditions and controls are practically decisive, indeed determining. It is the point which Marx's enemies can never forgive him for making, and that yet, from repeated practical experience – down to the contemporary controls exercised by corporate capitalism, most notably in the press – has quite relentlessly to be made.

Yet it is necessary even here to recognise socially specific and differential forms of determination. The weakest case is that which Marx actually goes on, in this passage, to make:

> The dominant ideas are nothing more than the ideal expression of the dominant material relationships, the dominant material relationships grasped as ideas, and thus of the relationships which make one class the ruling one; they are consequently the ideas of its dominance.[24]

The fact that this is often true, especially in systems of law and political constitution, but at times also more generally, should not hurry us into accepting the assertion that such ideas are 'nothing more than' the ideal expression of dominance.

For, first, the argument is too static. It is often the case, as even in law and political theory, to say nothing of natural philosophy and moral argument, that there are historical continuities and effects in certain bodies of thinking which make them more than locally determined by specific and temporary forms of dominance. None of them can ever be put *above* history, but the historical process, in this as in other respects, includes both *residual* and *emergent* forms of thought and belief, which can in practice enter into very complex relations with the more specifically and locally dominant. In any developed social order, we can expect to find not only interaction but also actual conflict between residual, dominant and emergent forms of thought, in general as well as in special areas. Moreover there is often conflict, related to this complexity, between different versions of the dominant, which is by no means always a ready translation of a singular material class interest.

This point connects, second, with the fact that, in class-dominated social orders, there are not only variable relations between different classes, with varied effects in intellectual work (of the kind Marx indeed later recognised in his observation that 'the existence of revolutionary ideas in a particular age presupposes the existence of a revolutionary class'[25]) but also complex relations between *fractions* of the dominant class, which in highly developed orders is more often a coalition or amalgam of particular material interests than a quite singular interest. This internal complexity, within dominance, has to be related to an internal division which Marx himself describes:

> Within [the ruling] class one part appears as the thinkers of the class (its active conceptualising ideologists, who make it their chief source of livelihood to develop and perfect the illusions of the class about itself), while the others have a more passive and receptive attitude to these ideas and illusions... This cleavage... may even develop into a certain hostility and opposition between the two parts, but in the event of a practical collision in which the class itself is endangered, it disappears of its own accord...[26]

This is suggestive but too simple. The division of labour between ideologists and active members of the ruling class is already subject to the fact of fractional interests. But also, within such a division of labour, specialised intellectual institutions come to develop not only their own local material interests but more crucially their internal intellectual criteria and continuities. These lead often to evident asymmetries and incongruities with more general institutions of the class, and indeed to conflicts, including internal and external intellectual conflicts. Very complex relations then occur, in much more than 'two parts', and these kinds of 'hostility and opposition' do not, on the record, 'disappear of their own accord'. Such relations are much affected by the fact of variable distance, as Engels later noted, between different forms of thought and direct political and material interests. But the complexity is not reducible to the facts of relative distance (as between, say, philosophy and law) alone; this can be seen, for example, in the serious internal divisions within modern capitalist *economic* thought.

Nevertheless, though needing these major qualifications as the means to any veridical analysis, Marx's central insistence on determining pressures, exercised by the material relations of a social order on both the practice and the nature of many if not all kinds of intellectual work, is to be welcomed as a revolutionary advance. Yet it is not only a matter of direct or indirect pressures. It is also, as the other crucial process of determination, a matter of practical and theoretical limits. Marx expressed this position in a remarkable analysis of mid-nineteenth-century France:

> What makes them representatives of the petty bourgeoisie (though 'according to their education and individual position they may be as far apart as heaven and earth') is the fact that in their minds they do not get beyond the limits which the latter do not get beyond in life, that they are consequently driven, theoretically, to the same problems and solutions to which material interest and social position drive the latter practically.

This is, in general, the relationship between the *political* and *literary representatives* of a class and the class they represent.[27]

This can be taken too simply, but it is the source of the important modern Marxist conception of *homology*, or formal correspondence, between certain kinds of art and thought and the social relations within which they are shaped. This conception can reveal determining relations at a quite different level from the bare proposition that 'ideas are nothing more than the ideal expression of the dominant material relationships'; among other reasons in the fact that something more than reflection or representation is then often in question, and art and ideas can be seen as structurally formed, but then also actively formed, in their own terms, within a general social order and its complex internal relations.

Marx's other productive emphasis, which can in general be taken as decisive, is his argument that dominant ideas (and, we might add, dominant artistic *forms*) take on, in the period of their dominance, the appearance of universality: a dominant class employs

an ideal formula, to give its ideas the form of universality and to represent them as the only rational and universally valid ones.[28]

The immense pressure of these notions of universal validity has been so major a factor in intellectual history, their deeply graved habits of mind so difficult to escape from, not only in intellectual work but in everyday practice and assumption (the ruling but in fact historically conditioned 'common sense' which Gramsci identified as the central element of *hegemony*, within and beyond direct dominance) that it is in this great challenge by Marx that much of his most general intellectual importance is to be found.

To learn from Marx is not to learn formulae or even methods, and this is especially the case, as has been argued, in those parts of his work, on art and ideas, where he was not able to develop or to demonstrate his most interesting suggestions, or was actually still limited by the dominant ideas of his time. The two areas in which this lack of development has been most limiting are, first, the history of the social and material means and conditions of cultural production, which needs to be established in its own terms as a necessary part of any historical materialism; and, second, the nature of language, which Marx recognised, briefly, as material, and defined as 'practical consciousness', but which for just these reasons is a more central and fundamental element of the whole social process than was recognised in the later propositions of 'manual' and 'mental', 'base' and 'superstructure', 'reality' and 'consciousness'. It is only from the most active senses of the material production of culture and of language as a social and material process that it is possible to develop the kind of cultural theory which can now be seen as necessary, and even central, in Marx's most general theory of human production and development. That he did not develop such a cultural theory, and indeed that from some more limited formulations misleading forms of 'Marxist' cultural theory were developed and propagated, in ways that actually blocked the inquiry, must now be acknowledged. Yet it remains true that the thrust of his general work is still, apart from social life itself, the most active inspiration for the making of such a cultural theory, even where we have not only to interpret but to change it.

1983

[1] S.S. Prawer, *Karl Marx and World Literature* (Oxford, 1976).
[2] Cit. *Marx and Engels on Literature and Art*, ed. L. Baxandall and S. Morawski (St Louis, 1973), p. 59.
[3] *Ibid.*, p. 60.
[4] *Ibid.*, p. 59.
[5] *Ibid.*, p. 61.
[6] *Ibid.*, pp. 60–1.
[7] R. Williams, *Keywords* (London: Fontana, 1976), pp. 76–82.
[8] K. Marx and F. Engels, *Werke* (Berlin, 1957ff), vol. 3, p. 539.
[9] K. Marx and F. Engels, *Historisch-kritische Gesamtausgabe* [MEGA] (Moscow, 1927–35), vol. 1, part 5, pp. 15–17.
[10] *Ibid.*
[11] *Ibid.*
[12] *Capital* (London, 1954), vol. 1, p. 178.
[13] MEGA, vol. 1, part 5, pp. 28–9.
[14] *Ibid.*, pp. 15–17.
[15] *Ibid.*, p. 17.
[16] *Ibid.*, p. 21.
[17] MEGA, vol. 1, part 6, p. 197.
[18] *The German Ideology*, in K. Marx, *Selected Writings*, ed. D. McLellan (Oxford, 1977), p. 189.
[19] *Ibid.*
[20] Cit. Baxandall and Morawski, *op. cit.*, p. 134.
[21] *Ibid.*
[22] *Theorien uber den Mehrwert* (Berlin, 1956), vol. 1, p. 381.
[23] MEGA, vol. 1, part 5, p. 35.
[24] *Ibid.*
[25] *Ibid.*, p. 36.
[26] *Ibid.*
[27] *The Eighteenth Brumaire of Louis Bonaparte*, in K. Marx and F. Engels, *Selected Works* (Moscow, 1962), vol. 1, p. 275.
[28] MEGA, vol. 1, part 5, p. 36.

A Defence of Realism*

The Big Flame is a play written by Jim Allen, produced by Tony Garnett and directed by Ken Loach for BBC television. I want to discuss it in relation to our understanding of realism. It should be clear at the outset that except in the local vocabulary of particular schools, realism is a highly variable and inherently complex term. In fact, as a term, it only exists in critical vocabulary from the mid-nineteenth century, yet it is clear that methods to which the term refers are very much older. Let me make just one obvious general distinction between conceiving realism in terms of a particular artistic method and conceiving realism in terms of a particular attitude towards what is called 'reality'. Now if, taking the first definition, we concentrate on method, we put ourselves at once in a position in which the method can be seen as timeless: in which it is, so to say, a permanent possibility of choice for any particular artist. Certain things can be learned from this kind of emphasis, but once we become aware of the historical variations within this method, we find ourselves evidently dissatisfied with the abstraction of a method which overrides its relations with other methods within a work or with other aims and intentions.

Let me give one or two examples of this. Realism would be an obvious term for that well-known episode within the medieval play known as the Play of the Townley Shepherds, which is basically a play of the nativity and the annunciation of the birth of Christ to the shepherds, and in that sense a characteristic religious form of medieval drama (indeed, largely written in that way). The inserted episode to which I am referring is that in which, before the annunciation, the shepherds, recognisably shepherds of the district in which the play was written and played – that

---

* The text which follows is transcribed from a version of a lecture first given by Raymond Williams at the SEFT/*Screen* weekend school on Realism held at the London International Film School on October 8–10, 1976.

226

is to say, offering themselves for recognition in these terms – discuss the problems of their own life as shepherds and represent themselves in that very specific situation. Then comes the annunciation. Now, you can look at this either way: you can say that the scene is inserted because it is of interest to the people who know of that life or are sharing that life and who recognise this as the life of shepherds in their own district, in which case this definition can be assimilated to a common later definition of realism; or you can look at it in quite another way and say that the establishment of the locality, the local realism, of these Yorkshire shepherds is a condition of that work as a whole, in that the annunciation, presumed to have happened to shepherds in Palestine, is a universal annunciation, and the condition of the local realism is a condition for the universality of the religious event. In other words, you can only finally determine the function of that realism, and thence the critical significance of a description of it as that, when you have analysed not only the local method but the relation of that method to other methods and other intentions within the work.

Or, again, consider those scenes which are often inserted in English renaissance tragedies, usually with a conscious social movement from the major personages of the drama, personages of rank, to persons of a different social order who speak in different ways, and who again, interestingly, are often recognisably contemporary English characters, even within an action which can be that of an Italian court, or a Roman forum, or of some much earlier period. The intention at these points is not the same as that within the Townley shepherds play, where the locality-with-universality is a very specific convention. On the other hand, in terms of method, we have to describe certain scenes as realistic: the written speech moves much closer towards the imitation of everyday ordinary life: all these are later seen as conditions of realism. Yet the scene inserted within this very different kind of play can be described as realism with any accuracy only if the relation to the intentions of the larger work is made. Here we have not the local/universal specificity of the religious drama, but a problem of interrelation and extending action in which the contrast between the modes of action and the modes of speech of the principal characters and these subsidiary characters is itself a function of the definition of the dramatic action as a whole. The contrast between this version of realism as method and the alternative version of realism as fundamental attitude can, I think, only be appreciated historically when, looking through the development of dramatic forms, we come to the unmistakable qualitative difference which occurs when the realistic method, often very similar to that used in these earlier particular scenes, is extended to the construction of a whole form, and when the play as a whole is conceived as not only using these methods but as embodying entirely different intentions. If we are to discuss those later intentions, there is a certain obvious loss if we set intention aside and discuss only method, or think that we can reduce the question of intention to the question of method.

The crucial development of realism as a whole form occurs in the drama in the eighteenth century, although there are precedents. There is a very interesting case, for example, in restoration prose comedy, which happened to have an unusually integrated relationship between plays, actors and audience within the quite extraordinarily class-limited nature of the restoration patent theatres. The life of a small class around the court is written about by dramatists who belong to that life, and plays for audiences almost exclusively of that life, and as a whole form, these are perhaps the first realist plays – according to one definition – in English. There is a concentration on contemporary everyday reality within the terms of that class. The modes of speech have moved towards the imitation of conversation with a much greater consistency than in any earlier drama. Moreover, this is accompanied by certain changes, themselves not wholly determined by artistic intention: substitution of actresses for boy actors in the playing of female parts is only one obvious example. And yet it is significant how often the title of realism is refused to that kind of comedy of manners, as it is now usually classified, because, although the method and the intention is in these broad terms realist, the later definition of realism as a whole form was concerned with different, and indeed consciously opposed, attitudes towards reality – it being assumed that the limited interests and the limited habits of this class, which found its embodiment in that particular dramatic form, are not in the full sense an engagement with contemporary reality.

It is indeed when we come on to this later drama, specifically the bourgeois drama of the eighteenth century, that we come to realism as a whole form, and that we need to identify certain defining characteristics. First there is a conscious movement towards social extension. There is a crucial argument in the early period of bourgeois tragedy about the need to extend the actions of tragedy from persons of rank, to whom by convention and precept tragedy had hitherto largely been confined, to – as it was put – 'your equals, our equals'. This movement of social extension – 'let not your equals move your pity less' – is a key factor in what we can now identify as a realist intention. Then, second, there is a movement towards the siting of actions in the present, to making action contemporary. It is remarkable that in most preceding drama it seemed almost a constituent of dramatic form that it was set either in the historical or in a legendary past, and the emphasis on the actions of the contemporary world is the second defining feature of this new bourgeois realism. And the third, which is perhaps in the end the most important, is that there is an emphasis on secular action, in the quite precise sense that elements of a metaphysical or a religious order directly or indirectly frame, or in the stronger cases determine, the human actions within the earlier plays. This dimension is dropped, and in its place a human action is played through in specifically human terms – exclusively human terms. This was seen as a loss of significance, as a narrowing of drama. It is often condemned as a sentimentalisation of the tragic action, and indeed in local terms this was often true. But it is impossible to overlook the connection between this conscious secularisation and the development of attitudes which we must associate with realism in a much wider sense than that of dramatic method, that is to say with the development of rationalism, of the scientific attitude, of historical attitudes towards society.

At the same time, within a specific situation, these general realistic intentions were limited by specific ideological features. Lello's play *The London Merchant* is an important example of this type. And yet, it is held within a particular local structure which has to do with the ideology of a particular class and not with these more general intentions; or rather these general intentions are mediated through the specific ideology. It is a story of the honest, hardworking, obedient apprentice who is contrasted with the apprentice who is seeking his own fortune and his own pleasure in his own way. This leads him into theft and murder, while the good apprentice marries his master's daughter and succeeds. The good apprentice and the daughter watch the execution of the bad apprentice and his mistress, and invite the audience consciously to mark their fate and learn how to avoid it. It is not surprising that this play was subsequently subsidised for annual performance to apprentices by a London guild of merchants, and that this went on for more than a century. And we can see that in a sense, just because of the ideological content, the realistic intention is obliquely confirmed. It is assumed that this picture of what happens is sufficiently clear and convincing in the terms of realism to be available as a lesson, a moral lesson, to people finding themselves in the same situation: they can directly apply the actions of the drama to their own lives.

The development of realism in the drama from these early bourgeois plays towards the important high naturalism of the late nineteenth century is slow and complex, and yet by the time, for example, that we come to Ibsen in the late nineteenth century, it is clear that what has developed from these three emphases is a new major form. The three emphases which are then often consciously described as realism are the secular, the contemporary and the socially extended. In a sense, those definitions have become so widespread, though never of course exclusive, that they have come to include within their overall definitions many local variations of method.

There is a complication here in that in the late nineteenth century there was an attempt to distinguish realism from naturalism, and it is worth considering this distinction for a moment. In fact, naturalism, even more clearly than realism, is not primarily defined as a dramatic or more general artistic method. Naturalism is originally the conscious opposition to supernaturalism and to metaphysical accounts of human actions, with an attempt to describe human actions in exclusively human terms with a more precise local emphasis. The relation to science, indeed consciously to natural history, the method of exhaustive analytic description of contemporary reality, and the terms naturalism and realism which have those philosophical connections, are for a time interchangeable, even complicated by the fact that in a famous definition Strindberg called naturalism the method which sought to go below the surface and discover essential movements and conflicts, while realism, he said, was that which reproduced everything, even the speck of dust on the lens of the camera. As I suppose we all now know, the eventual conventional distinction was the same but with the terms the other way round. Naturalism was seen as that which merely reproduced the flat external appearance of reality with a certain static quality, whereas realism – in the Marxist tradition, for example – was that method and that intention which went below this surface to the essential historical movements, to the dynamic reality. And within the terms of that distinction it is now a commonplace – it seems to be a picture that could be set up in type for every interview with a contemporary director or dramatist – that naturalism has been abandoned, naturalism in the sense of the reproduction of the appearance of everyday reality. It remains remarkable in view of all these declarations that the great majority of contemporary drama is of course the reproduction of everyday reality in precisely those terms, with really surprisingly small local variations. And realism, although permitted a wider extent because of the reference to dynamic movement, has tended to be swept up in this abstract and ultimately meaningless rejection – with various complications about psychological realism, neo-realism, and so on.

It is clear even from these few examples that we have to be especially careful about definitions which we have seen to be historically variable, and especially about definitions which abstract the method from an intention in ways that are finally insupportable in any substantial analysis. The best example I can give of this problem of the relation between a technical and a general definition is the case of the room on the stage in nineteenth-century drama. It is undoubtedly a quite specific historical development: the reproduction of the stage as *room*, or a room on the stage, which occurs during the nineteenth century in a wide area of the European theatre. Before that, even where rooms had been in question, the stage was still primarily a playing space. And of course given the nature of earlier actions, the room – the specifically domestic unit – was much less often used than the more public places of street, palace, forum, court. Now there is a familiar kind of technologically determinist history which relates the development of the room on the stage to developments in theatrical technology: the introduction of gas lighting, the improvement of stage carpentry, and so on. But it is in fact ludicrous to suppose that if people before the nineteenth century had wanted to create rooms on stages in the way that they were created in the late nineteenth-century and twentieth-century theatre they would have been technically unable to do so. The truth is that the production of the room on the stage was a particular reading both of the natural centre of dramatic action in terms of social extension and the emphasis on the contemporary; it was also as it happens in its later development a specific naturalist reading in the full sense of the indissoluble relation between character and environment, in which the room was a character because it was a specific environment created by and radically affecting, radically displaying, the nature of the characters who lived in it.

The true history is more complex than either a history in terms of increasing technical capacity, or a history in terms of this scientific version of a relation between character and environment. In fact, if you look at when the first 'box sets' with reproduced rooms were put on the stage in England (the English and French theatres moving at about the same rate in this respect), you will find that the rooms are there not to give any impression of recognition or demonstration of environment, but simply to display a certain kind of luxury. They are 'society' plays of a consciously displayed kind – of a fashionable kind, as we would now say – and most of the technology of the box set and the subsequent adaptation of theatres to the fully-framed box set, which was not complete until the 1870s, was more conditioned by this 'furnishing display' than by either of the other intentions. But there is a radical development, not so much in English drama as in Scandinavian, German, Russian, and then extending through Europe, of the room as the centre of the reality of human action: the private domestic room, which is of course entirely consonant with a particular reading of the place of human action – this is the life of the bourgeois family, where the important things occur in that kind of family room. All I mean is that if we are analysing a form of that kind it is not enough to note the method and relate it to some abstract concept of realism, or to assume that the reproduction of a room has some constant implication in overall dramatic intention.

This point is also relevant to the subsequent variable uses of film. It is clear that film could in certain ways more actively develop the reproduction of room, of mobility from room to room, of a variety of scenes conceived in those simple terms, than it could again move out of doors into the street, into the public places which on the whole the theatrical drama had left behind. At the same time, inherent in the fact of the camera was the possibility of the use of the image for quite different purposes. And since most uses of films were defined in terms of the received dramatic tradition, you find the same variation of message and intentions and variable combinations of methods and intentions, and the same variability – not to say confusion – of terms. It is in this sense that one can perhaps best approach the problem of definition of *The Big Flame* with a consciousness of inherent variation, and ask certain questions about it.

It might be worth asking first: how would the makers of *The Big Flame* themselves describe their work? Would they say that it was showing real life in the Liverpool Docks? They might. But I think that that is not all that they would say. One can see certain obvious continuities with the earlier history that I have described. In one sense, the movement to which this particular work belongs can be sited historically as a further phase of that social extension which defined the first period of bourgeois drama. When the bourgeois tragedians talked of moving out to a concern with 'your equals, their equals', they were moving towards their own class. Still there was very little extension towards a class beyond them. And there is a perfectly accurate way of reading the subsequent history of this kind of dramatic form in terms of its further social extension, one of the three key features of the definition of the bourgeois dramatic form. This is a conscious extension of dramatic material to areas of life which had been evidently excluded even from majority drama. And television was often conceived in this way as the site for a particular dramatic extension, since it had already a full socially extended audience. It was seen as the proper site, in conscious opposition to the theatre with its persistent minority audience in social terms and its much more limited class audience, of the alternative which allowed a popular audience and the extension to themes of a much more fully extended drama, that of the drama of working-class life, bringing the working class to the centre of dramatic action.

There are still not enough examples of this to indicate that the movement is complete. In the theatre it is a very late movement: I don't know that it happens before, say, Hauptmann's *The Weavers* in 1892, which is a classic in the naturalist theatre, and which is accompanied by certain conscious political intentions. It is hardly possible to conceive of an extension of this kind without a certain conscious political viewpoint in the at first relatively open terms of taking a much wider social life to a much wider audience. And yet you only have to see *The Big Flame* once to realise that something more than simple extension is involved. It is not, as in some cases of the extension to working-class life, the realisation of something that is exotic to the audience. There is a sense in which what was earlier called the drama of 'low life' is a minor intention of bourgeois drama itself, where 'to see how the other half lives', as it was often put, was in itself a particular intention, even a particular form of entertainment. Indeed, one of the questions which has to be asked about *The Big Flame* is whether it is interpreting the particular action within the docks to a wider audience, or whether it is interpreting that class to itself. I think there is evidence of both intentions in the work, and to distinguish between them is important in any complete analysis. On balance, I would say that *The Big Flame* belongs to a kind of realist drama for which a fourth term is necessary in addition to the defining characteristics of the socially extended, the contemporary and the secular; and that is the consciously interpretative in relation to a particular political viewpoint. It has an interesting cross-relation with, for example, the drama of Brecht. It is interesting that Brecht, although in many ways sharing the intentions and the philosophical positions which had underlain realism, had in much of his drama – although certainly retaining and increasing the secular emphasis – moved away from the contemporary. It remains a remarkable fact of his drama that so much of his work is set in the past, and the everyday is subject to that move. The intention of *interpreting* an event, which Brecht made so intrinsic a part of his dramatic form, distinguishing it from the form which offered an event for mere empathy, seems quite clearly evident in *The Big Flame*, and is probably even consciously derived from something of the influence of Brecht.

The Big Flame sets out to establish the level of existing working-class history and consciousness in a specific workplace. It is looking at the Liverpool Docks at the time of the Devlin report on the docks. It uses features of the developed realist film of this contemplative kind – that which had been developed in the Soviet cinema, for example, and indeed in the Soviet theatre in the early 1920s: the deliberate use of non-actors, of people 'playing themselves'. The locations are (or are in part) the locations of the historical action, the contemporary action, as well as being the locations of the dramatised action, and within these locally defining features a recognisable level of consciousness is established in the conversation of the dockers in the early part of the film. What then happens is perhaps inconsistent with the narrower definitions of realism in that, having taken the action to that point in this recognisable place, a certain dramatic, but also political, hypothesis is established. What would happen if we went beyond the terms of this particular struggle against existing conditions and existing attempts to define or alter them? What would happen if we moved towards taking power for ourselves? What would happen in specific terms if we moved beyond the strike to the occupation? Thus if we are establishing the character of realism in *The Big Flame*, we have to notice the interesting combination, fusion perhaps, and within this fusion a certain fracture, between the familiar methods of establishing recognition and the alternative method of a hypothesis within that recognition, a hypothesis which is played out in realistic terms, but within a politically imagined possibility. The thing is played through. It is not, incidentally, played through in a Utopian way. What happens in the move to occupation is of course a good deal of success, a good deal of exhilaration, the familiar idea of the release of energy when people take control of their own lives. But within it there are all the time movements towards betrayal, demonstrations of certain kinds of inadequacy of organisation, lack of preparation, the absence of any real warning against the eventual attack by the army; there is the insistence that against the demonstration of the workers' own power the forces of the State will act, and will act both by fraud and by violence, and in the end the particular hypothesis is shown as defeated, but defeated in terms of the local action, and not, while it is retained as a hypothesis, defeated as an idea. There is a very characteristic ending in which, although the particular action has been defeated, the organising committee replaces itself, and in the final scene boys come out from behind the men who are assembling to reconstitute the occupation committee: the boys of the next generation who will take over, and this within a teaching perspective that the working class must understand

and learn from its defeats as well as its victories.

It is interesting to look more closely at the specific techniques within this general movement. At first, the techniques are those of the realist film in the simplest sense: the camera is a single eye, there is no possibility of an alternative viewpoint, the viewer has to go along or detach him or herself, he or she has no complex seeing within the action. Indeed, a great deal is taken for granted in knowledge and recognition of the situation. The Devlin report is referred to, but whether it is known or not is in a sense taken for granted. Nothing is done specifically to establish it. What is established is a sense of militancy which is yet an incomplete militancy because it can only react negatively. The key transition from this limited militancy to the next phase of the conscious taking of power is introduced by an alteration of technique. The strong man with a clear view of what can next happen is introduced, again without much identification, and interestingly without much precise specification of political roots or relation to this action, but he comes in as the voice of a different consciousness, and there is a movement in that part of the film from the rather ragged discussion which is done within naturalist terms to the conscious voice-over presentation of an alternative point of view. The mode of the transition is the introduction of a convention which allows complex-seeing, variable viewpoints when the hypothesis is dramatised in terms of a recognisable action, again largely within naturalist terms. This convention is on the whole not used again, and at the end particularly this absence is significant because the learning from defeat is done by that final scene, insofar as it is done at all, by offering the implication that the class will renew itself in subsequent generations and in self-replacement, rather than by the use of conventions which would show the actual learning of lessons, the attainment of a new consciousness by analysis of what has happened – the convention which Brecht, unevenly but persistently, tried to establish in his kind of drama.

There is one local point here which is rather interesting to analyse. There is a quite effective short scene of a television interviewer who has come to discover what the occupation is about, but to discover this within the terms of his function as a reporter for a particular kind of television service. In fact, we are shown him falsifying in his summing-up what has been said to him, and this is an effective satiric presentation of what many working-class people feel about the function of television interviewers when they come to report events of this kind. As an isolated scene it is effective. Yet it is interesting also because of the general naturalist presentation. If we remember what we have heard outside that scene, we have in fact heard, though at a much more dispersed level than would give any warrant to the interviewer's summary, that kind of feeling: that the thing is too much effort, that people would like to get back to work. It is as if that scene was conceived as a satiric presentation in its own right. This use of yet another convention dependent on our awareness of the modes of television interviewing and its insertion into the dominant convention of the rest of the film creates a certain unresolved tension, even a contradiction.

Or take another problem of point of view, one which requires a more positive emphasis: one of the unnoticed elements of the production of meaning within what is apparently the reproduction of what is happening, the familiar media claim to be showing things as they occur. Here it is a question of the position of the camera when there is fighting between the police and others who are presented as engaged in some kind of social disturbance. It is quite remarkable, and of course the reasons are obvious, how regular and how naturalised the position of the camera *behind the police* is in either newsreel or in fictionalised reports of that kind of disturbance. The police are seen *with* the camera. The crowd, the disturbance, is object. It is significant that in *The Big Flame*, in contrast with the normality of this convention, the viewpoint is with the people being attacked. This is a useful reminder, both for an analysis of this film and for analysis of the many hundreds of examples which must be seen as working the other way round, of the way in which the convention of showing things as they actually happen is inherently determined by viewpoint in the precise technical sense of the position of the camera.

Another local point worth analysis is the scene in the court towards the end of the work, where there is a problem of undefined political viewpoint. I have already said that the work is a combination of the techniques of classical realism in its extended sense – of realism plus hypothesis – and of political intention in the broad sense, to understand the nature of the movement from one kind of militancy to another, the development of consciousness, which at this level is still, although a specific left viewpoint, the viewpoint of a rather broad left. What happens in the court scene is the development of something else which I think in fact is the result of a more specific, indeed sectarian, viewpoint within the film. The judge in his speech moves well beyond the conventions of the naturalist method which has sustained the rest of the work. He makes an extraordinary assertion about the relation between dockers and students: that it's all right for students to have ideas of this sort, but if working men get them it's very dangerous. The idea that it's all right for students is, I think, the product of a particular sectarian position which develops into an implication about intellectuals generally; and the judge is in effect made a straight man for this sort of sectarian point. It would not be so noticeable were it not inserted within a work which on the whole develops along more consistent conventions in which what is said is conceived as what is typical. The judge speaks more like a character in a Brecht presentation, and this inconsistency is significant not just as a problem about method and technique, but as an illustration of the way in which, as I think, inevitably, specific uses of method and technique are in the end inseparable from fundamental conscious or unconscious positions, viewpoints and intentions.

Towards the end of the film, there is the singing of the 'Ballad of Joe Hill', and this is worth a brief consideration. Obviously in one sense this is the classic ballad for the expression of a defeat from which new energy, new consciousness, can be derived: that Joe Hill was killed but never died, and the mood of the ballad moves straight into the mood of the final scene, in which out of defeat comes the slow new organisation, new consciousness, the possibility of the future. It is interesting because at one level the ballad and the mood are consonant, but it raises a very specific problem about the naturalist convention, because it is of course the introduction of a much wider history, a much wider consciousness of the working-class movement as a whole, a use of a song of another place, another time; and again it is a problem, as throughout in the film, of the matching (often the failure to match) of the most immediate kinds of naturalist reproduction and the attempted (and often successfully attempted) introduction of the consciousness, classically defined as realism in contrast with naturalism, of the movements of history which underlie the apparent reality that is occurring. This is so deep and permanent a problem of the methods of naturalism and realism that this local example has a very obvious general bearing.

Then, finally, the question of the use of the 'real people', the non-actors, indeed the dockers, among actors in this play about dock life and dock struggle. The use of non-actors was extensive in early Soviet film and theatre: indeed, the problem of crowds could perhaps within that kind of production only be handled in that way, not necessarily for more than logistical reasons. But again it raises a question about the method. It is interesting for example that in Hauptmann's *The Weavers* what emerges, which is most uncharacteristic of plays about the working class, is the shape of the class as a whole rather than the more familiar figures of the representative or, even more commonly, the leader. As this comes into the question of dramatic method, there are some very interesting differences to note. In the film, undoubtedly the overall intention is the presentation of the general life, and when the dockers speak as themselves it is possible for the trained ear to recognise that speech which is at once authentic and rehearsed. That is to say, it is authentic in that it is the accent and the mode of speech of men reproducing their real-life situations. It is also rehearsed in that it is predetermined what they will say at that point and in what relation to each other. This is of great interest, and Loach and Garnett have given us more valuable material for thinking about this than any others in their generation.

It is interesting to look into the detail of this at the point of production, because the relation between the producers and the people whom they are at once serving and reproducing and, it should not be forgotten, directing, is something we should explore and know more about, because there is a sense in which one can see the production of this kind of work developing into the gaining of consciousness by the producer rather than only, what the method implies, the reproduction of the development of consciousness according to an already finished script, which seems to be the dominant method. Indeed, we do need to explore, in detail and with many examples, the process of production on this precise point of the relation between the prepared script and the use of people who are, in the significant phrase, 'playing themselves' – but 'playing themselves' as roles within a script. There is also the problem in this reproduction of people in their own situations trying to understand their own conditions, developing their consciousness within the very act of production of the film, a problem of the relation between this and what is also evidently a kind of 'speaking to' both the real people finding themselves in their situation – presenting an argument to them about what they need to do next (because that, remember, is the hypothesis of *The Big Flame*; it is not what they have done but what they could do next), and the mode of speaking beyond them, to an audience, of what they could do next. There is a clear implication at the end of the film that the report of the occupation, although it is shown as defeated, is getting out to other people, and is shown as providing a model on which they could act. If we remember the period of the late 1960s in which the film was made – and indeed that period continuous to the present – then the movement towards occupation, the movement towards this new phase of working-class consciousness and action has been significant in British politics; it is perhaps the most significant contemporary action within it, and undoubtedly, I think, Garnett – who has spoken about this – would see the film as a whole (leave aside the dramatic hypothesis within the naturalist film) as a hypothesis within this larger relation of the work and the television audience. It is in that sense, feeling very much on the side of the makers of this film – that is to say sharing with them evident general political values, general dramatic intentions – that the problems, both the technical problems within the realist and naturalist modes and the problems of consistency within them, seem to me to deserve this kind of analysis.

What I have done is fairly preliminary, raising questions rather than answering them. But I wanted first to take the discussion of realism beyond what I think it has been in some danger of becoming – a description in terms of a negation of realism as single method, of realism as an evasion of the nature of drama, and the tendency towards a purely formalist analysis – to show how the methods and intentions are highly variable and have always to be taken to specific historical and social analyses, and then with that point established, to begin to approach this very difficult task of analysing what are at once the significant realist works and the quite unresolved problems of this kind of work. In our own immediate situation, if I have one final emphasis to make, it is that we live in a society which is in a sense rotten with criticism, in which the very frustrations of cultural production turn people from production to criticism, to the analysis of the work of others. It is precisely because these makers are contemporaries engaged in active production, that what we need is not criticism but analysis, and analysis which has to be more than analysis of what they have done: analysis of a historical method, analysis of a developing dramatic form and its variations, but then I hope in a spirit of learning, by the complex seeing of analysis rather than by the abstractions of critical classification, ways in which we can ourselves alter consciousness, including our own consciousness, ways in which we can ourselves produce, ways in which indeed if we share the general values which realism has intended and represented, we can ourselves clarify and develop it.

On Solzhenitsyn

(i) Literature and Revolution

We are used to thinking about two kinds of relationship between literature and revolution. There is the work of writers who precede a social revolution, who directly or indirectly expose the values of a society that needs radical change, and who sometimes succeed in articulating the consciousness that will surpass it. These writers are of many kinds, from the lonely, often isolated figures who offer new visions or definitions of humanity, to the more engaged, more negotiable and negotiating critics of society, whose reference to political change can often be taken as direct. From a Blake, that is to say, through a Dickens and a Hardy to a Wells. Characteristically, in belonging to a pre-revolutionary period, they can be seen in some historical perspective. We understand Turgenev and Tolstoy and Chekhov better because we have 1905 and 1917 as points of projection and of actuality beyond their work. We are indeed sometimes in danger, just because this is so, of subordinating them to history: seeing not works but phases, limited approximations to a more lately revealed truth. And this is especially so if we adopt unconscious evolutionary assumptions, that we ourselves (who are often not history) have arrived at some higher and ratifying point, from which we can look back in detachment at the struggle to create and to define.

Some retrospect is similarly available in the second familiar relationship: that of literature created in and by a revolution: the works of a disturbed and heroic, a transforming and liberating time. And here again there is considerable variation. There are the seized moments of absolute change: Blok's vision of Christ at the head of a Red Army detachment; Pasternak's recreation of the moment when it seemed that the gods had come down to change the whole world; Yeats's 'all changed, changed utterly, a terrible beauty is born.' Or the more recent:

Los poets cubanos ya no sueñan ni siquiera en la noche...

unas manos los cogen por los hombros,
los voltean, los ponen
frente a frente a otras caras
(hundidas en pantanos, ardiendo en el napalm)
y el mundo encima de sus bocas fluye
y esta obligado el ojo a ver, a ver, a ver

(Heberto Padilla)

Cuban poets don't dream any more, not even at night...

hands grab them by the shoulders,
turn them around, put them
in front of other faces
(drowned in swamps, burning in napalm)
and the world above their mouths flows by
and the eye must see, see, see

But then there are also these moments lengthened into history: not only the breakthrough but also the civil war; not only the liberation but the blockade, the waiting, the tension, the fatigue. By Russian writers, especially, we have been given these narratives: some monumental and in the end academic; others – say Sholokhov and Pasternak, for all their deep differences – engaged and alive in the revolutionary history. Writers and readers elsewhere can look back to these times, experiencing revolution through the power of a novel or a poem; sometimes experiencing it as a substitute, while their own actuality closes in.

But there is a third relationship between literature and revolution: not necessarily the most difficult but perhaps the most difficult to admit. A new society is created by a real revolution, and then, in the modalities of history, it lasts; it lasts fifty years; acquires its own developing and difficult history. Within that society, if literature is to live, the moment must come when the experiences of liberation and transition are not enough to write about. And what should happen then? For in the name of the revolution one kind of literature, one version of reality, has come to be consecrated. It has also come to be formalised. The writer who questions it, who goes on to his own new work, is writing how? *Against* the revolution? *Against* the revolutionary society?

It is how it will often be seen: from inside the society and, more bitterly, from outside. It is bad enough when such a writer is misunderstood, is even slandered, by his own contemporaries and countrymen. In writing his works he has joined, they say, the 'evil breathers', the slanderers of revolutionary society, the enemies of the

241

revolutionary state. It is worse when it has to be added that there are indeed such people, and that they are highly organised. A writer of this kind is exposed, almost at once, to a virtually unbearable tension. Slandered and then stopped in his own country, even directly repressed, he is simultaneously, and in ironic proportion, flattered, publicised, promoted by people and organisations who are indeed, and without equivocation, enemies of his society. But then one kind of writer, to whom all this happens, can collapse the tension; can move quickly to one of its poles.He may emigrate, physically or spiritually. And indeed if he is not, in any sense, a revolutionary writer, if in his ideas and values he truly belongs with his society's enemies, there is little real tension, though there may be plenty of difficulty and hardship. But the man who stays, and more important the writer who stays, is under extraordinary pressure. He does not belong with his colleagues who are slandering him nor with most of the people outside who are flattering him. If he is one kind of a writer, a radical visionary, his social situation may correspond with his literary situation, though it will still not be easy to bear. But if he is a writer of another kind – a realist novelist, overwhelmingly concerned with contemporary actuality, and with the actuality of his own people and society who are officially rejecting him, the tension and the challenge are obviously very great.

Alexander Solzhenitsyn is the outstanding example of such a writer in our time. Certainly in Soviet official terms, he is a dissenter. But he is in some important ways different, on all the evidence we have, from the group of dissenters with whom he is often identified. Some of these (and I do not hold it against them, I simply record it) are writers who would be reactionary in any society. That they have behind them and around them the experience of what happened to the Russian Revolution, of the long deformity of Stalinism, of the stagnation after Stalin, is documentary but not essential to any adequate reading of them. What they arrive at, what they value, how they see other people, is very familiar to us, not only in our reactionary but in much of our orthodox literature. We have to respect their difficulties but then leave their friends, for there are more than enough, to welcome them.

Solzhenitsyn, so far as I can see, is of a different kind. He is a very Russian writer, but then so are some of the others. He is also, more centrally, a realist and a humanist, and in his interests, his values and his methods is in some very important ways an identifiably Soviet writer: a definition that for all the difficulties still has some meaning. In trying to see what this meaning is, we may be able to understand him better, and to understand some of the unique difficulties of his situation.

Of course it would also be possible to indicate a different analysis. It would be possible to say that through the difficulties of its historical development the Soviet Union, half a century after its revolution, has many points in common with bourgeois societies after their revolutions, so that a writer like Solzhenitsyn is in effect a critical realist: paradoxically a critical realist, in the middle of an officially socialist society. I do not say that this may not prove in the end to be right. There are many things we still cannot know about him and his work. Yet I distrust any such category which would exclude the reality of the Russian Revolution. Its consequent history can certainly not be evaded: not while we are reading Solzhenitsyn. But neither can its original history: its new relations between men. Deep in Solzhenitsyn's work, so far as I can read it, are values which belong to the experience of that revolution, just as so much of his material, so many of his insights, belong to the experience of the revolutionary society which built prisons and labour camps on an almost unrealisable scale. This is all very different, it seems clear to me, from the modes of the nineteenth century critical realists. Solzhenitsyn's methods, too, belong to a society that has seen, even if it has then also been blinded to, the realities of a popular literature. Yet I leave the possibility in suspense. If it is not already true it may become true, given the extent of the pressures.

Meanwhile, however, there needs to be a different emphasis. Let us look at it first in terms of ideas: though first by reason of accessibility rather than by any estimate of final importance. From what ideas, to what ideas, is Solzhenitsyn's creative experience directed?

'Don't ever make this mistake. Don't ever blame socialism for the sufferings and the cruel years you've lived through.'

That is the voice of Shulubin in *Cancer Ward*. It comes in the tenth chapter, 'Idols of the Market-Place', of what is published in English as the second part of the novel. Shulubin is talking to Kostoglotov, the bitter, enduring, visionary man who is the pivotal character and at least in that sense Solzhenitsyn's own mode. Shulubin says it to him; Kostoglotov does not altogether accept it: that reservation is necessary and important. But still the whole discussion is of great directive importance. These are two men in extreme pain: victims of cancer, victims also of state repression. This is how Shulubin is seen:

Perched on his thighs he was so twisted that he seemed to be bent backwards and forwards at the same time, his arms stretched out and his interlocked fingers clasped between his knees. Sitting there, head bowed, on the lonely beach in the sharp lights and shadows, he looked like a monument to uncertainty.

It is in that essential context that the ideas are introduced. Shulubin is suffering more than even Kostoglotov, but then he has also done more, has been a time-server, even a book-burner. His physical state is now so terrible that he will 'lose the company of human beings'. And it is this man who can say:

> The man with the hardest life is the man who walks out of his house every day and bangs his head against the top of the door because it's too low.

Kostoglotov, by comparison, seems to have only his own pain. He didn't even burn books; he had none to read, in his camp. So:

> Don't ever blame socialism for the suffering and the cruel years you've lived through. However you think about it, history has rejected capitalism once and for all . . . Capitalism was doomed ethically before it was doomed economically, a long time ago.

What values, then, will men live by?

> I should say that for Russia in particular, with our repentances, confessions and revolts, our Dostoevsky, Tolstoy and Kropotkin, there's only one true socialism, and that's ethical socialism.

Kostoglotov puts the familiar materialist objection:

> Where is the material basis? . . . There has to be an economy . . . That comes before everything else.

Shulubin then introduces three names: Solovyov, Kropotkin, Mikhaylovski. From a distance these seem, at first, an unusual mixture. Solovyov (1853–1900) was an idealist philosopher: teaching the spirituality of all being and the possibility of universal brotherhood. Kropotkin, of course, was a scientific anarchist and prophet of mutual aid, guild socialism, the overcoming of the division of labour. Mikhaylovski (1842–1904) was a Populist leader, an idealiser of the peasant commune, and in the end a skeptical radical. They can be said to have much in common, as they are cited by Shulubin: a new society is created from known and reasoned values; it is not the consequence of economic developments, and it is an ethical rather than a political surpassing of material historical developments. All, in this sense, are opponents of Marxism. They are also (and the distinction needs stressing) obvious opponents of a discernible Soviet ideology of productivity and plenty leading to happiness. As Shulubin puts it:

> When we have enough loaves of white bread to crush them under our heels, when we have enough milk to choke us, we still won't be in the

least happy. But if we share things we don't have enough of, we can be happy today.

Or again:

> One should never direct people towards happiness, because happiness too is an idol of the market-place. One should direct them towards mutual affection. A beast gnawing at its prey can be happy too, but only human beings can feel affection for each other, and this is the highest achievement they can aspire to.

This is hardly a political programme. Indeed, as Shubulin puts it, 'no one should have the effrontery to try to plan happiness in advance.' But it is clearly and identifiably a social position: one of the original and still one of the most powerful critiques of bourgeois society and of capitalism; a widespread element, today, in the socialist and radical movements of the developed industrial societies. And the question I put (knowing the strength of the Marxist critique) is not first whether it is enough as the basis for a revolutionary movement, but what happens to a revolutionary movement or system which in developing beyond it, in understanding more of the process of historical change, has overlooked or discarded or come down to paying lip-service to its central and continuing human emphasis. It is not, in any case, a position from which one can 'come over' to capitalism, since capitalism is still the most absolute form of the disease it identifies. As a position from which a version of socialism can be criticised – a version in which there are socialist institutions of production but in which these are given priority over all other actual and potential socialist relationships – it has some obvious value. But this is to limit it to direct politics. The question we have really to ask is about its value to a writer: its usefulness, and limits, to a writer like Solzhenitsyn.

And what we have then to say is that Solzhenitsyn is not only Shulubin. I believe that Solzhenitsyn, if he had to generalize his beliefs, would make a summary very close to that which he puts in the mouth of this character. But as a novelist he sees this same man as a 'monument to uncertainty': these are intimations of value, within a process of suffering. And it is important to remember the fact of the dialogue with Kostoglotov:

> 'Oh no, I want happiness, you'd better leave me with happiness,' Oleg insisted vigorously. 'Just give me happiness for the few months I have before I die. Otherwise to hell with the whole...'

In the camps, in a kind of absolute scarcity, he and his friends thought there was a lot of good in private enterprise; it made things available, and they had nothing. This harder, more skeptical response is not a denial of the ethical argument, but it is its accompaniment. Through the detailed development of both responses, Solzhenitsyn shows something more than a debate; he shows a historical process: a widespread demoralisation; a glimpse of alternative values; the stress of actual relationships, from and towards both positions. The humanist writer is undoubtedly there, but so is the realist. The two modes of vision, the two processes, are continually active.

Solzhenitsyn's meanings, that is to say, can be seen more clearly in the substance of his fiction than in his arranged formal discussions. None of the discussions ever goes far enough to stand on its own, except as a general indication. The goodwill of the indication is obvious; so also, as in many related cases, may be its naivete. I will admit that there are times when I wonder if Solzhenitsyn is more than a documentary writer, who through an exceptional personal history has come into contact with material of such exceptional and yet general importance that he has only to recount it, and to add a few general ethical reflections, to be hailed in the West (as with that material would in any case be almost certain) as a writer of genius. This is in any case a question that has to be put, if we are to retain any critical integrity. In a fair amount of *One Day in the Life of Ivan Denisovich*, and again in much of *Cancer Ward*, some impression of this kind almost inevitably builds up. The characteristic method of loosely linked sketches can be related, of course, to the habit learned in the labour camps where there were no materials for writing and so incidents and anecdotes were memorised and habitually retold. But then this relation leads us back into the material, rather than out of it. It would be dishonest to suppose that by one kind of standard in fiction – the kind that in East or West gets abstracted as 'construction' – Solzhenitsyn's novels could not be shown to be loose, incomplete, suggestive, without sustained depth or context. Here and there, of course, this has been done. And any contrary position requires more than some act of affirmation. It requires detailed demonstration. What I want now to put forward is what seems to me to be the critical case, on two counts. I want to relate the 'documentary method', and especially the technique of linked sketches, to a position in experience which is in the end social and political, and which cuts across most of our received definitions of art and of formal social criticism. I want then to go on to argue that in *The First Circle*, which I think is very clearly his most important novel so far, there is a creative development of a very original kind which established him as by any standard a major writer.

The 'documentary' question first. There has been a profound tension, through this century, between the demands of received form and the demands of any extending social consciousness. In the West we know mainly the related tension: between received form and the fluidity of subjective experience. Most of our important and original writers have been remaking the novel towards that kind of subjective fidelity, and from within the exploration new forms have crystallised: Lawrence's *Woman in Love* was, in English, the outstanding transitional work. The shift was made, one might say, from what had been, essentially, a liberal social history to what is now, essentially, a liberal psychology. Form, which had been the balancing of a group and an environment, became internal and symbolic. Criticism followed. Few Western readers of *Cancer Ward* can resist asking themselves whether the disease is a symbol of the Soviet body politic: the growth cells becoming malignant. Or the prison camp: the human condition: the universe of the concentration camp. With effort, certainly, any of this can be sustained. But it is radically irrelevant. Cancer won't work as a symbol of a specific social disorder, when it is described as Solzhenitsyn describes it: a general and terrible human fact. Again, in real prisons there is more to do, as again Solzhenitsyn shows, than to project a victimisation as an abstract condition. The familiar starting points of modern bourgeois art are then in a real sense not only irelevant but damaging to Solzhenitsyn. Once the sympathy created by what has happened to him, in the camps and in his subsequent persecution as a writer, has been, even momentarily, set aside, it is clear that *by these criteria* he is not a major writer. We are looking in the wrong place for the wrong thing, quite as much as his official Soviet critics.

Certainly the liberal social history, as the basis for form, had to be gone beyond. But the particular direction in which, in our historical circumstances, this went left a whole area of human experience untouched. The concept of the group, in any active sense – and beyond it the concept of the sustained existence of others over and above any parts they may happen to play in our individual existence – was by now out of reach. Serious exploration, it came to be thought, cut away inwards, towards the crisis of a sensibility or towards its projection as an abstract, unhistorical condition. The recognition of others, let alone the searching out of others, became in itself problematic: a function, primarily, of the isolated sensibility or condition. And it is, then, very interesting that the description 'documentary' had to be coined for those writers and other artists whose imagination was intrinsically of an extending kind. Orwell went through this crisis as a writer, thinking he had failed when he was writing not 'art' – the received and temporary definition – but 'rapportage' and 'pamphlets'. It was in this work, however, and not in the attempts at 'art', that he became a significant writer. He found the liberating forms almost against his will; against the will of the assumptions by which he continued to be governed. Now the irony is, with Solzhenitsyn, that he inherited a different set of assumptions: those of Soviet revolutionary and popular art. The writer must go out to the people, see what is really happening, record everyday struggles and crises. There was never anything at all wrong with this emphasis (though to make it exclusive, especially in a transitional period, leads quite directly to bullying). What was wrong was what happened next: that if you saw what was happening you contradicted, violently, the official version of what was happening. Soviet fiction got a bad name, in the West, for two very different reasons, which need to be sharply distinguished. There was the hack fiction, some of it very professional, which was at best selective reporting and at worst deliberate manipulation. But there was also the popular fiction which, by what it was trying to do, outraged (it is still so; it is so with some of our own radical writers) the social and artistic assumptions of late bourgeois art. Not only by what it did but by what it was trying to do: the description of people at work, the emphasis on ordinary experience. The bourgeois jokes about tractor-fiction are very significant. That is a world of work and of working people which has to be declared 'not art', which has to be dismissed as 'propaganda' or at best 'documentary', because the admission of its emphasis would, very thoroughly, challenge and eventually break up the bourgeois novel. And then just as this point might be seen, the other part of the process occurred. Much of the fiction began to betray itself in its own terms, becoming not what was happening but what in the official picture, with just a blemish here and there, was supposed to be happening.

Dudintsev, in *Not by Bread Alone*, was at a limit of this process: setting ordinary values, of work and loyalty, against the muddle and corruption of the system which was supposed to embody them. That, if you like, is critical realism. But the contradictions were much deeper than that, and at their centre were the camps. Solzhenitsyn, as I see it, had behind them, when he came to write about the camps or about the exiles in hospital, all the real strengths of revolutionary popular fiction, but now with this deep irony: that they were recording, at a significant centre, the character of the post-revolutionary regime. Or not quite, at this stage, the character of the system. The writer comes across people, rather than discovers them. There is this abnormal isolation: the dominating environment of the camp or the hospital. There is a central figure who defines one kind of value: a hard-strained, unsentimental, truth-telling survival. That figure is then the tendency of the narrative: its governing stance. But form, beyond that, is deeply extending and in one important way casual. People are met and known, lost sight of, moved on from, seen again but without highlight, crowded out, as all are, by the no less significant reality of others. It may have happened, at first, without conscious planning: this form was, after all, a real experience. But this concept of, as it were, the negative group, which is yet sharply human, individualised, needing absolute attention, is the organising principle of *Ivan Denisovich* and *Cancer Ward*. To have constructed them differently would have been – it is what bourgeois form now is – to exclude. A documentary fiction, a fiction of sketches and encounters, tales passed from mouth to mouth, interrupted yet always urgent histories, is in this radical sense a fidelity: a basis for humanism and for realism, neither self-centred nor exclusive, holding to that reality of the human person – that socialist reality – that we are indeed individuals and suffer (as bourgeois art can record) but also that we are many individuals, and that the man next to us who irritates or comforts us is also a centre and has beyond him innumerable centres: all subjects, all objects; a recognition that forbids any formal emphasis which would reserve centrality or significance, by some principle of selection, to the more human among humans.

Thus *Cancer Ward* begins with the arrival of a minor administrator, Rusanov, who has a large tumour on his neck and is put in the cancer wing. We see the place through his eyes: an observation of others who are suffering, in this old, overcrowded hospital. He is without sympathy and sees people in ugly ways. The intrinsic suffering and the ugliness of exposure are seen through a mind which is in part shocked by the terrible physical thing that has happened to him, in part accustomed to a distaste and contempt for others, an habitual but now disturbed consciousness of his own privileged position, which we would know as a class feeling and which is in fact a familiar viewpoint in Western fiction of this kind. It then moves to his neighbour, Kostoglotov, a political prisoner now in perpetual exile, who has been brought in almost dead but who is responding to radiation treatment. This other mind, which becomes dominant in the novel, is in a different way bitter: seeing as much of suffering and exposure, with that inevitable observation which comes from being shut up with it: politically skeptical at a depth which takes over from ordinary politics and becomes a whole crisis of belief; but also, with his returning energy, capable of seeing what Rusanov never sees –

the humanity of the others, the endless and selfless work of the doctors and nurses, the goodness of ordinary life and experience as against the obsession with social position and material success of Rusanov. These contrasted viewpoints, and the suffering that is seen through them, are the basic success of the novel. Then towards the end of the first part, though also more briefly elsewhere, the novel moves to see the same scene through yet other eyes, in what is really, in its brief development, a series of sketches, and it ends with an obviously staged discussion of sincerity in literature: the tension between telling the uncomfortable truth of the present and the doctrine of imagining, within this, the seeds of a different life.

It is thus a difficult novel to read, let alone to judge. What we see with Kostoglotov, or with the nurse Zoya, or the doctors Dontsova and Gangart, is of course painful, in so much suffering, death, humiliation of the body, but life flows in this, deeply involved and felt. To see with Rusanov is sickening, and it is only relatively late that the novel succeeds in defining his distorted consciousness: not only the self-pity, the contempt for others, but these as the weakness which have made him that kind of administrator: a cold, frightened, self-interested manipulator of others, in the name of a system. And by that time, in fact, we have also got what connects but is sickening in his consciousness: the naked ugliness of others who are suffering and who disturb one's own suffering.

It is untidy of course. It has the awkwardness of any radically new emphasis. The wrought works of an older sensibility make it look unfinished, tentative. People ask not only where is the familiar form – the continuity of attention – but where is the new consciousness? Where, say, is the socialist consciousness of this revolution that builds prison camps? Almost a child can do it; read, rehearse and repeat the theoretical explanations. Beside them, certainly, the gestures to 'ethical socialism' can seem velleities. But this is cutting deeper back. For cannot theory of an advanced kind coexist with the most absolute, willed and unwilled, failures of human recognition, of the kind that here, sentimentally and unsentimentally, is the first of all values? The touch in the dark of a corridor of a cancer hospital; the feel of sun on the hands and on other hands; the pity that must be more than pity for a disease not only seen but shared. And to put it in terms of ideas, if Solzhenitsyn believes that this kind of close, absolute human recognition was more present in the 'ethical socialism' of the nineteenth century than in the 'Marxism' which for sound economic and political reasons seemed to surpass it, I for one think he is right, though I doubt whether we could recover the recognition by going back on the historical insights; we would have to go on from them, and that is where many of us, in very different societies, now are and move.

It is a dangerous passage. Human recognition, as an idea, has a version that betrays as well as a version that saves. It can shrink to recognition of people like ourselves; ourselves multiplied; a bourgeois humanism. Or, perhaps even more dangerously, to a recognition of absolute others: poor devils of others in camps and hospitals; men not like us, victims of our enemy; men whose suffering is to be pitied and exploited – the exploitation in the pity – as we hold them at arm's length and see not them but, in our terms, a system. In getting beyond pity – in his roughness, irritation, anger, laughter – Solzhenitsyn is honest, emotionally, in an exceptional degree. He stays with his people and with what is happening to them because in a deep way he is one of them: not an observer or a mirror, but a man in this collective: a surviving individual in this surviving, decimated group. It is the survival of the people, under so heavy an experience, that comes through as a value in the surviving, articulate, bitter and compassionate man.

Except that *The First Circle* is different. Its experience and organisation are different. Unless I misread it, a much harder idea than a realist humanism is there as its form. The design is there in the title; that is why I think I have read it correctly, though there is always room for doubt. For the method at first seems the same: linked sketches of people, seen, lost sight of, reappearing, disappearing. All that is continuous is the common and dominating environment: the special prison for intellectuals. I have said already, about the earlier work, that the collective is in a sense a negative group: they relate, often positively, but within fixed lines, not of their own choosing, that are the limits of their freedom. Yet the idea of the negative group, once established as the general situation, is left in the background; the immediate recognitions are more important.

In *The First Circle*, very differently, the idea is central. The linked sketches are not illustrative of casual, involuntary meetings and discontinuities within a dominating environment. The very absence of real links – voluntary, positive, aiming at continuity – is now the defining quality of a system. It is not so much the negative group, in that earlier sense, as a kind of seriality: all the links arbitrary and in a more profound way negative; the seriality, the lack of real connections, including the imprisoning as well as the imprisoned, the dominators as well as the dominated. The thread of narrative is connected to just that idea. What is being done, centrally, is work on the human voice, work on the very medium of recognition and discovery. Ostensibly this is to serve state security: to allow scrambled messages, that limited betrayal – the service of official secrecy – which is still only the tip of the iceberg. For the really dangerous and dreadful discovery is a means of recognising individual human voices, in quite new and specific ways: recognition of anonymous telephone voices. Not just the passive state secrecy but the active state investigation. The most positive value of all, this absolute value of recognition, is now so transvalued that it is the means of men's betraying each other, betraying others they have never even known or seen. It is easy to talk, abstractly, about the perversion of a system. This, concretely, is a systematic perversion of terrifying depth. Knowledge, kindness, loyalty, self-interest, fear, ambition: all feed, in this serial system, into mutual and collective betrayal. The ethical contrasts, though not at all renounced, are back in a different world. Ethical criticism, we say easily, when we are telling the story of our intellectual development, developed, and had to develop, into social criticism. It is a much harder process than we ordinarily imagine. It is not a surpassing of ethical values; that leads straight to the terror. It is a perception of ethics as relationships over so wide a range, from the temporary affair to the state institution, that most of our ordinary points of reference dissolve.

That the connections in *The First Circle* are arbitrary, at first only a restless shifting from this person to that, is in the end the meaning: a series of arbitrary connections which compose an objectively arbitrary reality. The work on the voice has a central irony, as we have noted: that detecting, understanding, scrambling voices is being done by men who need to speak in their own voices, to describe their common condition. But then, the irony goes deeper, into the construction of the novel itself. For what happens in it, in its essential form, is also a kind of scrambling, in which a human society (that connected community which is the ordinary form of the realist novel, and which had even survived, through the emphasis on recognitions, in *Ivan Denisovich* and *Cancer Ward*) is fragmented into pieces of sound which can be understood only when they are put together again in a particular way: when the series is surpassed and the real connections made clear. Yet these connections are themselves negative. Characteristically the novel ends with a misreading, by an observer, of a conventional sign. The vans used to convey prisoners around Moscow are painted to look like bulk food trucks, with MEAT in four languages on their sides. As the prisoners are being driven away to the distant camps, a foreign correspondent sees their van and makes a note:

... clean, well-designed and hygienic. One must admit that the city's food supplies are remarkably well organised.

This is the kind of false decoding – a false decoding of signals both true and false which can no longer, within the system, be distinguished – in which all the characters are involved, and which is then the characteristic form of social relationship. In a more profound sense than that in which we ordinarily use it this is a system of alienation, at the very roots of meaning.

What is false must be corrected; must be replaced by truth. That is one characteristic form of dissent, of critical dissent, and in part, certainly, it is Solzhenitsyn's role. But there is a more radical dissent: not the correction of a system, but the finding of human values beyond it. Inside that van something of this kind happens:

The prospects that awaited them were the taiga and the tundra, the Cold Pole at Oi-Myakio and the copper mines of Jezkazgan, kicking and shoving, starvation rations, soggy bread, hospital, death. No fate on earth could possibly be worse. Yet they were at peace within themselves. They were as fearless as men are who have lost everything they ever had – a fearlessness hard to attain but enduring once it is reached.

It is the kind of fearlessness which Solzhenitsyn himself has so consistently displayed. But in the van it is different:

Half-listening to the noise of the engine the prisoners said nothing.

The end of this work on the human voice is this kind of silence; a fearless silence; a coming out on the other side of suffering. It is, then, not critical realism; nor is it, in its silent waiting, a revolutionary realism. Clearly it could go quite another way: 'at peace *within themselves*'. We do not yet know. It is a moment of silence, after so many false messages, after the ending of ordinary hope and of all conventional reassurances.

'For a country to have a great writer is like having another government.' This is said by one of the characters in *The First Circle*, and the idea is in the great tradition of Russian realism: literature as another source of information and values; another centre of decision and truth. Historically, such realism has preceded a change; it is not the change in itself. Hanging on in his own country, where he can no longer be published; reaching back for this kind of conviction and commitment; finding and exemplifying a courage that may endure because it has known and faced terror: this is where Solzhenitsyn now is.

(ii) Russia Betrayed: A Note on **August 1914**

Any new novel by Solzhenitsyn would be an event. His earlier work, *One Day in the Life of Ivan Denisovich, The First Circle* and *Cancer Ward*, is important enough for that. It is still necessary to look very closely at the relation between these novels as records of the experience of repression under Stalin and their achievement as literature. There can be little doubt that the work has been politically exploited, by opponents of the Revolution who rejoice in this evidence of its degeneration. But Solzhenitsyn is, very specifically, a Russian writer. He does not work within the conventional separation of politics from art. The question he makes us ask is an unsettled question, with the Russian and much of our own literary tradition on the one side, and Western modernist literary theory on the other. Is there some formal line between a record of experience and a work of art? Is there any necessary formal distinction between artistic and social or political purpose? When the politics are convenient, as in the case of the novels of repression, the question is often slurred in the West, or is apparently resolved by weak adjectives like 'powerful'. And since Solzhenitsyn now as a writer is the direct object of political discrimination within his own country the confusion can be prolonged, even in the case of *August 1914*, where the story of the defeat of the Russian Imperial Army in the invasion of East Prussia is in Solzhenitsyn or in official Soviet history very much the same: a corrupt and indifferent regime and high command which betrays the Russian soldier and the Russian people. It is surely strange, as we read such a story, to see British television commercials, in the name of an apparently serious newspaper, with a KGB man saying dramatically: 'this manuscript must not reach the West'.

It is then very difficult to disentangle the novel from its inevitable or its arbitrary associations. But it has to be attempted, for this is no occasional work. Its subject has been in effect Solzhenitsyn's lifelong interest, and it is announced as the first in a series of linked novels, of which the next will be set in 1916 and the one after that...? Doesn't 1917 come closer: the revolution and the society it created: the way of life that led to the cancer ward? Something like this can be guessed, but we can not yet say. It is difficult to read a historical novel if the historical date you are really interested in comes after the events described. Yet without 1917, and without the whole pressure of the Solzhenitsyn case, who would read *August 1914*? Who would call it a great novel?

I for one can not. I believe *The First Circle* is indeed a great novel. But *August 1914* is not as good as, say, *Cancer Ward*. It has several literary resemblances to that part of his previous work: the unusually episodic and discontinuous construction, with the unity resting in a kind of negation – the existence of an overpowering general situation, of a fatal kind, just beyond the limits of the action. In *The First Circle* there was a successful attempt, through the idea of research on the human voice, to identify and materialise this overpowering alienation. In *August 1914* the general name is Tsarism, as the general name in *Cancer Ward* was Stalinism; but each is only a name, an undiagnosed general condition of which we see, though then vividly, only the symptoms. Behind each condition, moreover, is a quality that should, in the most popular sense, have recommended Solzhenitsyn to his fellow-countrymen: an intense love of Russia and the Russian people, so intense as to be almost inarticulate, at the point where that kind of love turns into this kind of despair.

August 1914 begins with a few chapters in which an idea of enlightenment is being lived, with difficulty, in the confusion of Imperial Russia at the beginning of the war. This theme is only briefly resumed, in a few later chapters; it may be picked up again – it is the only good reason why they are there in quite this form – in later novels in the series. But the main weight of the novel then moves to the campaign. It includes some memorable episodes: the bombardment of the Vyborg regiment; the suicide of General Samsonov; Colonel Vorotyntsev's stand and his dreadful reception at General Headquarters. But in other chapters it is like being inside bound volumes of military memoirs: a war seen from staff maps. This surprised me most, since Solzhenitsyn's ordinary position is, if anything, populist. We stay with the incompetent or confused generals, over so much of the action. The counter-movement is in the able and frustrated junior officers, against a largely general background of the bravery of the ordinary soldiers. It is as if the impulse of the history is meritocratic, against a groundswell of despair that rank and confusion always triumph although they are destroying a country and a people. Anyone who has served in a mobile war will know much of this feeling: Tannenberg, in this sense, reminded me of Arnhem. But as the shadows of the history lengthen it is a very limited point of view: a matter of competence rather than of ultimate consciousness and commitment.

Perhaps it will come clear in the later novels. But there is no point in telling less than the truth about this one. More than any writer in the world Solzhenitsyn stands for telling the truth. Our necessary solidarity with him is a solidarity in the light of that absolute stand.

Review of *August 1914* by Alexander Solzhenitsyn, translated by Michael Glenny.

Commitment

Most writers' statements for or against 'commitment' are now understandably subjective; it is the fashionable tone of the time, at most levels from serious creation to publicity. By contrast, when 'commitment' became the local name for an old kind of argument, in the nineteen-forties, the fashionable tone was more public – in the atmosphere of the war and the resistance. So that the first question is not which tone we prefer. We have rather to ask what issues are placed and displaced by the terms and tones being used.

Ironically 'commitment' itself, in the older public tone, had strong elements of subjectivity. It normally presupposed a writer who was in a position to choose, consciously, his alignment. And of course Adorno was right to point out that if this is all that is being said, it is 'politically polyvalent'. This needs to be remembered if we are to reconstruct the complex history of the argument. Theoretically there can be no doubt that Adorno is right. But the original argument for 'commitment', in Sartre, was profoundly linked, historically, with the values of the resistance and with his democratic and socialist conclusions from them. Thus the argument for commitment was usually taken as an argument for being a Left writer. Because of this local and periodic situation, you can find later writers arguing against 'commitment' and yet giving a lot of their time to arguments and fictions against socialism or communism, and for the specific relationships and systems they generalise as 'freedom'. The polyvalent ghost of Orwell, even, is often invoked against 'commitment', that is, against 'time serving propaganda-writing for the Left': Orwell, who once said, of course incorrectly, that every line he had written had been for democratic socialism. It is still worth saying that 'no commitment', in literary pronouncements, often functions like 'no politics' in conservative political arguments. The only bad commitments are to that other side; on our own side we are simply writing the truth as we see it, free and honest individuals all.

256

But then if you go back to the substance of the original case for 'commitment' you will find that it is an oddly chosen word, and that what Sartre was arguing for (in prose; he exempted poetry, which he did not understand) could have been better described as 'involvement':

> If a written sentence does not reverberate at every level of man and society, then it makes no sense.

It was an argument of what to write about, rather than how to write or with what social or political line. And while this is then indeed, as Adorno said, politically polyvalent, it does catch up identifiable problems of choice: Solzhenitsyn writing about the labour-camps; Yashar Kemal writing about the migrant cotton-pickers; rather than other things in their experience which they could have written about, and which other literature has in fact addressed itself to. 'Commitment', there, is a choice of the most significant material within a writer's grasp.

'Commitment', as you would expect from Sartre, thus depends on this element of conscious *choice*. It is what an individual decides to write, of course with the corollary that the involving decisions are better than the deflecting or withdrawing decisions. It is in the development of this corollary that much of the damage is usually done, by those who claim to know in advance (as Brecht accused Lukács) what kind of work should be done, and how. This sort of claim becomes significant when it is backed up by political and administrative injunctions, or by commercial priorities and preferences, or by a prevailing climate of critical opinion. It is then understandably not difficult to get a majority of writers declaring themselves against it, even though an overlapping majority of writers are at the same time submitting to their own local form of it, while being very fierce against other forms. For the record I am against all such forms, and I am glad that it was Brecht, a communist writer, who made one of the first and most eloquent attacks against these 'enemies of production'.

'Commitment' implies conscious choice, and thus voluntary choice. This makes it sound almost liberal, and it is indeed, in one sense, a profoundly liberal idea. It presupposes writers who, as it were, survey the spectrum and decide to which part of it they will move. It also presupposes a natural state of innocence, free of ideology, from which a writer may or may not choose to move, committing himself, if he moves that way, to a set of acquired positions and values. Historically this is the bourgeois concept of the individual, who exists, as it were, free and formed, before he decides to enter into relationships, associations or contracts, or, in the extreme case, to refrain from doing so or to enter into as few as he can. This concept still dominates the popular modes of self-interpretation and explanations of careers.

There is obviously some truth, and some important truth, caught up in it. But in its ordinary forms, it is, like most debates about 'commitment', naive. No writer is ever free in that absolute sense. He is, especially as a writer, specifically and significantly shaped by his native language, however reciprocal the process, before any possibility of choice becomes relevant. In a wider area, he is into family relationships, a social and physical environment, a mode of education, before he can ever exercise choices as a free sovereign individual. Thus we are all, as writers, significantly situated before we even come to write. We are also, I would say, significantly aligned. We see writing through the resources of our given language, through the inherited forms of our literature, through the institutions in which it is practised. And if this is true of our specific situation as writers, it is also true – often much more deeply than we realise – of our values, our perspectives, our assessments of significance. Indeed it seems to me clear, and valuable, that all of us, as writers, are carrying a much larger freight than our single selves, though if we succeed in making it into ourselves, or ourselves into it – processes of social identification, or of (for some) unproblematic internalisation of our inherited culture – we can appear to speak as sovereign subjects. This is, it seems to me, why we get the common situations in which, 'speaking only for myself and in the name of the free individual', many of us succeed only in saying what we all already know. And a good deal of important literature, it should be noted, does no more than that. What we all already know are the (in fact locally and socially generalised) 'timeless truths of the human condition' or 'the fundamental agonies of human existence' or 'the insights beyond the mere babble of the time', as well of course as more immediate knowledge such as that 'socialism is liberating/repressive' or that 'culture is class free/dependent', when the 'we's begin to break up a little. By observation, anyway, what we all already know is quite sufficient for an actual majority of writers, although in periods when the subjective stance is dominant we have to be careful to claim – and, more, to believe – that we have discovered it quite by ourselves.

What then, from this position, is 'commitment'? In most of its senses, it is that practical commitment to what we already are. But this, which seems by definition valuable, can be contrasted with what those others are, and, when the temperature rises, the condition of those others can be seen as if it were some merely wilful or arbitrary forcing of the 'true self' (one like our own) or the 'authentic literary sensibility' (writing like ours) into somebody else's straitjacket.

Yet much, perhaps most, writing is in an important sense socially determined. Quite a lot of it, indeed, is determined in the hardest sense of that word: the inherited forms write it; the dominant institutions commission it. But in any full sense determination is a much more complex process: not absolute and inevitable pre-forming, but a set of dispositions: pressures to think and feel and write in a certain way; limits on certain other ways of thinking and feeling and writing. It is only, in my view, in relation to this complex process, and as a matter of relevance to only an actual if diverse minority of writers, that commitment, as a substantive issue, arises. For of course we make some, and at our best many, real choices. We may begin the long unravelling of what we have been formed to be, and we may then choose to confirm it in new ways, or to begin the painful process of changing ourselves. Again, in a shifting time, we may experience a collision or a tension between our formed selves and quite new experiences and circumstances, and we can resolve that, or try to resolve it, often by writing our way through it, in various ways, some of them involving conscious and indeed very deliberate choice. If much important literature is confirmatory, much, also, is the consequence, indeed often the process, of these profoundly unsettling encounters. There are periods in which what emerges, in some writers, is an energetic new commitment: to a new kind of writing; to new selections and emphases of subject; to a social or political cause with which these can be associated, by its closeness to this selection or emphasis or subject, or by its actual or foreseen change in the relations between writers and readers, which can make the new kind practicable. Our own period is a more mixed case. What I find mainly valuable in it is in fact of this kind: especially some television and theatre drama, some fiction, some poetry, which because of some change in the social origins and locations of writers is attempting to respond simultaneously (and not without serious formal difficulties) to the actual enlargement of an audience for drama and literature and the connected selection and emphasis of working-class experience. But in many more continuous forms, and with some powerful backing from some central institutions and perhaps especially literary education, the movement is quite the other way; and the expression of a threatened subjectivity (itself, confusingly, very evident also in some of the other nominally new work, for which it can be mistaken or substituted) is surely dominant: not a confident mode, as in some earlier periods, but an anxious and often bitterly defensive one.

Well, a discussion of commitment will not resolve these profound differences of formation and alignment. But I wish we were mainly discussing formation and alignment, and with them the comparatively rare cases of conscious commitment beyond their received terms, rather than opposing commitment to Commitment, as if between sovereign subjects and willing slaves. Or, to put it another way, a commitment to examining our most settled commitments might be the most literate thing we could attempt.

Brecht

Bert Brecht, the Communist poet and playwright, has become a cultural monument. Is it then not time, he might ask, to consider blowing him up?

One of the problems is this kind of tough talk. A certain recklessness of language, a down-to-earth bluntness, has been widely received as his most valuable legacy. It is what makes him, some say, an essentially popular writer. But that difficult term takes us back to his period, which is essentially that of the 'twenties and 'thirties. 'Popular', then, was an apparently unproblematic defining term of the Left. There was also tough straight talk from the Fascists, but both were beyond the received intellectual consensus, with its endless qualifications and balancings.

In fact, this was only true, even then, of the most literate levels of the culture. Since the invention of wide-distribution capitalist journalism, in the second half of the nineteenth century, all positions, including the most orthodox and deferential, had made use of at least a simulacrum of popular talk. In our own world, a version of down-to-earth, colloquial, knockabout and name-calling talk can be found every day in the tabloid papers, some of which once held the middle ground but all of which are now hard for power and wealth and the *status quo*. It is depressing to trace some of the tones and devices of Cobbett, a genuine radical and popular journalist, to many of his stylistic successors who are now evidently and proudly part of the Great Wen, of the Thing. It is just as depressing to pick up so many echoes of that 'Brechtian' talk – both hard and coarse, anti-sentimental and cynical, angry and merely irritable – in a contemporary dramatic argot. Some of it, certainly, is still in the minority radical theatre, but just as much of it is associated with that essentially conformist tendency – 'shit to beliefs' – which is one of the forms of cultural adaptation to power. In fact, as the history shows, that style, after the confusion of the 'twenties in Germany, went as readily into Fascism as into any radical cause.

Style, that is to say, in its usual formalist version, is often the enemy of history. This is the problem, now, about the image of Brecht. For there is what we can call an English Brecht, just as there has been an English Chekhov. That mocking analyst of the historical failure and inertia of his own class was turned, in the English theatre, into a charming chronicler of whimsicality and eccentricity. This analytic and teaching dramatist is detached from his specific intelligence and viewpoint, and is then all tough talk and open stagecraft. In one influential version he is even further reduced. For he becomes, in that most persuasive of English recommendations, uncertain, and therefore interesting. Thus he is all human heart but Marxist head. He belongs to Western culture, yet (as it was recently put) has an Eastern ideology. In either version, that anti-sentimental talk, that general diffusion of doubt, that Modernist exposure of the mechanics of action, are profoundly acceptable, but only as a style. In the most reduced version, he is a vital force in the theatre, but what you can expect to see, past it all, is that engaging old muddle of the mysterious, messy human condition.

So wasn't Mother Courage, in spite of everything, a tough old bird, going on with the war? And wasn't Galileo, again in spite of everything, deliciously earthy, fond of his goose, bowing to the inevitable and giving his authority to a lie, but still, like a real professional, getting on with his work? As for the villains of the *Threepenny Opera*, aren't they a damn sight more vital, more human (like our own dramatic Cockney cops and robbers), than most of the solid citizens you see creeping around nowadays, and Christ! don't they just vibrate in the theatre?

It is almost useless to quote Brecht himself against any of these readings. English Brecht, like other English orthodoxies in field after field, has taken care of that. Of course he *wanted* to think differently, but his heart, his guts, wouldn't let him. He knew what we are all really like, after the talk stops: trade, adaptation, entertainment; the war, the goose, the lively and stylish crimes and frauds. Of course we all want to live differently, we all want a better world, but what Brecht shows us, again and again, is how it all goes wrong, how easily we deceive ourselves, and yet, after all, how human life keeps bobbing up.

This reading is persuasive because it corresponds, in exact detail, to the dominant structure of feeling of the last thirty years. It is the Orwell version, but now more habitual and resigned. And this explains what would otherwise be the puzzling fact that the two major influences on English theatre in the last twenty-five years have been those polar opposites, apparently – Brecht and Beckett. Beckett's icy clarity leaves no room for doubt. The human enterprise is doomed; we play games while we wait for the end. When Brecht encountered *Waiting for Godot* he wanted to write a play in reply to it: the wish came too late.

But then a different process took over. Beckett's perspective was wholly desperate, but in the theatre, skilfully played, it had its own entertaining vitality. And this was evidently a game that many could play: black despair, entire self-deception, an inevitable violence waiting in the wings: but still, a stylish and entertaining evening at the theatre. It was what Brecht had noticed and raged against in the German theatre of the 'twenties, and he would probably not have been surprised to find his own work absorbed into the new dominant structure. His central intention was always to explain why things had gone wrong, and thus to provoke us into thinking how to avoid the same old mistakes. But shift that emphasis just a little, involve us with the errors, humanise and naturalise them, and the trick is turned. Of course we all want to live differently: the trouble is that we haven't yet found out how. The errors could have been avoided, but they were not. Endgame.

English Chekhov was never mere fantasy. It was a matter of playing up certain tones, playing down others. English Brecht is a similar case. The last scene of *Galileo*, in which the manuscript of the *Discorsi* triumphantly crosses the frontier, but in a closed coach, while the boys whom Galileo might have enlightened are still talking about witches, has only to be omitted, as has often happened in production, to tilt the play towards a quite different meaning.

Yet the problem may be deeper than that. Brecht looked for historical instances and for parables as a way of teaching us lessons, not only about history, but about the contemporary world. The method quickly engages us, but in the case of Galileo, for example, the problem now is to find anybody who doubts that the Earth moves round the Sun, or who thinks that it is socially or morally disturbing to say so. He is thus available to everyone as, in spite of everything, an intellectual hero and indeed an all-purpose liberal. Brecht's underlying argument is of course more complex. The highest value is not knowledge, or even, in that limited sense, truth. The central question is what the knowledge is used for, and Galileo's deepest betrayal, in Brecht's version, is to cut the links between knowledge and the education and welfare of the people. From this betrayal came the difference and irresponsibility that allowed scientific research to present politicians and generals with an atomic bomb. Conclusion: Galileo was wrong, though in the immediate and local argument, about the Earth and the Sun, he is not only shown, but we know him already, to be right.

It is then necessary to distinguish between two kinds of cultural effect.

English Brecht is a relatively obvious incorporation. The dialectic has been reduced to a method of open staging: as he put it himself, 'the theatre can stage anything; it theatres it all down.' But in Brecht himself there is a more difficult problem. Like most of the Left in his period, he believed in popular common sense. Yet this went along, as in orthodox Leninism, with the not readily compatible belief that intellectuals had a duty to bring the truth to the people, and to resist, in this use, all the powers of church and state. Galileo appears to fit the model exactly: he discovered the truth but he failed to resist the authorities. But where then is popular common sense? Still talking about witches.

The difficulty lies in the initial rhetoric. It is true, as Brecht so often insisted, that real knowledge is gained by practice, and that working men, seen as merely ignorant by princes and prelates, have their own basic knowledge of the material world in which they work. But this is very different from saying that there is any comparably adequate understanding either of the material world in which they do not work and learn by observation and handling, or of the political and economic world which organises and disposes of their labour. The gap that keeps people from the first kind of knowledge can be bridged by science and education: that is the Galileo model, and in Brecht's version the measure of his failure. The gap that keeps them from the second kind of knowledge is evidently different, to be bridged only (as in Leninism and more generally in the socialist movement) by political organisation and education. Brecht's image of Galileo, in which the two kinds of gap are connected and could have been bridged in the same operation, is entirely characteristic of the socialist thought of his period, in which natural science was seen as the leading edge of a more general enlightenment and emancipation. The historical version of Galileo as scientist stays relatively close to the record. The version of Galileo as failed general emancipator is not historical, but is a projection from the later form of thought.

The screw was then turned. Fascism, not only a very brutal but a very old political philosophy, was using advanced technology. Ignorance and demonology were being diffused by powerful modern means. At the same time, natural science was reaching what could be taken as its triumphant climax: learning to control the most inward secrets of matter; splitting the atom and discovering the technology of atomic power and the atomic bomb. And meanwhile where was popular common sense? Was it a force against these new destructive powers? If it was not, there must have been a betrayal, and there he was again, Galileo, the founding figure of the default.

It is significant that Brecht turned so often to the past for what were intended to be contemporary lessons. In his own time, the intellectual Right turned regularly to identify the Renaissance and the Reformation as the beginning of the decline into modern barbarism. He did not support this, but in *Galileo* he went to the same historical period and drew what was apparently the opposite conclusion: it was the check of those movements, the failure to carry them through, that gave barbarism its new chance. It was a generous response, and his popular sympathies were never in doubt. But the element of projection is very obvious, and it delayed the facing of any of the harder questions.

It produced, in its way, a new demonology. There has been a very deep shift, on the left, in attitudes to natural science. From the leading edge of emancipation it has become, in some influential propaganda, at best a mixed force, at worst, as with nuclear weapons, a destroyer. To watch a production of *Galileo* in which, over the final scenes, there are projections of the images of Bikini Atoll and Hiroshima is a dreadful test of nerve. It is much better, of course, than the naturalised image of this engagingly greedy old man who had discovered, in spite of those silly old priests, that the Earth goes round the Sun. That is simple indulgence: the easy heroics of retrospective radicalism; the even easier conceits of retrospective truth. But from Galileo to Hiroshima is also an indulgence: an ignorant if well-meant evasion of difficulties and responsibilities. It would be much better, if we want to face the problems, to look at the dramatisations of Oppenheimer and of Sakharov, but even then we would be displacing. It is what happens when, in conceit or revulsion, any intellectual is set centre-stage. Praise or blame can be heaped on him, but while we are twisting and turning about his private conscience, the major social and historical forces are given leave of absence, or are introduced only in the convenient forms of stupid bureaucracy and generous if ignorant – or let us not quite say that, let us say 'ill-informed' – people.

Brecht fought very hard, with the weapons of his time. He remains a quite different figure from orthodox or incorporated Brechtianism. Instead of using theatre to reconcile us to failures and errors, he worked untiringly to expose error and to show that the action could be restarted, at any time, and played differently. That is still his challenge, and the only good way of responding to it is to judge everything, including his own work, in these hard and open terms. We have then to say that in his most historical plays, like *Galileo*, the challenge is weakened. It is only in the wildest voluntarism that we can see that action being replayed: and the false conclusion that is then waiting, in the dominant structure of feeling, is that the weight of inherited failure is just too appallingly heavy. The Brechtian exposure of error, stopped at that point, becomes a coarse acquiescence, with the talk getting rougher, for its own sake, as the sense of hopelessness settles in. An insulated colloquial vigour is then beside the point. It finds all too easy a congruence, under its label as 'popular', with the hard-pressed, resentful, cursing and cynical language of subordination. We all know what the world's like but with any luck, keeping our heads down, we'll get the occasional goose.

'Eats first, morals after.' But that savage summary of what is at once bourgeois ideology and a version of popular common sense has been stood on its head, under the polite name of the 'consumer', now the agreed point of orthodox social reference. An entire social order is organised to define this version of human destiny, and to protect its existing supplies and privileges. The morals, as indeed always, come with the eats. But then imagine a scientist who tells us untraditional truths about the limits on resources, about hunger and population, about the pollution in so much of our production and consumption. Imagine a political scientist who tells us the uncomfortable truth that these processes are locked into a social and economic order, and that this is protected by a vast system of propaganda and of weapons. Do the princes and prelates, the electoral bandwagons, listen? Does common sense listen?

Brecht defined the new drama as one in which the spectator can sit at his ease and listen – critically, of course. It is now time to shift this relationship, to move beyond this version of critical consumption, to start to see ourselves where we have always in fact been – on the stage and in the action, responsible for how it comes out.

1980

Lukács: A Man
without Frustration

It is still very difficult, in the English-speaking world, to focus the work of Lukács. Any full understanding of it depends on a familiarity with classical German philosophy and with the intellectual development of Marxism which is still relatively uncommon in our language. The intricacy of the current international discussion of various phases of his thought contrasts very sharply with the few relatively general impressions which most of us have been able to register, even through careful study of those more readily accessible works which are said to be his most significant. Three of these impressions can be recorded as a measure of our distance. First, that he is one of the more interesting and tolerable Marxist critics of literature, in the breadth of his learning and in his relative freedom from dogmatism. Second, that as an opponent of Brecht and of Modernism, and a defender of classical realism, he belongs to an old and fruitless kind of Marxism and can even be fairly taken as a cultural representative of its Stalinist phase. Third, that he is a major example of the 'humanist fallacy' in Western Marxism, in his reliance on notions of 'man as subject' and more directly in his kind of socialism, which is more properly a 'romantic anti-capitalism'.

I doubt if any of these impressions could be fully sustained, in any extended study of the extraordinary range of his writings between 1906 and 1971. Yet the situation is familiar from many other cases. Why should anyone, for substantial reasons, begin so long and difficult a study unless there are some strong preliminary indications that it is likely to be of real value? It is relatively easy to understand the preoccupations of that brilliant group of his pupils, many now in exile, who are impressively represented in the essays edited by Agnes Heller. Yet it is only if we judge, as I do, that at least some of their questions about Lukács connect significantly with more general and contemporary questions of theory and practice that the rest of us can tread in that shadow. Again, there are crucial questions, for anyone still living in

Hungary or in the rest of Eastern Europe, about his intricate and controversial relationships with various phases of political and intellectual life: his service as Minister of Culture in two unsuccessful Hungarian revolutions, in 1919 and 1956; his years of 'adjustment' in exile in Stalin's Moscow; his controversial final years, in which those closest to him contrast his elevation to cultural authority with the effective dilution or dismissal of his most important and still oppositional thoughts. It is difficult to judge any of these relationships from a distance, yet some of them, if they can be properly understood, have a much more general importance than a settling of particular accounts.

'If they can be properly understood': that is the central question that follows from the most fascinating of these books: the tape-recorded and edited interviews conducted by Istvan Eörsi while Lukács was in effect dying. This kind of composition, especially when it is not merely based on 'prompt' questions but approaches, however gently, the really difficult and critical issues, is often a revealing and especially accessible form. On the other hand, much depends on the kind of mind that is being questioned or interrogated. The problem can be indicated by what he said in another interview, with *New Left Review*, reprinted here as an appendix:

> I can say that I have never felt frustration or any kind of complex in my life. I know what these mean, of course, from the literature of the 20th century, and from having read Freud. But I have not experienced them myself. When I have seen mistakes or false directions in my life, I have always been willing to admit them – it has cost me nothing to do so – and then turn to something else.

This reminds me, perhaps wrongly, of a general perception of Lukács which comes through in the following exchange, dealing with the period of his imprisonment in Rumania after the defeat of the 1956 revolution:

> Int: I heard another anecdote according to which a Rumanian prison warder was assigned to convert you ideologically.
> G.L.: That is possible. I did in fact know a guard like that, but it was a completely harmless business.
> Int: The story went that after a few weeks' discussion he had to undergo treatment in a psychiatric clinic.
> G.L.: I can no longer recall anything about that. When I left Rumania, he had not yet gone into a psychiatric clinic.
> Int: Was he an intelligent man?
> G.L.: At party level such people are thought to be intelligent. That is all, but it isn't very much.

It is easy, at least from a distance, to see in the character of these responses a very specific and important kind of mind, raised to an extraordinary degree of interest by its quite exceptional ability. It is, or is presented as, the mind of a man wholly dedicated to pure thought, who can indeed abandon and move on from positions and affiliations without significant disturbance, and who moreover from that practice moves without difficulty into the kind of hard confidence, which can be interpreted as arrogance, of such judgments as that 'at party level such people are thought to be intelligent.' Thus far it is the mind of one kind of high intellectual, who knows and accepts and keeps his distance from what others see as substantial everyday life, and who can in fact rely on being judged, eventually, solely by the quality of his work.

Yet in fact this is, or is presented as, the mind of a man who reached distinction early as a bourgeois intellectual from a rich family; who then joined, quite suddenly, a Communist revolution in his own country and became an active commissar; who following its defeat became an underground organiser and exile, travelling through many years on a false passport; who in exile in Moscow was repeatedly involved in controversy and during the worst years of Stalin had strong reasons to fear for his life; and who, when he later returned to Hungary, went through a whole series of controversies and dangers, including his membership of the government of the eventually executed Imre Nagy. It is perhaps the major case, in the twentieth century, of a classical intellectual, of an older, late nineteenth-century kind, who can be seen as moving by the phases of his own thought towards the extremities of revolutionary politics.

'Can be seen as moving': the qualification is necessary because many others have seen his intellectual development, especially in his middle years, as a series of compromises and prudent adjustments to the forms of revolutionary power to which he had committed his life, even when he had seen clearly, as in the case of Stalin, what these forms had become. The full record is still relatively obscure, and many who begin from this judgment of him will not be persuaded by his retrospective account. The man without frustrations or complexes, able to change by taking thought, will be seen as a figure constructed to cover a more complex history.

I can see the possible force of this, but quite apart from problems of method there is simply not enough evidence to move in one now familiar Western way, towards a form of psychological reconstruction and explanation. A good deal must be allowed for the habit of that generation of intellectuals, which can be found again in so different a figure as Beatrice Webb, of delineating a sphere of public intellectual life from which merely personal matters are excluded. Lukács himself at times talks in that way in the interviews, but there is a different and very positive tone in his autobiographical notes for 'the decisive year 1917–18': 'growth of a new attachment: unfathomable, but I had the feeling that for the first time in my life I was in love: complementarity, solid basis for life (a touchstone for my ideas) not opposition.' He had been deeply moved by an earlier relationship, with Irma Seidler, who had committed suicide in 1911: 'After that I published my essay "On Poverty in Spirit". This contains the account of her death and the expression of my sense of guilt.' But the later relationship with Gertrud Bortstieber, whom he eventually married (in secret) when they were both exiles, is presented in a different dimension:

> Gertrud's importance in this transition: for the first time in my life. Different from previous occasions (Irma, Lena): my policy always clear; relationship – even love – within the given line of development. Now with every decision, Gertrud strongly involved: particularly in human, personal decisions. Her reaction often decisive. Not that I would not have turned to communism without her. That was something that was contained in my previous development, but nevertheless the complex questions surrounding the actual decision and the highly important personal implications of that choice would quite certainly have had a different outcome but for her.

He goes on to instance her 'instinctive rigour in intellectual matters', but then broadens the whole analysis:

> What was at stake was my need to fuse my intellectual and practical aspirations with the contemporary world situation in such a way as to make my efforts bear fruit (not just objectively and practically right, but also favourable to my personal development). At this point the situation pointed to something qualitatively new: the choice between two world systems. No one – with the exception of Lenin (in quite a definite sense) – has understood that the two processes are ultimately identical: that is, the social development of the new man is in effect a synthesis of all the individual aspirations to come to terms with the novel reality in an honest revolutionary way.

The conclusion to this analysis seems to me quite central to Lukács's thought. It is from this project of a 'synthesis of individual aspirations' – not any aspirations, but those learned from and centred in a changing reality – that his important work in ethics and aesthetics and literary history, but also his most general philosophical and political theories can be best seen to proceed. Yet it is easy to see how from a different and more familiar position the project can be reduced to a projection. This is in effect the position chosen by Lee Congdon in *The Young Lukács*: 'In his earliest years, he despaired; regarding alienation as the *condition humaine*, he espoused a tragic conception of life. Only when, out of the crucible of a great personal tragedy, he came to believe that alienation might be overcome, did he begin his own existential and ideological 'quest for community' that would end only with his marriage to Gertrud Bortstieber and his studies in Marxist dialectics.' I am not greatly surprised that an analysis begun on this reductive principle, in which the world to which Lukács was responding is theoretically subordinated to forms of psychological and intellectual history, should end with a description of Lukács's most important work, *History and Class Consciousness*, as 'a blueprint for tyranny'. But the issues are much too grave and complex for that kind of general short-cut, which actually contrasts with the detailed care of much of the rest of Congdon's informative account.

It is not surprising, again, when Congdon ends with a reference to the supposed 'portrait' of Lukács as Naphta in Thomas Mann's *The Magic Mountain*. That characterisation has been generally influential in Western perceptions of Lukács, and it is interesting now to be able to read his own reflections on it: 'If Thomas Mann had asked me in Vienna whether he might use me as a model, I would have agreed, just as I would have done had he said he had left his cigar case at home and asked me for a cigar.' This is fair comment. Lukács was lending something for Mann to use. In fact, there were complex interactions between their writings as far back as *Death in Venice*, of which a manuscript is said to contain literal extracts from Lukács's *Soul and Form*, without quotation-marks. But it is in any case clear that the fictional transformation of an impoverished Marxist émigré – as Lukács was when they met – into an elegantly dressed 'half-Jewish pupil of the Jesuits with crass views' is a matter to be primarily related to Mann's novel rather than to the substantial character of his supposed model.

This kind of deflection merely delays the necessary encounter with the central problems of Lukács's thought. These begin, as I see them, if we relate what Lukács said about 'the choice between two world systems', in his decisive affiliation to Communism in 1918, to what Istvan Eörsi offers as his last word: 'Both great systems in crisis. *Authentic* Marxism the only solution. Hence in the socialist states Marxist ideology must provide a critique of the existing state of affairs and help to promote reforms which are becoming increasingly urgent.' This can be seen as some kind of deathbed appeal, though decidedly not deathbed repentance. What matters to the rest of us is the intellectual route by which Lukács reached this conclusion, and in what sense 'authentic'

Marxism can be distinguished from its orthodox or surrogate versions.

In relation to Lukács there is no better guide than Agnes Heller, whose remarkable essay on the later philosophy concludes *Lukács Revalued*. She offers an exceptionally interesting analysis of what has been seen as the most important intellectual event of his life: his repudiation of the still influential *History and Class Consciousness*. This has usually been taken as an act of accommodation to the (inferior) orthodoxies of the party to which he had wholly committed himself. But there is also an intellectual explanation, of more general significance. In *History and Class Consciousness* Lukacs had seen a specific historical agency for the 'synthesis of individual aspirations': the proletariat, which it is generally said he idealised along a known Marxist path. The position can be carried forward to contrasts with the actual development of the proletariat, and especially of its party and nominal regime. The idealisation is then broken down, as in successive phases of rejection of Marxism by former Marxists.

But Heller shows that the distinctive development of Lukács was a form of return to Marx and therefore to an 'authentic' Marxism. When he read the *Paris Manuscripts* in 1930 he was struck by Marx's concept of 'the human species' and of 'species-essence'. What followed, he concluded, was that '"class" cannot take the place of "species"': the precise substitution, or identification, which he had made in *History and Class Consciousness*. Heller is unsparing in her analysis of the twists and turns and masquerades which, during his exposed years in Moscow and beyond, followed this shattering realisation. It was only in 1953, at the end of the period of the worst official orthodoxy, that the central inquiry could be directly resumed. What comes from this new phase is the major work, *The Specificity of the Aesthetic*.

This is an important clearing of ground. Indeed I believe that for all but specialist historians this is the Lukács who has now to be focused and considered. Yet the difficulties begin with the very title, intended to be the first of three volumes, which seems to indicate specialism. On the contrary, the ambition is general. As Heller interprets it, 'Lukács outlines in his *Aesthetics* a philosophy of history within which the unity of individual and species appears as the truth of history... In and through art the question of the truth of history emerges and is solved.' The general reasoning behind this assertion is as follows:

> The category of reflection is replaced by that of mimesis... Mimesis is used in the ancient sense of the word: the imitation of 'ethos'. 'Ethos', in Lukács's understanding, is 'species character' that becomes manifest through individual deeds and destinies. A work of art is mimetic if it

grasps the species in the individual and represents thereby the sphere of the so-called 'particular' (*das Besondere*)... Through his intensified subjectivity, the artist attains to objectivity; through his extremely profound and sensitive experience of time he reaches the level of species. This experience of time... constitutes the eternity of the temporal, the universal validity of what has emerged in the historical *here and now*... It is in the 'particular' that individual experience, risen to the level of species, becomes form.

Insofar as this position is new, for it carries some remarkable resemblances to a familiar nineteenth-century idealism of art, it is in the linking to historical process and to the culmination of this process in the general human liberation which works of art already prefigure. This can in some senses be tracked back to Marx, and especially to the Hegelian element in Marx. It is now a strong tendency in radical cultural philosophy.

It is a tendency from which I, at least, wish to take my distance. Edward Said wrote an interesting essay, 'Travelling Theory', in which he traced the passage (and change) of some ideas from Lukács through Goldmann to my own work in Cambridge. I think what actually happened was an intersection of certain ideas, within an assumed common frame of reference, which on closer examination turns out to have been no meeting of minds at all. I think Lukács was right, in his later work, to insist that a theory of art is not something to be added to historical materialism: rather it is something already latent within it. But I find it significant that he did not go on to write the proposed second part of the *Aesthetics*, which would have applied historical materialism to the problem. I think Heller is right in saying that he had already written it, in his own terms, in the first volume, since with that version of history there is no space for any other kind. What is actually latent in historical materialism is not, in Lukács's categorical sense, a theory of art, but a way of understanding the diverse social and material production (necessarily often by individuals within actual relationships) of works to which the connected but also changing categories of art have been historically applied. I call this position cultural materialism, and I see it as a diametrically opposite answer to the questions which Lukács and other Marxists have posed.

The argument will continue, and in some areas – most notably, I think, his sustained critique of 'objectified' capitalism – Lukács will remain an important point of reference. But in another sense that whole phase is ended, or ought to be ended: that movement of high intellectuals, with their own curriculum and preoccupations, towards the labour and democratic movements. Their memory can be honoured as a way of understanding and beginning to reverse the relationship, until 'the return to everyday life' is not a categorical conclusion but a hard and contested starting-point.

1983

Review of *Record of a Life: An Autobiography* by Georg Lukács edited by Istvan Eörsi (1983), *Lukács Revalued* edited by Agnes Heller (1983) and *The Young Lukács* by Lee Congdon (1983)

Sources

I

My Cambridge – from *My Cambridge,* edited by Ronald Hayman (1977), pp.55-70

Seeing a Man Running – from *The Leavises: Recollections and Impressions,* edited by Denys Thompson (1984), Cambridge University Press, pp.113-122

Fiction and the Writing Public – from *Essays in Criticism,* Vol. VII, No. 4 (October 1957), Basil Blackwell, pp.422-8

Desire – from *The London Review of Books,* 17 April 1986, pp.8-9

Distance – from *The London Review of Books,* 17-30 June 1982, pp.19-20

Writing, Speech and the 'Classical' – Presidential Address delivered to the Classical Association at University College, Cardiff, 10 April 1984

Community – from *The London Review of Books,* 24 January 1985, pp.14-15

Wales and England – from *New Wales,* No. 1, 1983, pp.34-8

The City and the World – from *RIBA Journal, 80,* 5 August 1973, pp.426-31

II

A Kind of Gresham's Law – from *The Highway,* Vol. 49, February 1958, Workers' Educational Association, pp.107-10

Middlemen: The Arts Council – Given as the 1981 W.E. Williams Memorial Lecture at the National Theatre, November 1981, for the Arts Council: Politics and Policies

Gravity's Python – from *The London Review of Books,* 4-17 December 1980, p.14

Isn't the News Terrible? - from *The London Review of Books*, Vol. 2, No. 13, 3-16 July 1980, pp.6-7

The Press and Popular Culture: An Historical Perspective - from *Newspaper History*, edited by G. Boyce, J. Curran and P. Wingate (1978), Constable and Company Ltd./Sage Publications, pp.41-50

British Film History: New Perspectives - from *British Cinema History*, edited by James Curran and Vincent Porter (1983), Weidenfeld and Nicolson, pp.9-23

The Future of 'English Literature' - from *News from Nowhere* 3, May 1987

Adult Education and Social Change - Tony McLean Memorial Lecture, September 1983, Workers' Educational Association South East District

The Red and the Green - from *The London Review of Books,* 1982

Communications, Technologies and Social Institutions - from *Contact*, edited by Raymond Williams (1981), Thames and Hudson, pp.226-38

III

Marx on Culture - published as 'Culture' in *Marx: The First Hundred Years,* edited by David McLennan (1983), Fontana, pp.15-55

A Defence of Realism - published as 'A Lecture on Realism' in *Screen*, Vol. 18, No. 1, Spring 1977, Society for Education in Film and Television, pp.61-74

On Solzhenitsyn: Literature and Revolution - from *Literature in Revolution*, Special Issue of *TriQuarterly*, No. 23/24, Winter/ Spring 1972, pp.318-34; *Russia Betrayed* - from *The Guardian*, 21 September 1972, p.14

Brecht - from *The London Review of Books*, 16 July-5 August 1981, pp.19-20

Lukács: A Man without Frustration - from *The London Review of Books*, 17 May-6 June 1984, pp.14-15

Index

INDEX

INDEX